REMEM

….NEVER JUDGE A BUCK BY ITS COVER!

The Accidental Shopkeeper

Author Patrick Limming

First published in Great Britain by
Patrick Limming

ISBN 978 0 9929468 0 7

Printed by :
Welland Print Ltd.
West Marsh Road
Spalding
Lincolnshire
PE11 2BB

The Accidental Shopkeeper

Reminiscences, Recollections & Ramblings from over forty years in retail.

Acknowledgements

All the staff at Holbeach Library
Carol Tasker at Lincolnshire Archives
Christine Hanson
Pete Boekestyn & Sue Cooper of Welland Print
Vicky & Cliff for their encouragement
Illustrations by Mark Wood & 'Naughty Netty' Santry
Rosie Limming for sorting my many mistakes!

Dedicated to

Jack & Anne Limming,
without whom none of this would have been possible.
Also to Alice, for putting up with all the compromises
being a shopkeeper brings.

Thanks also to all the people who have helped me carry on what Jack & Anne started.
There are many I haven't mentioned, but without your contribution,
this would be a very short book!
(Exceptions to the above apply; you know who you are!)

Introduction

I started on the very bottom rung of the shopkeeping ladder, before I had reached my teens, and then spent the next 40 odd years climbing my way up it. I guess that makes me a very slow climber, as the ladder isn't very tall; but now I am at the top, I thought I would share the view with you, together with a few of the experiences I have had on the climb.

The journey takes us from the beginnings, in the shop created in the sitting room of the family home, through the heady days of expansion and success, to the far more troubled high street of current times.

The chassis of the book has been constructed from the diaries I have kept since I was 16, whilst the bodywork is formed from memories buried deep in the partial void between my ears.

Although it may not seem like it at times, this is not a work of fiction, and all the characters are real people, who have been a part of my life over the years, although in many cases their names have been withheld!

I hope you will gain an insight as to what it is like to run a small business, but I have also tried to share some of the lighter moments with you; hopefully none of which will get me arrested!

Contrary to what some people think, I do actually have a life beyond the shop doors, and have included some of my 'out of shop' experiences, to give you some time away from the shop too!

So; I hope you enjoy sharing my journey; it's been a funny old ride!

Patrick Limming May 2014

Chapter 1 Life Before The Shop.

So; there you are thinking should you invest your money, or indeed your time in this book. Well, I can't promise you will learn much, unless you are thinking of becoming a shopkeeper of course, in which case I can save you a lot of time, and a bit of money: don't do it, get a proper job! I must also confess to the book being quite repetitive: there are only 26 different letters in the whole thing! On the other hand, there may hopefully be a few laughs along the way, and if you stop now, you may never get to know about Kev and the toothbrush! On balance, I think it's worth a punt, but then I would say that, I'm a shopkeeper; albeit an accidental one.
It may appear I have an encyclopaedic memory, but truth be told, I have kept a diary every day since I was 16 years old, and as Mae West put it. "Keep a diary and someday it'll keep you". Now while I don't suppose for a minute my diary is as interesting as hers, it does seem a shame to have spent the best part of two months of my life writing it and then just leave it to gather dust. So, here you have it, complete with warts!

I suppose 'accidental shopkeeping' runs in the family, but to explain this we really need to go back a couple of generations. Both sides of my family have lived and worked in the Lincolnshire Fens for enough generations for us to be considered locals, even by the stringent criteria of the area. We don't quite have the webbed feet that are alleged to signify a fully fledged Fen dweller, but otherwise we qualify! My mother, Anne, was born into the Harrison family in 1916. They were farmers in the small hamlet of Holbeach St Johns, and were what you might call comfortably off; that is to say they owned their own land and house, and even had a Horse and Trap! She was the second of five children, Connie being the eldest, with Frank, Meg and Jean following on after mum, although Meg sadly died at just 22 years of age.
My father, John, or Jack, as everybody called him, came from a slightly less settled background. He became the meat in a sandwich

consisting of older brother Sid, and younger sister May, in 1913. His father, Herbert Limming, was a farm manager, in the days when the landowner did exactly that, and the manager ran the farm for him. This arrangement would work just fine, until the person who merely owned the land, dared to have an opinion that differed to that of my grandfather's as to how the farm should be run. From what I heard many years later, from people who had worked with him, said landowner would be told that if he wanted to run the place he had better get on with it, (or words to that effect!), and that would be that! Apparently my grandmother used to dread the dramatic entrance followed by the announcement 'Pack up the cart ma, we're leaving'. It was probably one such incident which led to the first Limming foray into shopkeeping, as for a while they kept a shop in the village of Whaplode (Coincidentally, this is the village where I now live!). It appears however that granddad soon tired of this new way of life, leaving poor old grandma to look after the shop, whilst he returned to farm management. Obviously she did not have shop keeping in her blood either, and complained about the constraints it brought. All of which meant that the budding entrepreneur of the family, dad, was often conscripted into tending the shop, so that granddad could placate his wife by taking her out for the day.

JOHN (JACK) WILLIAM LIMMING IN HIS 'ROMMEL CHASING' GARB!

The consequence of all granddad's flying off the handle was that the family got to move about a fair bit. I realised just how much when people who had grown up all over the area would come in the shop and tell me how they remembered my father from school. It seems strange in these times when everybody seems to think they have a right to go to University, almost regardless of their ability, or indeed their actual need to, that even though dad had been awarded a scholarship to go to Grammar School, his father would not countenance it, on the grounds that he needed to be available to help out on the farm, during the busy periods, and therefore couldn't spare him for something as unimportant as a Grammar School education! This trait of not being told what to do is something which seems to run through the generations unfortunately, which is probably why we don't seem to settle too well in proper jobs; but I digress!

ANNE LIMMING (NEE HARRISON) IN HER NURSES' UNIFORM.

It was whilst living near Bourne, when in his teens, that two events occurred which influenced dad for the rest of his life. The first was being taken by his father to see Bourne Town football club play. As he stood there, cold and bored beyond belief, he vowed never to watch another football match as long as he lived, which as far as I know, he never did! The second event had a far more positive effect. At that time, local hero Raymond Mays, was competing very successfully in races and hill climb events, from his base in Bourne. In those days the local roads were lightly trafficked, and the enforcement of traffic regulations a little less draconian than they are today; so the straight between Bourne and Twenty was often used by Mays as an improvised test track. My father would hear the car bursting into life in Bourne, (looking at the age dad was at the time, it would probably have been one of May's Bugattis, or the Vauxhall-Villiers he ran later.) and the race was then on to try and bike up the track from the farm to the main road, before Mays went flashing by in full flight! He would then turn round at Twenty, and do a repeat run in the opposite direction. The excitement of seeing this powerful car and the fabulous noise which bellowed from its open exhaust instilled him with a love of speed and motor sport, which stayed with him the rest of his life.

Mum and dad first met at a fete in Carters Park, Holbeach. Both were there with friends, but seemed to hit it off together straight away, apparently it was dad's sense of fun and his somewhat unusual line in humour that attracted her! She was 18 at the time, and still living at home and helping out on the farm. My father was 21, and by now working as an accounts clerk at Birchnals Mill, in nearby Spalding. Soon they were spending a lot of time together, much to the disapproval of mum's father, who saw dad as quite unsuitable, with his tuned up motorbike, and 'reckless' lifestyle! Later in life he told me how fortunate he felt he had been to have had his bikes at a time when they could be enjoyed, without the constraints of both traffic and legislation. Most mornings, on the way into work, he would happen upon this same likeminded adversary to have a race with. Apparently the other chap's bike was a tad faster down the straights, but dad's Norton was better in the corners, and so he could usually overtake him on the final twists and turns, before town!

There were various motorbike incidents during this period, one of which probably started my father's lifelong mission of winding up mum's eldest sister, Connie. She had been a fun loving girl in her earlier years, but she then became involved with, and eventually married, Arthur, who was a strict Methodist, and frowned upon anything which might be construed as fun! This meant that Connie had to take on this very straight laced demure, but I always felt that under this veneer there still lurked the Connie of old, something which dad did his best to unleash!

DAD ON HIS BSA. IT WASN'T LONG BEFORE HE HAD PROGRESSED TO HIS BELOVED NORTONS.

On one particular occasion, Connie needed a lift to somewhere, and was duly inserted into the sidecar attached to dad's motorbike. Needless to say the contraption was ridden in the usual flat out manner, accompanied by a constant flow of admonishments from the sidecar. Some way into the journey they caught up with a heavily laden furniture removals wagon, its load spilling out onto the tailgate, which had been fixed in the horizontal position, to accommodate it.

This opportunity proved too much for dad to resist, and before Connie could utter a threat strong enough to deter him, she found herself under the tailgate, with dad on the motorbike hanging out to the side, supposedly waiting for a safe opportunity to overtake.

Needless to say that opportunity did not present itself any time soon, and legend has it that they travelled for quite some distance like this, with Connie's ranting becoming more extreme, until dad could no longer pretend he was unable to hear her! It seems she was not in a hurry to travel with him again! It is always the duty of any self respecting brother in law to aggravate his sisters in law of course, a tradition that I try to uphold to this day, although buying my current wife's (I like to call her that, it keeps her on her toes!) youngest sister some anti wrinkle cream for her 40th birthday was pushing my luck a bit! Sorry, I have wandered off again!
Other incidents involving dear old Connie which spring to mind include the rather cruel fridge wind up. At that time fridges were not as commonplace as they are today, and Connie had not seen one before she set eyes on our new acquisition. She opened the door, to carry out an internal inspection, but when she closed it again, dad said he was sure the light hadn't gone out; so Connie duly opened the door to check, and sure enough there was the light still glowing away! There followed many more opening and closings of the door, with dad somehow managing to keep his composure, as Connie tried her damdest to extinguish that light! I think it was mum who eventually put her out of her misery.
Occasionally dad did overstep the mark a bit; one such occasion was when we were on the way to a family wedding in our trusty Triumph Herald. Mum and dad were up front, with Uncle Arthur and I on either side of Connie, resplendent in a suitably oversized hat. The wedding was taking place at Whaplode Drove, and on route there just happened to be a humped back bridge. I don't really need to relate the rest, do I? Said bridge was duly negotiated at a velocity most inappropriate for the wellbeing of any oversized hat. I can still see poor old Connie, as she parted company with her seat, only to return a second later, with her hat now placed somewhat lower on her head than before. I seem to remember words were said!

A customer told me, several years after his death (that's dad's death, not the customers; I'm no clairvoyant!), that another favourite trick of his was to ride through town, late at night as the pubs were closing, conducting his motorbike from within the sidecar. Apparently he had modified it in such a way that he could operate the controls from the sidecar, so that if he went by the hapless victims with the bike closest to them, it looked to all intents and purposes as though they were witnessing a riderless motorbike! It would appear it gave several drunks quite a start. This may seem a little irresponsible, but I just think it was his way of encouraging people to drink more moderately.

MUM & DAD'S WEDDING. FROM LEFT WE HAVE : EDITH & HERBERT LIMMING, MEG, JACK & ANNE LIMMING, REG ROWELL (I THINK), CONNIE CRAWFORD, ARTHUR AUGUSTUS (GUS) HARRISON, ANNIE HARRISON.

Anyway, to return to the plot; after a courtship of about three years, Jack William Limming married Anne Harrison in 1937, presumably her father having realised by now that he wasn't going to go away!

They moved into a rented house, in Windsover Road, Spalding, something which years (and chapters!) later would complete a string of coincidences.

DAD AND FRIENDS ON NEWBURY STATION. HE IS ON THE THIRD ROW BACK, FOURTH FROM RIGHT.

Unfortunately their time together proved short lived, as Hitler was about to start his uninvited tour of Europe, and dad signed up for the Army. The financial position this put mum in meant that she had to give up the family home, and move back in with her parents at Holbeach St. Johns. The war meant there was a need for more nurses, and so mum ended up in Chesterfield, I believe looking after soldiers who had suffered serious burns, although that might have been elsewhere.

It seems incredible now, but mum would bike from Chesterfield to home for her rare weekends off, a distance of about 90 miles each way. Those Tour de France boys don't know they're born!

I find that people who served in the war generally seem to fit into one of two categories. Either they are keen to relate their experiences, and relive battles fought, and victories won, or they regard it as a phase of their life which was necessary, but is now past, and see no need to return there. Unfortunately, in some ways, my father was in the latter group, and was always far more interested in what could happen in the future, than what had happened in the past. I suppose you stand some chance of influencing the future, but stand no chance of altering the past!
All he would say, if questioned on the subject, is that he spent the war chasing Rommel up and down the desert!
I did find out bits and pieces from various sources, over the years, and so know that he was in the 8th Army, and served mainly in the Middle East. I also know that although he was supposedly in a clerical position, he used to get so bored that he would volunteer to drive the fuel tankers up to the front line. Mum also let slip, many years later that he had promoted himself to the rank of Sergeant, albeit with good cause! He had been acting Sergeant for some time, but had never been officially made up, and so it would appear he did the necessary paper work, and somehow got it all formalised. I don't know how true this is, but I do know that the documentation that I now have contains writing which is uncannily similar in style to dads'!
He did once confess his love of rough seas was due to an experience whilst being evacuated from (I think) Greece, where the craft they were in was tossed about like a cork, as the captain seemed almost telepathically to avoid the missiles that were raining down around them.
After he was demobbed dad returned to clerical work, and life started to settle down again; that is until 1947, when my eldest sister Jacqueline arrived to shatter the peace; she was joined two years later by Rosemary, so you would have thought by now they would have learnt their lesson, but alas not; so after many years deliberation, I came on to the scene, some eight years later, in 1955. Thinking of which, I have been very remiss in not

introducing myself! My name is Patrick, and I complete the trio of junior Limmings. Being the youngest brought with it many burdens of course; being lowest in the pecking order, and having to wear all the cast offs: a situation made infinitely worse by my siblings both being girls!
In the midst of all this dad had a change of career, as he joined Hix & Son, a local Estate Agent and Auctioneers. I mention this for no

ME POSING OUTSIDE JACQUES AMANDS PREMISES ON WASHWAY ROAD, DURING TULIP TIME. THIS SITE IS NOW OCCUPIED BY INTERGREEN.

other reason than this part of his life would play an important role, some years down the line. Eventually he decided the Estate Agents life was not for him, and he wound up at Jacques Amands', as manager for the Dutch born flower bulb merchant, who had operations in both Holbeach and London. Mr Amand was a larger than life character, very flamboyant, and in typical Dutch style, a real risk taker. Consequently, his business fortunes did not always follow the smoothest of trajectories, but when times were good he knew how to enjoy himself, something which was instrumental in

dad acquiring a taste for the finer things in life, many of which were sampled at the likes of the Strand Palace Hotel, whilst visiting the company's London headquarters.
This would prove to be something of a problem once he and mum were working for themselves, for on the *very* rare occasions that we did go out, mum was always conscious of the cost, whereas dad's attitude was that if he couldn't have what he fancied on these rare occasions, then he would sooner not go at all! Therefore, a typical meal out for the three of us (my sisters were living away by this time) would go something like: Dad to me. "I don't think you've tried smoked salmon yet have you?" Me. "No, not yet". Mother. "Oh, you wouldn't like it, it's just like eating old leather, have the soup instead". It soon became apparent to me that dad had a much better idea of what I would like than mum, little realising at the time that poor old mum was merely trying to keep us solvent!

During this period the Limming family had moved to Holbeach, and were now resident at The Crescent, on Spalding Road. Things were going well, dad had a steady job, they had two healthy girls, and the austerity of those early post war years was fading into the past. What could possibly go wrong?
Well; it just so happened that one of dad's old colleagues from the Hix & Son days was auctioning off this house in Fleet Street, and so dad thought he would go along and have a look, (although quite why he did so has never been made clear!). The bidding was not going terribly well, and so dad thought he would help his old friend out and move the bidding along a bit. Perhaps not the best idea he ever had! And so it was that he became the accidental owner of 17 Fleet Street, Holbeach.
To say mum was not best pleased when told the news would be an understatement of some magnitude. I believe the conversation went something like. "Did you have a good day dear?" "Yes, thank you." "Did anything interesting happen?" "Well, I bought a house." "You bought a house! Where?" "In Fleet Street." "In Fleet Street! hope it's not that dismal old place that Goodacres used to live in."

"Well; yes, actually it is." As I said, not best pleased!
And so it was that we moved into the house that I was to live in until I was married, many years later. The house had been extended and generally knocked about over many years, its best feature, from a small boys point of view, being the cellar, which doubled as a somewhat chilly swimming pool during the wet winter months, when the water table would rise, and gradually fill the cellar! Still, having an indoor pool was quite something for Holbeach in those days. (Still is, come to think of it!). It wasn't actually deep enough

DESPITE WHAT THE CAPTION CLAIMS, THIS IS ACTUALLY FLEET STREET, NOT HIGH STREET, BEFORE THERE WAS A 'LIMMINGS'. THE BUILDING WITH THE MAN UP A LADDER IS No 17, WHERE IT ALL STARTED, BEFORE EVENTUALLY SPREADING TO ENCOMPASS N^{OS} 19 TO 25.

to swim in, but it still sounds impressive. Despite mums reservations, the front room was nice and bright, with its' south facing aspect, and there was a dining room, and good sized kitchen, with a pantry. The spacious front entrance hall contained a staircase, which led up to the four bedrooms, and a bathroom. (I know I am starting to sound like an estate agent, but it will help you later!). Being from an earlier era, the property had such novelties as a wash house, and even our very own well. On the minus side, mains sewerage was yet but a distant dream, so visits from the infamous 'Dilly Cart' were a regular occurrence. Still, at least the actually toilet was inside, so we didn't have to endure the 'Lincolnshire Longdrop', a contraption still in use today, in some of the counties more rural locations!

By this time my grandma Harrison had passed away, and granddads health was deteriorating, so he came to live with us. I can just about remember him going to Boston market and me running up to meet him off the bus, hoping he would have brought a fresh crab for tea. I also remember he had this lovely rose gold wrist watch, the chronograph function on which used to fascinate me. Granddad & grandma Limming were still going strong, he now having run out of land owners to disagree with, and tending his garden and allotment in Church Street, Holbeach.

I suppose that as this Holbeach place keeps cropping up, I had better expand on its many claims to fame! It is a small market town, in South Lincolnshire, about 20 miles from the nearest civilisation. (Peterborough!). Considering its size, it has spawned more than its fair share of famous people. There is Geoff Capes; one time Olympic shot putter, and Worlds Strongest Man, sports commentator, Stuart Storey (who was also coach to Geoff, in the early days.), Boz Burrell, bass guitarist with Bad Company and Sir Norman Angell, winner of the Nobel Peace Prize in 1933. In fact, Holbeach is such a happening place, that even Biff Byford, front man of Heavy Metal group, Saxon, lived here for a few years!

Anyway, once again, order seemed to have returned to the Limming house hold. Things must have been good, as we even went on a family holiday to Clacton. Dad had hired an Austin Metropolitan from the local garage, complete with convertible roof, so we really thought we were the business! Dad was a stickler for punctuality, and if he said the car was leaving at 8.00am, that is

THE WHOLE FAMILY TOGETHER, ON A RARE HOLIDAY TO CLACTON.
MUM & DAD BACK ROW, ROSIE, ME & JACQUIE SEATED.

when it would leave, and it was up to you to be ready! As far as I can remember, this is the only time we went on holiday as a family, although there may have been others I've forgotten.

Meanwhile, things had taken a bit of a downturn at Amands', and so it was that dad handed in his notice, and decided to become a shopkeeper.
Now, one of the prerequisites of being a shopkeeper is that you actually need a shop in which to shopkeep: Quite how the subject was broached, I do not know, but before mum knew what had hit her, the dining room was full of the furniture from the sitting room, and some blokes were knocking a gaping hole in the front wall of her once cosy room. Soon there was a large display window installed, a door inserted next to it, and some steps, to span from street level to the elevated room; sorry, shop.
The conversion work was completed on 23rd February 1960. The reason the date can be recollected so precisely, is that mum never tires of telling us that she spent one of her 44th birthdays scrubbing the floors, ready for opening the next day. I say 'one' of them, because, as she was born at midnight, she always celebrated her birthday on the 23rd and the 24th. She even used to con two presents out of dad! He, by the way, was 46 by this time, and was about to start working harder than ever before!
I was too young to realise it at the time, being not yet five years old, but life was never going to be the same again.
Not long after the shop opened, granddad Harrison passed away, leaving mum a decent legacy. Now, any right minded couple would have put a nice bit by, ready for the inevitable expense of three growing children, and maybe splashed out on a new telly. But we are, of course, not dealing with right minded people here; we are dealing with that frankly unhinged entity, the wannabe entrepreneur, and so it was that mum's nest egg ended up being invested in the new enterprise.

Chapter 2. The Early Days

In its original form the shop was a very mixed bag. Basically, anything that they thought they could make a shilling on was in; so there was pet food, fancy goods, sweets, cigarettes, gardening bits and bobs, fruit & veg and anything else that could be crammed into the 16 feet by 13 feet space!

It was obvious right from the start that this venture was only going to succeed if the pair of them put everything into it, and then some! As all granddad's money had been spent on stock, a regular income was still needed, as in the early days any earnings from the fledgling business would all have to be re-invested to keep building up the stock levels, to the point where mum and dad drew just £156.00 between them in that first year.

So, to make ends meet, the shop would be open from 7am to 7pm, 364 days a year, the exception being Christmas Day, when they took things easy, by opening at 10am and skiving off at about 3pm, so that Christmas dinner could be enjoyed in some sort of peace and quiet. Dad also had jobs taxi driving and delivering school meals. Mum would be left to hold the fort whilst dad was away doing his 'proper' jobs, and then after the shop closed, dad would settle down to do the book work. This would typically take until about 9pm, after which he would then cook himself something to eat, (often fat bacon and fried potatoes as I recall!) and then it was time for bed, before a 6am alarm call, to start it all over again; and that was how it was for quite some time.

Mum was a bit of an unsung hero in all of this, as apart from her role in the shop, she still had all the usual household chores to do, and three children to look after.

Somebody obviously thought that she was doing even more than she actually was, as the tax office received a tip off that Mrs. Limming was doing book keeping for other people 'on the side'. This led to an investigation, which they could well have done without at the time. Dad was called upon to give an explanation. "Mr Limming, can you prove that your wife is not running a business, providing book keeping services." Dad's reply was typical of the man: "No, I can't prove it, but I'll let you into a little secret. I'm not running a Fish and Chip shop in Sutton Bridge; but I can't prove that either!" The point was taken, and the spurious allegations were dropped. If one thing was guaranteed to wind him up it was misguided officialdom. His view was that having spent some of the best years of his life supposedly fighting for freedom, he wasn't about to have somebody telling him how to run his business. This attitude, and the aforementioned Limming trait of not being told what to do, would see him have many run-ins with officialdom over the years!

One such incident was when the tax office queried the amount dad was declaring for personal spending. They wanted to know how he paid for his entertainment, holidays, motoring etc. Wrong person to ask! He furnished them with his work schedule, and then asked when exactly they thought he did this holidaying etc. That was another one that went no further.

I suppose dad's idea of entertainment was a bit left field anyway. He very rarely watched television; I remember him coming into the room once, when mum was watching Coronation Street. He stood there for a few minutes, looking aghast, and then left the room muttering something about an insult to human intelligence! He preferred to listen to the police radio, whilst doing his book work. I have to admit it could be quite entertaining. One night there were bursts of laughter, followed by dad's characteristic snort, emanating from his office. (Known to the rest of us as 'the kitchen') I went to see what could have provoked such an outburst, and it appears a message had come over: "Be on the lookout for a male, wearing a dark overcoat, six feet." There was a pause, and then the reply came back. "Six feet. He shouldn't take a lot of spotting then!" The other officer, obviously devoid of a sense of humour, just retorted: "Not been in the force long, have you son?"

Being the age it was, there was nothing so grand as central heating in the house. A coal fire took the worst of the chill off the sitting room, whilst a Rayburn in the kitchen performed both heating and cooking duties. As for the upstairs, there was no heating at all, which meant that in the winter ice on the inside of the bedroom windows was pretty much the norm, and you soon perfected the technique of getting dressed in bed! This situation was just about bearable in a bedroom, but in the bathroom it was a definite no, no. Luckily, Health and Safety had not been invented then, so on particularly cold days, (for me that would generally include any which fell between October and April!) the Morphy Richards convector heater would be put in the bathroom, and then an extension lead run to the nearest socket in the bedroom/storeroom next door. I would generally give it about 20 minutes to ensure the water didn't freeze as it came out of the tap, and then I would complete my ablutions in the shortest possible time. Needless to say, the drying off procedure was carried out in as close a proximity to the heater as possible. This arrangement worked absolutely fine, until the fateful day when I bent down to dry my legs, and my tender backside made firm, if very brief, contact with the fine mesh grill on the front of the heater. The result was a perfect facsimile of the grill, branded onto my buttocks. I don't know which was worse, the severe discomfort every time I sat down, or the fact that my mother thought of it as some kind of work of art, which had to be displayed to all and sundry. I was really pleased when it started to lose its definition, and I was spared my freak show type ordeal!

Obviously the shop was a somewhat unconventional environment for a young child to grow up in; but to me it just seemed normal: didn't everybody have a stack of chocolate in their hall, and a selection of vases in the bedroom, or have to squeeze up half a staircase, being careful not to dislodge the stock stacked precariously on the other half? It was very much a case of making your own entertainment, as 'quality time', (an expression I never have liked!) or indeed any sort of time, with my parents was necessarily rare.

Much of my free time was spent with a pedal car replica of an Austin A40 Devon (The Austin J40, for those detail obsessives

A BUDDING STIRLING MOSS WITH AUSTIN A40 PEDAL CAR.

amongst you!). This really was a cool car in its day, with two seats, pneumatic tyres, working lights, (well, they were until I pranged it!) and even a hooter. I also had all the right gear, courtesy of an old fancy dress costume, comprising racing overalls, goggles and crash helmet. I was allowed as far as the Central Fish Bar, about 200 yards from the shop, where there was a nice wide bit of pavement on which to turn round for the return trip. Any pedestrian traversing what I considered my personal race track needed their wits about them, as the Austin was conducted at break neck speed, with my little legs flailing back and forth like the pistons on a steam train. Anybody stepping into my path would have been bowled over like a skittle! The only saving grace was that progress was accompanied by the nearest my still immature voice could muster to the sound of a racing engine, this at least giving some warning of the approaching missile.

Another thing the Austin taught me at a very young age was that girls tend to like nice cars too. It was not long before I was peddling down to North Parade on a Sunday to pick up Susan Morefoot, who would then be conducted in great style to Sunday school. I think the novelty must have worn off eventually, as I seem to remember the arrangement coming to an abrupt end one week, when I refused to take her home after the class! It's worth noting that a good J40 can now fetch well over £1,000, so that's another one I should have hung onto.

Whatever the sacrifices, clearly mum and dad were doing something right, as the shop became busier by the week, which brought its own problems; where to store the ever increasing amounts of stock. I don't know if any boundaries had been agreed with mum before the shop took over her home, as to which parts of the house were 'business' and which were 'private', but I have a feeling that she hadn't envisaged quite the level of intrusion that resulted!

Stock spread throughout the house like some sort of cancer. Shelves were screwed to any spare bit of wall, the lovely entrance hall, now redundant as such, the front door having been barricaded with stock, was reduced to half its former width, as it was crammed with old packing crates, containing sweets and cigarettes. The chaos continued up the afore mentioned staircase, turning left at the top, to invade what had been the fourth bedroom.

Mum really must have been a saint. I know she wasn't fond of the house in the first place, but I really don't think these additions helped the cause. There were other sacrifices as well. With so much time spent at work, it meant their social life became virtually nonexistent, which was a shame, as they had previously had a good circle of friends. There was still the occasional contact, but it would usually involve the friends coming around to our house after the shop had shut on a Saturday night, although even then you could not guarantee what time that may be.

Shops in a small town such as ours, tended to be more than just a place where you went to spend your money; they were very much

an intrinsic part of the community, and people would come in for a chat, to catch up on the local gossip, or even seek advice on matters totally unrelated to the shop itself. One customer in particular would always wander in, often with his young daughter in tow, just before closing time on a Saturday night; much to the annoyance of my mother. You then knew you were in for a late night! On occasion, he used to stay that long, that the daughter, who was no more interested in the state of his sweet williams than I was, would join me in the room, to watch television.
This somewhat flexible approach to opening hours was taken to the limit on one of the rare Saturday evenings when we did have visitors. As the area to the rear of the house had also succumbed to the ever spreading stock cancer, it was not a safe place for those unfamiliar with the terrain to venture after dark. The safest option therefore, was to show guests out via the shop. Now; opposite the shop was the Ram pub, whose hours tended to be as flexible as ours. (I remember one particular night, after the landlord's sons, Mick & John Horsepole, had gained a podium place in the sidecar race at the Isle of Man TT, the party spilling out onto the street, complete with piano, at 1am!). It was well gone 11pm, as dad opened the shop door to let our guests out, unaware that the light had been spotted by a customer leaving the Ram. Said man strode into the shop, and without a moment's hesitation, greeted dad with: "Evening Jack; Twenty Players please. I didn't realise you were open this late". Totally unfazed, dad just went behind the counter, served the man with his cigarettes, and off he went!
We used to sell flowers, plants and fruit & veg, in those early days, and it was decided that it would be a good idea to produce some of it ourselves. We already had the indoor swimming pool, which provided the perfect environment in which to bring on hyacinths, ready for the Christmas trade, but it was felt a greenhouse would also be a good move; so, one was hired, just around the corner from the shop, and mum found herself with yet another side line! What was even more amazing about all this is that although I didn't register the fact at the time, mum was also a volunteer at Holbeach

Hospital, and would go on Sunday evenings to help out. I just don't know how she found the drive and energy to do it all.
One summer's evening my good friend Mo Mosley and I were supposedly helping round at the greenhouse, but having an attention span typical of kids of that age, we soon wandered off in search of something more interesting to do. We realised that the metal gates to the site made an excellent improvised swing, and we set about seeing how fast we could get them to swing back and forth. Luckily my mother happened to notice that the whoops of delight seemed to have turned to something a bit more plaintive. Upon coming to investigate, she was greeted by the site of Mo and me lying on the ground, with the gate on top of us, and the brick pillar on top of that. Cue a trip to Boston hospital, Mo with a broken arm, me with a badly bruised leg, complete with dent, where one of the gate's rods had gone in.
I was very fortunate with my friends and neighbours, as they were aware of my situation, and would sometimes include me on their days out, the Mosley's even taking me on holiday a couple of times. One such trip was to sunny Holme on Sea, where we stayed in a caravan. Mo and I shared a bunk bed, he on the top, me underneath. This state of the art accommodation had all mod cons, including the provision of a small potty, tucked away under the bunk, in case of night time emergencies. I did indeed have such an emergency, and duly made use of the potty. Later on in the night Mo had a similar call of nature. My bladder capacity was not such that I could fill a whole potty, so not a problem: or at least it wouldn't have been, had I not left it at the foot of the steps. I think I need elaborate no further, suffice to say that finding his foot wedged tightly into the offending receptacle, being lapped by my still warm offering, did not improve my chances of being invited again!
Things had now reached a stage in the shop, where there was not even a cranny, let alone a nook, to squeeze any more stock into, so there was only one thing for it, make the shop bigger. Now I don't think even dad would have dared suggest knocking through into the

THE ORIGINAL 'FRONT ROOM' SHOP.

sitting room, nee dining room, so the only way was outwards. The proximity to the pavement meant that this would only be a small extension, but crucially it would mean that the shop front would now stand proud of the rest of the building, with a window at each side, with which to catch people's attention.
Trying to run a shop in the middle of a building site was not ideal, but the alterations were duly completed. This additional 12 feet by 4 feet area meant we could fit in a window board, on which goods could be displayed; bulbs in the autumn, gift items at Christmas, and so on, we really were going places!
Eventually even dad had to accept that there was a finite amount of stock you could fit into a house and stay married, so something needed to be done. Luckily fate intervened in the shape of No 19 Fleet Street, the adjacent property to the shop, otherwise known as 'Dirty Dicks', by way of reference to its former use as a 'doss house'. This property was one half of a pair of once grand, semi-detached Georgian houses, which were now in a very dilapidated

state. Looking at the deeds, some years later, it was clear that these houses had quite a chequered history, with more than one of the previous owners having ended up in Lincoln Prison. This may have gone some way to explaining their now sorry appearance.
The continuing growth of the business meant that even workaholics like mum and dad could no longer cope, and so it was that our intrepid shop keepers moved into the realm of employers. This brought with it a whole new level of responsibility, as they now needed to take enough money every week to sustain somebody else's livelyhood, a considerable amount when all the costs associated with an employee are taken into account. So the need to grow became even greater. You can never stand still in business, for if you are not going forwards, then you will most surely go backwards!
In those days a huge number of local people would have a piece of land with which to earn a bit of extra money. This would be used to pay for holidays or other treats, and was an important part of the local economy. If the strawberry crop was good this would also mean a harvest for the local shops.
Having this large pool of potential customers made a move into the supply of horticultural sundries to the local small holders and allotment keepers a logical step. This also meant yet more storage was required, and it occurred to dad that if the outer walls of the out buildings of No's 17 & 19 were utilised, it would not take too much more construction work to link the back of No 19 to these. I have no doubt the appropriate permissions were sought, before a functional, if somewhat rudimentary building was constructed, referred to affectionately as 'the back shed'.
It wasn't long before the new addition was crammed full with produce nets, canes, seed potatoes, chip baskets, (funnily enough for strawberries, not chips!) and anything else that would turn a profit! But still there was not enough space, so when the opportunity arose to rent the grand sounding Park Hall, in Park Road, Holbeach, it was too good to miss. This 25feet by 75feet building had previously seen action as a dance hall, a cinema, and

latterly as warehousing for none other than dad's old boss, Jacques Amand.

By this stage more staff had joined the firm, and many more lines had been added to the stock inventory. I was by now old enough to start taking a bit of an interest in the goings on, and would be given various tasks. One of the more interesting was the 'stock control' of the tortoises! These would arrive, packed in wooden cases, containing 50 of the poor creatures. It seems incredible now that such things went on, but back then it was considered quite acceptable. Anyway, the tortoises would be corralled in a compound on the back lawn, made of chitting trays, (wooden boxes, used for putting potatoes in, so that they form shoots or 'chits,') and would be fed on lettuce and other greens. Checking in the original 50 would not be a problem, as you just counted them as you took them out of the crate; the problems started when you came to check them later. Now they may have a reputation for not moving very quickly, but I can assure you that when you are trying to count them, they move plenty fast enough! I am also convinced that we must have had the rare 'Houdini Strain', as the blighters were always escaping! The furthest I can remember rescuing one from was Woolworths, which must have been a good 300 yards from the shop. Fortunately it was well known that we had them, so if an errant tortoise was spotted in town, we would usually get a phone call, or the escapee would be returned by some honest soul.
Business was done in a very different way in dad's time, and especially for him, as the shop was his work, his hobby and his leisure; in fact it was his life! You tended to have much more of a relationship with suppliers, and loyalty, on both sides, was far stronger than it is today. Once you had built up the relationship with a supplier, you would tend to stay with them until they either ceased trading, or did something to upset you. This meant that many of the reps also became friends, and where and how business was conducted was dependent upon the strength of that friendship. Mr Dawson for example, would sometimes arrive late in the day,

so that on a summers evening we could go down to the marsh, at Shep Whites, to collect samphire. (Which, despite what those posh townie chefs on telly try to tell you, is pronounced samfa, not samfire, as they like to suppose!) I remember once tagging along, for some strange reason wearing a suit, which was just asking for trouble. Sure enough, I fell into a muddy creak, which did not go down terribly well upon returning home, despite my two guardians doing their best to clean up the mess before we confronted mum. Mr Dawson would stay overnight, and the ordering would be done the following morning. Another favourite was Mr Mudge. Dad and he had a lot in common; they were of a similar age, their war careers had been similar, and better still, he was a huge motor racing fan. These attributes qualified him for 'special lunch' status! I really used to look forward to these visits, as it not only meant that mum would do a really good meal in honour of Mr Mudge, with something exotic like roast pork, but it also gave me the opportunity to talk to someone who actually went to the British Grand Prix! The final member of the 'inner circle' was Reg Pywell, who dad later helped set up in business on his own. It is a sign of the depth of these friendships, that Reg sent mum flowers on the anniversary of dad's death until he passed away himself.

Another business relationship that blossomed into a lasting friendship was that with Bill & Vera Cauley. They had a shop, not dissimilar to ours, in Eastleigh, Hampshire, and dad used to take Bill around the local bulb growers, to source his stock. Again they hit it off, as Bill had been a Spitfire pilot, which dad found very interesting; it was also nice for mum to have Vera to sympathise with about shop life! The relationship also had benefits for me, as in my early teen years mum and I would go down to their lovely little cottage at Hook by Warsash, near to the Solent, and have some time away from the shop.

Another aspect of business in those days was that it was actually quite enjoyable. By that I mean the bureaucracy had not got to a level where everything you did had some rule or regulation attached to it. Today's Health and Safety used to be covered by a thing called common sense, and I have to say that it seemed to work just fine, from what I remember, or perhaps you just accepted risky situations a bit more readily in those days! I do have to admit that carrying 12 stone bales of peat from the lorry, down the yard, and then stacking them 6 high, probably had a lot to do with my spine now being a funny shape, but there you go!

Another practice which probably wouldn't have stood up to a risk assessment, was the method used to unload strawberry punnets at the Park Road warehouse. These would arrive in rigid lorries with box bodies, about 600 cases at a time, and it was something of a challenge to see how quickly we could decant them into the warehouse. We got this down to a fine art, and a four man team could empty a load in about 45 minutes. The first job would be to build a series of pylons out of punnet cases. On to these would be placed roller conveyers, down which the cases would whiz at great speed. Given that every inch of space in the warehouse needed to be utilised, the stack had to be built right up into the roof of the building; we even packed them around the beams in the roof! The system involved the lorry driver loading the cases onto the roller, one person at the end of the roller, who would throw the cases to the man half way up the stack, who in turn would throw them to the stacker, who could be as much as twenty plus feet up! There was no let up in proceedings, and everybody would get into a rhythm. Any hesitation by the stacker could spell disaster, as each box would be launched by the man below at a few seconds' intervals, and if you were not ready to catch it, then chances are it was going to hit you! As none of us were overly keen on heights, the job of stacker used to get shared around. We still look back on those times as the 'good old days', but I'm not too sure I would want to do it now! I say 'we', as amazingly, one of the members of staff from those days, Tony Machin, is still with the firm today!

I suppose another thing which would be frowned upon now is the amount of exposure I have had to what I suppose would be deemed 'hazardous substances'. You may remember many years ago, all the furore about a chemical called DDT. This was used, amongst other things, for dusting strawberries, to protect them from insect infestation. Well, being a supplier to the local growers, DDT was a stock item. The trouble was that it came in 4 stone bags, and many of our growers were in a small way, and did not need that amount. This meant I spent many an hour, in the basement of No 19, weighing out DDT into 7 and 14 pound bags. As it came in the form of a fine dust, it would all puther up as you scooped it into the bags, no matter how gently you tried to perform the task. This, combined with the very low ceiling, (I could not stand up straight in the room) meant I would stand there, wreathed in a cloud of DDT dust! Whether it has done me any harm in the long term, I do not yet know, but looking on the bright side, I have never been troubled with greenfly! Although DDT was by far the most unpleasant of the weighing up tasks, I also have scooped more than my fair share of derris dust, dried blood, bone meal, and fish, blood & bone, none of which were the most pleasurable of experiences!

So, the Limming Empire kept marching on, and another bit of the jigsaw slotted into place when Mrs Andrews, the occupant of No 21 Fleet Street for many years, finally passed away. As she had done nothing by way of maintenance to the house for many years, it was not the most salubrious of properties, which probably helped dad acquire it without too much competition.
The obvious thing to do was to make No's 19 and 21 into one unit, so that you could move freely between the two. Naturally a full structural survey was carried out before removal of the adjoining walls, whereby everybody gave them a bit of a thump, before declaring them non structural! As they were only constructed of lath and plaster, they probably were not contributing too much to the structure of the houses: so, out came the saws and hammers, and that was job done.
All this new found space meant the stock inventory could grow even more, it also meant there were even more rooms in which to lose things! It's a good job we were all younger then, and still had decent memories, for although rooms were categorised, (there was

the hosepipe room, tool room, chemicals room etc.) there were always those cross over items, which never quite had a proper home. Usually there would be someone who remembered where the poultry spice had been put, for example, or even if not, you would start in the most obvious room, and work your way through them, until you stumbled across it.

Dad was well aware that this rambling collection of buildings was not the ideal working environment, and his thoughts turned to re-developing the site. Plans were drawn up, but unfortunately he never did manage to raise the funds to achieve his ambitions.

By now the horticultural supplies part of the business was becoming well established, with the most important time of the year being the strawberry season. It is hard to imagine now just how many were grown locally, but the competition to supply the packaging was very intense, and you had to make sure your prices were very keen, as the growers would not pay a penny more than they need. This was in the time before the now universal plastic punnet, and in those days they were made out of wood pulp, by a company in Yarmouth called Hartman Fibre. As mentioned, they would come packed 250 to a box, with a lorry full consisting of roughly 600 boxes, depending on how good the loaders were at the factory at stacking them in the lorry; all done manually in those days, of course! If we had finished the previous day low on stock, it was not uncommon for dad to set off at 4am for Yarmouth, in our trusty VW truck, to be at the factory for opening time at 6am. He would then load the truck with as many cases as he dare, and rush back to the shop, so that we had enough stock until the main delivery arrived from the factory, usually at about 10am. We would then stack the first load of the day outside the shop, all along the pavement, and by the close of business we would put what few cases remained away in the stores. Any further loads would be sent to Park Hall. This scenario would go on throughout the season, from June to August.

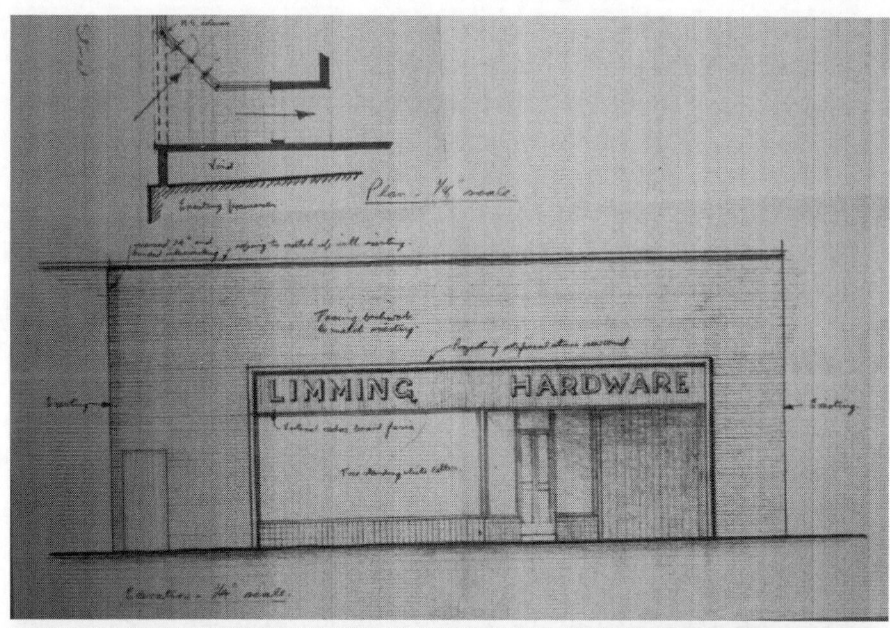

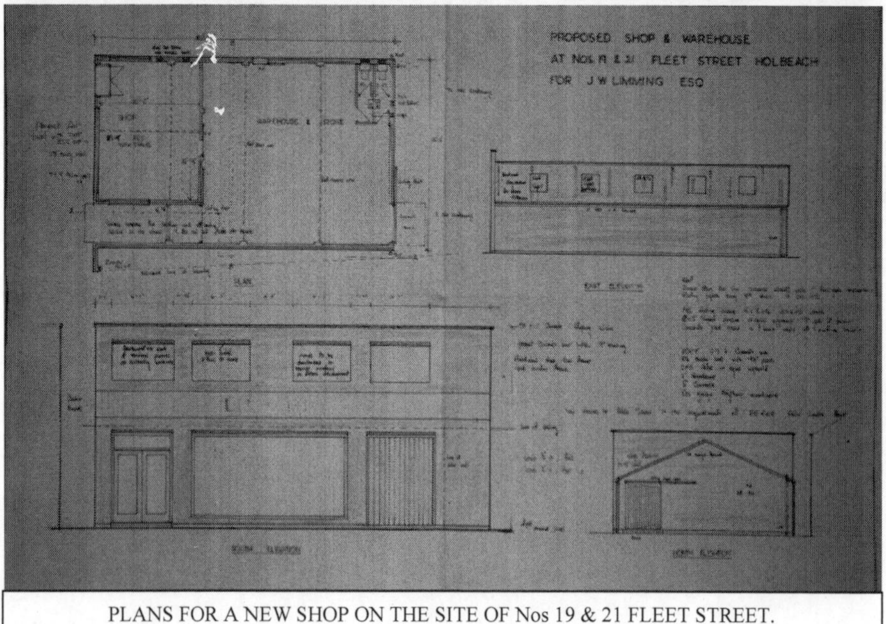

PLANS FOR A NEW SHOP ON THE SITE OF Nos 19 & 21 FLEET STREET.

Aside from the more serious aspects of the business, dad also liked to have some fun during his working day, I suppose you have to remember that it was both his livelihood, and his hobby. One such diversion was his branching out into selling jokes. Of course, for a boy of a certain age this was marvellous, as obviously someone had to try them all out! Apart from the usual severed fingers and plate lifters, we did rather a good line in stink bombs. A favourite trick used to be to wait in a phone box, pretending to make a call, and then when somebody else came to use it, you would end the fictitious call and vacate the box. The trick was to crush the stink bomb under your heel just as you exited the box; this usually then gave the unfortunate victim long enough to dial their number and part with their money before the stink bomb pervaded the air with a truly stomach wrenching smell. You were then treated to the sight of somebody trying to hold a conversation from outside the phone box, with the handset stretched to its furthest extent, whilst trying to imagine what the previous occupants most have eaten to produce such a smell. A bit naughty I know, but I put it down to lack of parental supervision! As I remember, after one too many stink bombs being let off in Woolworths, (not by me, I hasten to add!) the police 'requested' that we stop selling them, so that put an end to the fun.

Another thing which used to keep dad amused was thinking up things to put on the sign board, which used to stand out on the pavement. There were such gems as: 'we are giving our fruit a weigh today' or 'etceteras from 6d', all of which made him chuckle, even if people didn't really get it most of the time. On one occasion people could have been forgiven for thinking it was another wind-up, as the message on the board advertised 'free ice creams', only this time it was a genuine claim, as the shop freezer had broken down, and there was nothing for it but to dispose of the stock. The local kids thought it was great as they descended in droves to help us out. At least it was good PR.

As money became slightly less tight, (and I do mean slightly, as nearly every penny earned was still being ploughed back into the business) we would occasionally go out for a late Christmas lunch, after the shop had closed. I remember on one such occasion we went to a local pub, and whether through over indulgence with my selection box, or some other reason, I was not feeling too well. The first course was tomato soup, not a favourite of mine, as it comes into the category of 'hot drinks' as far as I am concerned, something which I do not consume, even to this day! Anyway, as I was presented with this delight, things came to a head in the poorly stomach department, and suffice to say, the bowl of tomato soup took the brunt of it. I was terribly embarrassed of course, but dad didn't bat an eyelid, he just calmly said "Never mind, they will just send it back out as oxtail." Perhaps not in the best of taste (the comment or the soup), but it is something I have never forgotten; he could usually see the funny side of most situations.
I suppose it was also about this time in my life where my entrepreneurial instincts started to emerge. There was not a lot in the way of entertainment for kids in Holbeach at that time, (still isn't, come to think of it!) so there was an opening for somebody to provide some. A friend and I constructed a den, in what passed for our back garden, and this then became the head quarters for our activities club. It was the ideal venture for a youth of limited means, for with no more than a box of chalk, doubtless 'on loan' from the shop's stock, you could organise a game of 'Tracker'. For those of you who had interesting childhoods, this involved one group setting off armed with the chalk, with which they would have to leave marks as to their route. The trick was to put the marks in an obscure place as possible, to slow down your pursuers, who would set off to track you down after a suitable amount of lead time had been allowed. Sometimes there would be quite a gang of us, and at sixpence a day, or whatever it was, it was quite a good little earner. The stores were also an excellent venue for hide and seek.

Another opportunity presented itself when the old cottages behind us were demolished, leaving behind a collection of little hillocks. We salvaged some of the old linoleum which had been left behind, and placed this on the hillocks. We then marked out a track in-between them. All that was left to do was strip Rosie's old bike down to the bare essentials, drench the lino with water, and we had our very own cyclocross course! It proved to be great fun, if a little hazardous, as the lino had all the properties of sheet ice, so you could perform spectacular slides, jumps and crashes for hours on end.

Bikes played a very important part in my formative years, as they provided my first taste of freedom. I am never quite sure if we lived in a less dangerous society then, or if it is merely that the media is so full of stories of things happening to children these days, that we just assume that to be the case. The only incident I can remember being reported were the 'Moors Murders', but it may just be that a less sensationalist media didn't report the less high profile cases. Either way, I am not convinced that things have changed as much as we are led to believe, it's merely that the modern media brings it to our attention more.

Whatever the perceived risks, my friend Richard and I used to bike everywhere together, and would think nothing of biking the 25 miles to Wootten Woods, tearing around in the woods all day, and then making the journey back home again, with neither our parents or ourselves fretting about 'what might happen'. Irresponsible? Foolhardy? Maybe, but I know it was certainly good fun, and taught me a lot about self reliance.

Although growing up amidst a 7 day a week operation had its disadvantages, there were also some up sides, for although, as mentioned, leisure time with either parent was a very rare occurrence, at least dad did try to make sure we got one day out somewhere together each year, even though it would usually mean mum having to hold the fort. The good thing about this was it would usually involve cars, and once away from the shop, dad knew how to enjoy himself! He was also of the opinion that if you wanted to go somewhere, or do something, you should just go for it, and if you maybe shouldn't be there or be doing whatever it was, somebody would more likely than not inform you of the error of your ways at some point. He applied this philosophy on many occasions, which resulted in me doing such things as driving around the Oulton Park racing circuit one evening in his Triumph 2000, after we had driven down for the Gold Cup race the next day. I suppose I would have been about 13 at the time, so it was a real thrill, and I managed a few laps before an official started remonstrating in a manner which suggested we should maybe make for the paddock! The attitude was very much that if you were going to have a day out, then you needed to make the best of it, and the usual tight budgetary constraints would be forgotten for the duration of the trip. On occasions this would get him in hot water with mum. None more so than when we were supposed to go to the London Motor show for the day, returning that evening. The only trouble was that he happened to see a poster as we were leaving the Motor Show advertising that Tommy Cooper was appearing at the Palladium Theatre that evening. Now, Tommy was a huge favourite of dad's, so the next thing I know we are at the box office, buying tickets for the show. Of course it would be too late after the show to consider travelling home, so the next stop was the Strand Palace Hotel, which he knew from his days with Jaques Amand. On enquiring after the price of a room for the night he quite rightly decided that the price was a bit rich for the likes of us, and we wandered back out onto the street. After a short walk we entered another hotel, and as we walked up to the reception, it all looked a bit familiar. It transpired all we had done was walk round the corner, and re-entered the same hotel by a different entrance! After a quick bit of negotiation we were booked in. I will never forget that phone call home. I could only hear one side of it, but I could well guess the responses that were emanating from the other end. "We won't be home tonight," pause, "At the Strand Palace," much longer pause, "We're going to see Tommy Cooper at the Palladium." Poor old mum; that was likely the house keeping

budget for the month gone!
Another favourite trick of his was to sell things not actually belonging to him. I suppose he just couldn't help himself, but I well remember the occasion when a customer enquired as to whether we sold bread, which of course we didn't. Undaunted he went into the kitchen, where he discovered the loaf bought earlier by my mother for that nights' tea. Before you could say toast a deal had been done; yet another satisfied customer. Come tea time his misdemeanour was discovered, and needless to say mum was not impressed! She became even less so when she discovered that he had sold it for less than she had paid! He also caught my sister Rosie with the same trick. For some strange reason, she liked to spend her summer holidays scratting about in the ground for stuff people had thrown away centuries before. She had bought a can opener in preparation for one such expedition, and unfortunately for her, dad had a request for just such an item. Once again he failed to turn a profit, Rosie's one shilling and eleven pence can opener changing hands for just one and six. Of course, to him it was all profit, not having had to outlay anything in the first place.

SHOP FRONT IN 1968, SHOWING GALAXY VENDING MACHINE & FAMILY CAT.

Talking of my sisters, they were of course quite a bit older than me, (still are, come to think of it) and so before I had reached my teens they had both left home. Jacquie had gone off to Lowestoft, to train as a Nanny, and Rosie to London, to study Mathematics at University. Once qualified, Jacquie's choice of employer would cause quite a fall out between us. She had the chance of three jobs, one of which I can't remember, but the other two were with

Edmund Vestey, of Dewhurst butchers fame, (amongst other things) and Graham Hill, of motor racing fame. To me it was a foregone conclusion that she would go for the Graham Hill position, and I had already envisaged myself, hobnobbing with the Hill family at the British Grand Prix: this was going to be my way into racing, it was obviously fate!

To my utter disbelief, however, she took the Vestey job, using the defence that we had family friends living not far away from the Vestey pile. This seemed like a very poor excuse for ruining my future career prospects, and we didn't see eye to eye for quite some time after that! I suppose the Vestey situation did teach me something, as on the occasions we went to visit, Mr and Mrs Vestey were always friendly and welcoming, in a posh sort of way, even inviting us to join them for lunch on one occasion. Ever since I have always thought that if somebody in their position could accept plebs such as us, then nobody else I ever came across should have any excuse to look down on me. I formed the opinion that whilst I may be no better than anyone else, neither was anybody better than me!

At the dawn of the 70's dad was still pursuing his quest to buy up the whole of Fleet Street, and this time it was Nos 23 & 25! These properties had been occupied by various businesses throughout the years, including one of the many pubs in Holbeach, a hardware store, and latterly Gordon Woodman's electrical shop.

The owner of the business had decided to retire, and so the landlord, a local character, known as 'Piggy Dawson', offered the property to dad. The name Piggy came from his main occupation as a pig farmer, although he seemed to have his finger in a lot of pies, including running a finance company: so, not only did Piggy sell dad the property, he also lent him the money to buy it with, which seemed a pretty shrewd move to me.

This latest acquisition actually came with a proper shop front, and two display windows, although on the minus side, the fabric of the building left a little to be desired. No matter, we could now display

a wider range of goods, and expand the more profitable retail side of the business. It is interesting to think that at about the time we acquired Woodmans, as it was known, we started selling 'Super Ser' gas cabinet heaters. I remember they seemed to cost a king's ransom at £100, complete with gas cylinder. In 2012, over 40 years later, we were selling a similar item for just a few pounds more, so not everything has gone up as much as we suppose!
Woodmans also meant that dad could at last have a proper office, although he never did fully give up his night time kitchen office, as I think the lure of a cosy Parkray was too great on those cold evenings. Of course no office would be complete without a nice calendar, but not for dad the usual scenic or naked offering; no he had to have something much more mischievous, and the introduction of Value Added Tax in April 1973, (which replaced Purchase Tax, at a rate of 'just'10%) gave him the perfect subject matter! I don't know how or why, but at some time after its introduction, he had found himself in the vicinity of the VAT headquarters, an organisation he despised even more than the other tax collecting agencies, so he decide to take a photograph of the building. Apparently this was not allowed, and the security man came scuttling out to him. Somehow dad managed to persuade him that he had not yet taken the photo, and thus escaped without handing the film over. I suppose you have to remember that VAT inspectors had been given previously unheard of powers, which didn't sit well with many business owners, my father being one of them! I know the fact they were empowered to enter your home at any time of the day or night, without the need for a warrant was one thing that particularly irked him; even the Police couldn't do that! Also, I suppose in an effort to establish their authority, some of the inspectors were a little over zealous, and seemed to start with the assumption that you were trying to fiddle them, an attitude which did not exactly endear them to my father! One young inspector even had the audacity to suggest that the level of detail dad applied to his book keeping was far greater than required for their purposes: not a wise move!

Anyway, somehow the photo ended up being made into a calendar, which was placed directly behind dad's office chair, in direct line for the person sitting opposite. Come the next VAT inspection, and the officer was duly placed where he would get the full benefit of dad's masterpiece. It was obvious that the calendar had caught the inspector's eye, so after a suitable time had passed for his curiosity to get the better of him, dad said "I see you like my calendar. It's from a firm I do a lot of unpaid work for, so they sent me that as a thank you!" As with Queen Victoria, he was not amused! It's perhaps not surprising dad didn't used to hit it off with them, as I don't think a sense of humour was exactly a prerequisite for the job. It has to be said that as the years have passed, the attitude of the VAT inspectors has mellowed somewhat, and they seem to now understand that along with every other thing you have to be an 'expert' on, in order to run a business, it is possible that you may make the odd genuine mistake when it comes to their particular subject. In any case, there are so many anomalies with VAT, that even they don't really know all the answers! A case in point was when I asked about how we should treat rabbit food for the purposes of VAT. It had always been accepted that if the rabbit was being reared for food, then anything fed to it could be sold as zero rated, and no VAT charged. However, if the rabbit were to be a pet, then its supper would be liable for VAT. The dilemma for me was how large a bag of food did a customer have to buy before it could be assumed that bunny was supper and not part of the family. After much deliberation, the official response was that as long as we did not 'hold the rabbit food out for sale as a pet food', to quote the exact response, we need not charge VAT! So, henceforth we always sold plain 'rabbit food', and never 'pet rabbit food'.

By this time the supply of pet foods had become quite a big part of the business. A lot of it went to our farming customers, who found it convenient to buy in bulk, and put it on their account, as you obviously needed a guard dog on the farm. Some of the products are still on sale today, such as Bonios and Spillers Shapes, but in those days most of them came in four stone bags (25 kilos, for any of you lucky enough not to remember the old weights!), and were stacked in the cellar of 'the old houses', (no's 19-21). This was all very well, apart from the fact that there were rather too many points of access for our little four legged friends. Now we're not just talking about the cute Tom & Jerry chaps here, we also played reluctant host to the 'Big Boys', and none came bigger than Fred! I know people are prone to exaggeration about the size of fish and rats, and other things, come to that, but trust me, Fred was a big boy. Suffice to say that I went to pick up what looked like a perfectly normal bag of Shapes one day, only to find it was completely empty, with just a gnaw hole in the base to identify the culprit. Worse still, Fred was not frightened of us, a feeling which was not reciprocated: one day he just sat there in a 12'' flower pot, staring me out, I don't mind admitting, I was petrified. I suppose my cause hadn't been helped by a customer who always had great difficulty speaking, as he had no voice box. He had somehow learnt how to speak after a fashion, using his diaphragm. I had always assumed he had been the victim of throat cancer, but he eventually told me the real cause. He had been mowing a dyke side with a scythe, when he encountered a rat; before he knew it the rat had locked onto his throat, and that was the end of his voice box. So as you can imagine, I was not too keen when it was decided that Fred had to go, but there again, neither was anyone else, as we were all aware of the voiceless man's story! It was agreed that Robert would bring in his air rifle, and he, Tony and I would go big game hunting, Holbeach style. Off we set, in order of timidity, Robert leading, Tony cowering behind him, and myself, quacking at the rear, one hand over my throat, a big stick in the other. We knew that Fred liked to spend much of his time in amongst the flower pots, so we sought him there first, but to no avail. I think it was to the great relief of us all that we never did encounter our quarry that day, and eventually it was decided to call in the local rat catcher, who distributed some pretty lethal stuff around the place. I still don't know if the poison killed him, or whether he ate one too many bags of Shapes, and just exploded, but we never did see Fred again, although he still lives on in my memory as vividly, and terrifyingly as ever!

Whilst all this empire building was going on, the poor teaching profession was trying its best to bestow me with at least a rudimentary education, although they had their work cut out! As is the case for most children, adults were always trying to tell me that my school years would be the best of my life, so make the most of them. I remember thinking that if these were to be the best years, then I wasn't looking forward to the rest of them much!

I wouldn't go as far as to say I hated school, it was just that there wasn't a lot of the curriculum that interested me.

My initial schooling took place at Holbeach Infants School, just a short walk from the shop, and as far as I can remember, this phase of the process passed without anything of note happening. Next stop was Holbeach County Primary School, where again I muddled through, doing just enough to be considered 'quite bright', whilst still not being exactly wowed by the whole three R's thing. As the 11 plus exams loomed, I realised that a decision would have to be made, as it was quite possible that if I put the effort in, I would most likely be capable of passing them, and going to the Spalding Grammar School. This scenario had two major draw backs. Firstly it would mean partaking of that culinary delight known as school dinners. Now, I was quite a faddy eater at that stage in my life, so this thought most definitely did not appeal. Secondly, Spalding was an eight mile bus ride away, which would

I ALWAYS THOUGHT I WAS QUITE BIG FOR MY AGE!......

mean a much longer day than if I opted for the George Farmer Secondary Modern School, in Holbeach, and longer school days wasn't what I was looking for.

When the results came through I had indeed failed to reach the required standard, so that was job done, as far as I was concerned: the only trouble was that I hadn't accounted for the interview scenario. In those days, if it was felt you were capable of passing the 11 plus exams, they sent you to an interview board, where you were assessed to see if you really were worthy of a Grammar School place. I will always remember being drilled on how to conduct myself, and to make sure I convinced them I wanted to be a teacher, or some other profession which would justify the placement. I took all this on board, and when grilled as to my future job aspirations, proceeded to tell them all the reasons why I wanted to....race cars for a living! This didn't seem to be quite the speech they were expecting, and I think my card was marked accordingly.

THE GEORGE FARMER SCHOOL, HOLBEACH. DEMOLISHED AND REPLACED WITH A NEW BUILDING IN 2013

Oh well, at least I had been honest with them, as by now I was in no doubt as to what I wanted to do with my life: in fact I had known ever since I went to my first motor racing meeting. A love of cars, and fast cars in particular was bred in me, and that was all there was to it. Even at that age I was thinking about when I could get my first car, and every penny I could muster went into the fund. So it was that I found myself under the stewardship of Joe Fathers at the good old George Farmer. As things turned out it really was for the best; a Grammar School place would have been a waste really. Joe was disliked by a good many people, mostly because he ruled with a rod of iron, and would not stand any breaches of discipline whatever: and his idea of a major breech was walking down a corridor two abreast, or wearing a watch, so woe betide you if you did something unspeakable, like running up the stairs. For my part I found him hard, but very fair, an opinion that I had plenty of opportunities to validate, as I seemed to spend a fair amount of my time in his office! Most of the visits were not really my fault. As previously mentioned, dad and I used to have our annual outing, and in my later school years this was usually a trip to the British Grand Prix practice day, which happened to be on a school Friday. Now, most parents would have avoided possible repercussions by writing a letter saying little Jimmy had Malaria that day, or some such tale. Not dad! He would pen a letter explaining exactly where we had been, and then await the inevitable fall out! Joe may have been formidable, but dad was no less so when he felt his was a just cause. Joe (I didn't actually call him that to his face at the time, you understand!) would summon dad and me to his office, and then sternly explain how there were very severe penalties for taking a child out of school

DREAMING OF BEING THE NEXT JIM CLARK.

without good reason. Dad would then counter that there could be few better reasons than a trip to Silverstone, and that I would learn far more there in a day than I ever would at school; a sentiment with which I fully concurred! At the end of it all dad would make it quite clear that he would continue to take me to Silverstone, and would continue to tell the truth about where I had been. Although Joe had to make all the right noises, and threaten me with being stripped of my prefect status, nothing ever came of it, and I think in reality he appreciated the honesty. My other visits were due to a long running feud with 'Bodmas' the maths teacher, but that's another story altogether; let's just say I was as stubborn as he was vindictive! Eventually the situation became untenable, and it was decided the only solution was for me to move to another class, which meant studying for CSE maths instead of the previous GCE's. This was a shame, as I was actually quite good at maths. Suffice to say I spent most of my two years in this new class helping out the teacher with some of the less able students, as compared to the GCE syllabus, the CSE one was, in all honesty, pretty simple.

Probably the only incident that should have earned me a visit to Joe went unpunished. As I said earlier, we used to have a good line in jokes, and one of them was a packet of little jelly sweets, which were virtually indistinguishable from the then popular 'Jelly Tots'. I say virtually, as they were actually slightly more domed; oh yes, and filled with very hot pepper! Our history teacher at the time, Mr Siddle, was not long out of teacher training college, and as such maybe a little more modern in his approach than the old hands. This made him a perfect victim, for if he caught you eating in class, instead of sending you to the main man, he would merely help himself to whatever it was you had. As I sat there, being careful to select the genuine article, I knew it would only be a matter of time before he pounced; and pounce he did, demanding I hand over the packet. He tipped a good sized portion of the sweets into his hand, before tossing them into his mouth in one fateful action! He knew almost instantly he had been had, but to his credit did a reasonable job of disguising the inferno that was now raging inside his mouth, although it was a while before he regained his composure. He never did ask me for any more sweets!

I HAD ALWAYS BEEN IMPRESSED BY THE LOTUS ELAN; I WOULD HAVE TO WAIT MANY MORE YEARS TO REALISE MY DREAM OF OWNING ONE.

Although my academic achievements were underwhelming, they were nothing compared to my sporting ones! I had the same interest and talent for ball sports as a horse does for knitting. Whilst football seemed merely pointless, cricket was to me downright dangerous!

I always recall Graham Hill being interviewed by (I believe) Michael Parkinson, and he was asked what was the most frightening experience he had ever had. Some tale of circulating Spa in the pouring rain, or having a rear wing break at 160 miles per hour was awaited, but instead Graham recalled a charity cricket match, in which he had been persuaded to take part, where, in his words, some maniac threw this missile at you, and all you had to defend yourself with was this stick! My sentiments entirely. I never have understood the point of a sport which goes on for 5 days, and yet there is still no winner. Surely one lot must have run up and down more times than the other, or hit the ball more times; there has to be some way of sorting a result out! A drag race only lasts about 5 seconds, but they still end up with a winner!

This lack of interest in 'normal' sports made me something of an oddity; I didn't even support a football team, which was thought

very strange. Back then, in the late 60's, motor racing was very much a minority sport, and was only just emerging from being the pursuit of wealthy amateurs. It was watched by a small number of enthusiasts, and received virtually no television or mass media coverage. There was thankfully one other pupil at school with whom I shared my interest, so at least I had an ally. Our shared indifference for football meant we would both end up being put in goal, where I suppose it was thought we would have the least influence on the outcome of the game, each side having a player of little or no use. As often as not we would wait until the teacher had gone to supervise another game, and then wander to the centre line, to have a chat about something of more interest to us. We figured that if neither team had a goal keeper that was fair enough! I eventually found out there was one other motor racing enthusiast at the school, a young female English teacher. That alone put her pretty high in my estimations, but when she arrived one day in a Lotus Elan, and a convertible one at that, she attained hero status. This was also the time when I saw my first Elan stripped bare! I was on the way to school one day, and there on a trailer, outside Lefley's Garage, was a brand new Lotus Elan, in kit form, which Neil Lefley had just collected. (Colin Chapman, the founder of Lotus, had realised that if you sold the car in kit form, the customer did not have to pay Purchase Tax on it! The only snag with this was that as any car sold in this way was supposed to be 'self built', it was illegal to supply instructions on how to assemble the collection of bits. However, with typical Chapman lateral thinking, he realised that there was no law against providing disassembly instructions! Problem solved, you just started from the back of the book, and worked forwards) I stood there for ages, trying to work out where all the bits would go, and thinking it was just the coolest car I had ever seen. And so it was that the Lotus bug slowly started eating its way into my consciousness, very stealthily, but very surely.
By the time I was 15 I had my first car, an Austin A30, which I used to drive as fast as it would go around my friend Richard's dad's stubble field. When the stubble had been ploughed in the car

would be brought back to the shop, where I would drive the girls in the next door hairdressers mad by testing the modifications I had made to it with a series of acceleration runs, down the short yard that adjoined the Woodmans property. I had a lot of fun with that car, until one day the brakes, which were never a strong point, suddenly seemed to have become much better. This improvement was however short lived, as the next thing I knew everything came to a very abrupt halt, and the driving position had become somewhat more reclined. When I eventually managed to force the door open, the cause was immediately obvious, as the propshaft was sticking into the ground, with the car now looking decidedly banana shaped! At least that explained the braking improvement, as the rear brakes were cable operated, and they had been the only things holding the car together, this extra load on them taking out all the slack, and therefore improving their effectiveness. Once they cried 'enough' it was literally game over.
It was also at this time that I was left in charge of the shop for the first time. Dad had to run my mother and Mrs Cauley to the station at nearby Spalding early one morning, and so I was given the responsibility of running the show until the staff arrived. I am not too sure as to the legality of the arrangement, as a lot of our early morning customers were land workers, who mostly wanted cigarettes, but I suppose as no link between serving cigarettes and cancer had been established at that time, it was deemed to be OK.
Another landmark in my 15th year was the first holiday without parents involved. My friend Martin (Mo) and I were dropped off at Skipton station for the start of a week's biking, staying at various youth hostels. The group leader soon assessed which members of the party needed supervision, and which could be left to their own devises a bit more. After a couple of days we were allowed to go off, together with a couple of like-minded lads, armed with an Ordinance Survey map, and were left to find our own route to that night's hostel. Being young and enthusiastic, this usually meant we would go over the top of any hill on route, rather than taking the easier route through the valley. We figured the long slog upwards

was well worth it for the thrill of the high speed dash down the other side. On one occasion we had built up an unadvisable amount of speed when we encountered a cattle grid. Up to this point we had either dismounted, or gone over them very slowly, as we were aware that a damaged wheel would not be too helpful this far from civilisation. However, on this occasion, it soon became obvious that slowing down to anything resembling a safe speed would not be possible in the distance remaining, (we had been going fast enough to overtake several cars on the descent!) and so a split second decision was required. Mo, who was leading, decided to bail out, and turned left, onto the grass, where he promptly hit a small hillock and performed a manoeuvre Evel Knievel would have been proud of. The sight of him flying through the air convinced me that taking a chance with the grid seemed the better option, so I held on tight and took it at full speed, followed by Chris and Ian. This was of course the best way to negotiate a cattle grid, as you merely skimmed over the top of it. Lesson learned; all cattle grids were taken at full speed thereafter, especially by Mo!

Back at school the time had come to think about a career. It had become clear even to me that it was unlikely any of the Formula 1 teams were going to come looking for me straight out of school, so I thought I had better try and do things the Graham Hill way. He famously went to work for Colin Chapman and then traded labour for drives, which enabled him to get noticed, and eventually reach Formula 1.I managed to amass sufficient O levels to be considered for an engineering apprenticeship, and Lotus were duly contacted, but were not setting any apprentices on at that time. Ford was however, and an interview was duly secured. We had to go to London, and an intensive examination and interview session ensued. I probably set my sights a bit too high by revealing that I really wanted to work at their Advanced Vehicles division, which prepared the competition cars, but either way, I didn't get a position. Although my racing ambitions were starting to look unlikely for the time being, one thing I was sure of; I wasn't going

to be a shopkeeper; no way! Despite all this uncertainty, it was decided that I should enrol for the Mechanical Engineering course at Kings Lynn Technical College, at least then I would be moving in the right direction. A position was also secured at a local garage, who claimed they wanted a young lad who could be properly educated, and eventually run the workshop. In those days garages tended to be somewhere you went to work if you had good practical skills, but were maybe not too academically gifted, and as such, many of the mechanics had learnt on the job, the idea of gaining formal qualifications being quite new at that level.
My first day didn't quite go as I had expected. I had been given to believe that I would learn the practical side of the job alongside an experienced fitter, and then attend college one day a week. What actually happened was the boss greeted me with the question "Do you know anything about Minis?" My response was that I knew a bit, meaning I knew where the engine was, and which way around it sat, that sort of thing. Without further ado he said "well, the one over there needs a new rear sub frame on it." And that was my first job, not that I had a clue how to go about it!
It quickly became apparent that I was not cut out for life in a workshop. I hated being cooped up inside all day, and although I loved tinkering with cars as a hobby, it soon lost its appeal as a daily task. I stuck it for three weeks, but I was becoming more and more miserable, and so threw the towel in. As the shop was still expanding, it was decided I should help out, until something more suitable came along. As for the college bit, I still carried on with that, and after the seeming irrelevance of most of the subjects at school, it was a real revelation. Here at last you actually applied mathematics in a practical way, there was a purpose to it all! I really thrived in this environment, and now I could see some point to it, actually applied myself a bit. This resulted in the rather bizarre situation of a chap who served dog biscuits ending up winning the college prize for Mechanical Engineering! I had intended just to do the first year, and then call it a day, but as the dream of working for a racing team was still niggling away at me,

and with pressure from my father and lecturers, I decided to do another year, and see where I was then.
By now the administrative side of the business had become so time consuming that even a workaholic like dad found it too much to achieve in just the evenings, so the momentous decision was made to close on a Sunday, so admin could also be done then. This was a move welcomed by mum, who relished the idea of being able to have at least one meal a week as a family, without the usual trips back and forth into the shop, or answering the phone. Great in theory, not quite so good in practice! I am sure there was indeed the odd Sunday when we would chomp our way through the roast beef and yorkshires unhindered, but there were many more where there would be the ominous sound of footsteps, followed by a knock on the back door. Invariably you would answer it to the request for a couple of boxes of rubber bands, or some such thing. Of course, you couldn't politely refuse them, certainly not if you wanted to retain their custom, so off you would go, and so that undisturbed lunch would remain as elusive as ever it was. It always perplexed me how somebody could plant daffodil bulbs in September, watch them grow for 6 months, see them reaching maturity, and yet still not realise that they would, at some point, need a rubber band to put around them, until lunch time on a Sunday!

Dad was always full of good ideas for promoting sales; some more effective than others. One which did work well involved the Galaxy chocolate bar vending machine, fixed to the wall near the entrance door. This was quite a crude, but effective device. You simply inserted your sixpence in the slot, turned the rotary knob, and out dropped your chocolate. The gimmick however, was that every eighth bar had a sixpence taped to it, so you stood a one in eight chance of getting your treat for nothing. This proved very popular with the local children, and the scheme ran for many years. Presumably inflation wasn't so rampant in those days, as I don't remember the price ever altering, or maybe that's just my rose tinted glasses clouding less endearing facts! Another campaign,

which wasn't quite so well received, was his proposed advert in the local paper promoting the Esso Blue brand of paraffin we used to sell. The strap line simply asked the question 'colour prejudiced?', and then went on to urge the reader to buy our blue paraffin, instead of the pink alternative. The paper was adamant that there was no way they could run such an inflammatory advert, and much to dad's disgust, flatly refused to print it!
Another innovation was the purchasing of Green Shield savings stamps and cigarette coupons. For those lucky enough not to remember such wonders, in the case of Green Shield stamps, you could obtain these with purchases, I seem to remember it was roughly twenty stamps to the pound, and when you had filled enough books, they could be exchanged for gifts. A lot of our customers were far more interested in cash than gifts, so dad would purchase the books at a percentage of the redemption value. Similarly, several brands of cigarette would contain a coupon, which could also be saved for gifts. Dad had a redemption scheme for those as well! I remember my tent, sleeping bag and no doubt other presents I wasn't aware of, coming courtesy of the 'ciggy coupons'.

Sometimes dads humour would be completely lost on people, which although it probably said more about him than them, was still a shame! On one such occasion we had gone to a local pub for something to eat, as was the custom (on just one of the nights!), when my mother was away visiting Vera. Some of the fixtures and fittings had seen better days, and we were seated next to a particularly unsightly hole in the carpet. When the young lady came to see if we wished to order anything, dad said "well we've just come to see the floor show really", whilst glancing at the offending piece of concrete. His razor sharp wit failed to elicit much in the way of appreciation from our hapless waitress, but, as was usual in such circumstance, he had a good chuckle, and to my shame, so did I.

Amidst all of this, the day was at last in sight which I had been counting down to for as long as I could remember; my seventeenth birthday. This event was significant for no other reason than it meant I could at last become a complete human being and obtain a driving licence. This momentous event had required detailed and meticulous planning, not to mention a fund raising campaign that had bordered on the fanatical. Research had suggested that I would need about £300 for the purchase of a Mini Cooper 'S' and a further £100 or so to insure it. Fortunately there were always 'piece work' jobs to be done at the shop, and none was more mind numbingly monotonous than pinning box sticks! In those days flowers were still sent to market in wooden boxes, and to stop them leaping around in the box, a wooden stick, with a 'pin' in each end, was fastened across the box, so holding them firmly in place. The 'box sticks' were made for us by a workshop in Boston, which provided work for people with learning difficulties, or other disabilities. They came to us tied in 100's, and then we would have to nail not 100, but 200, of these tiny pins into each bundle. Each stick was only about 7mm square, so it was all delicate stuff, and even with a pin hammer, it was very difficult to keep your fingers out of the target area. That really was hard earned money! My prized model car collection also had to go in order to fund the real thing. I used to set up stall outside the shop on a Saturday, and would then become the Arthur Daley of the model car world, accosting any likely looking punter as they tried to pass by. Seeing the prices some of these models fetch now, I maybe should have hung on to a few: but needs must.

Chapter 3 The New Employee

When I finally became an official J.W.Limming employee I suddenly had the princely sum of £7.13 at my disposal each week. After some tough negotiating it was determined that I should hand over £1.00 per week to my mother for board and lodgings, which I then calculated left me 13 pence blow money, if I was to meet my savings target by the time I was 17. I kept rigidly to my routine, and as soon as I was paid it was off to the bank to deposit my six pounds. By this time my friends were all mobile with mopeds or scooters, and I was feeling a bit left behind, but I never let this divert me from the main goal.

As the time drew nearer I booked my driving lessons and started looking seriously at the car and insurance situation. After many phone calls, it became very clear that I would not be starting my motoring career in a Mini Cooper 'S'. Nobody would even consider insuring me, let alone give me a price! Eventually I found a company willing to take me on for a less powerful Mini Cooper at £70.50, so that was what it would have to be. The driving lessons duly commenced, and after six my instructor felt I was ready for my test, which I had always assumed would be a formality, seeing as how I was a budding racing driver.

Come the day and we chugged around Spalding for a bit, and then I sat there waiting to be awarded the freedom of the road, only to be told I had failed; and worse still, for going too slowly! Or, as the examiner put it, not making sufficient progress. My one fear had been that I would go too quickly, but my paranoia had led me to do the opposite. Worse still, I would have to wait over a month to get another test. This really did knock the stuffing out of me, I had been dreaming of this day for so long, and then I had messed the job up.

A couple of weeks later I finally saw a Mini Cooper advertised at a price I could almost afford, at a garage in Dersingham. It was six years old, and had obviously been well cared for. The asking price was £355, but luckily for me the garage had not been in business long, and was keen for a quick turnover of stock, so a spot of tenacious haggling eventually secured it for £305. I was so proud of my new acquisition: the only problem now was that I could only drive it under supervision, which was really frustrating. I would harass anybody I knew who was qualified to accompany me; and one such person was poor old Clive. Off we set, me keen to show off the capabilities of my girl, he to survive the ordeal. As we rounded one bend I was surprised to see a 'T' junction loom up unannounced. There next followed a lesson on what happens if you brake sharply with two wheels on tarmac, and the other two on a load of loose road chippings! The car turned sharp left, and into the adjacent field. No problem I thought, we will just cut across the corner of the field, and rejoin the road. Which indeed we would have; had there not been a drainage ditch on the projected exit route! As we hung there, upside down in our seat belts, I thought things couldn't get much worse. Wrong again; for who should be at the house we went to for help, but the local Bobby. He wandered down, had a look, and promptly booked me for driving without due care and attention!

So there I was, 48 days into my driving career, having failed my driving test, wrecked my car and gained three points on my licence! Not an auspicious start. And I had still to face my father. The police officer gave me a lift home, and I asked him to relay the news, as I thought it might soften the blow a bit. I expected an explosion, followed by a deserved telling off and lecture. What I got was the complete opposite. Dad just looked up from his work and said he was not in the least bit surprised; and that was it. I think he was well aware how crest fallen I was, and realised that no further confirmation of my stupidity was required! The only bright spot in all of this was that I did pass my test at the second attempt, 10 days later. As every penny had been spent on acquiring the car, there was no money left for a repair, so I had to run around in the firm's Mini truck, until I had amassed sufficient funds for my pride and joy to be repaired.

A year after my first accident I had another, more pleasant one; for

on May 3rd 1973 I met what was to become my first 'proper' girlfriend, although neither of us knew it at the time! I had gone round to invite an old school friend, who had been away in Holland studying, to my 18th birthday party, but was somewhat distracted by his rather attractive sister. Naturally it was only polite to invite her to the party as well.
As with most 18th birthday parties, the consumption of alcohol somewhat exceeded sensible limits, which was perhaps not the best state in which to try and persuade Alice (as I now knew she was called!) that I would be good boyfriend material. However, despite what was apparently a rather unusual 'chat up' approach, she agreed to see me again, so I guess that says something about both of us!
In those early days there seemed to be even more week left at the end of the money than there is now, even though the Mini could be filled with petrol for £1.50, and there was 4p change out of a pound for 6 pints of Lager! So, any opportunity to supplement my earnings was quickly grasped. One good earner for me was the delivery of bulbs for a merchant, who used to set up shop in a local grower's sheds, and then ship bulbs back to his native Cotswolds region. We used to do the deliveries for him, so last thing in the day I would load our trusty Volkswagen truck up with a ton of assorted daffodil and tulip bulbs, ready for a silly o'clock start the next morning. I would usually be at my first drop in Stratford upon Avon at 7am, and then would embark on a scenic trip of the Cotswolds, taking in such places as Broadway, Evesham and Stow-on-the-Wold. By the time I returned home it was usually about 7pm, with anywhere up to 350 miles having been covered. There would sometimes be two or three runs a week, so good for the bank balance, if not the social life.

At the start of 1974 I moved off the bottom rung of the ladder at work, as Tony Machin left the company; again! He had been one of the early employees, but had left to take up a factory job, prior to getting married, in order to earn more money. He rejoined us, but

then had the chance of a management position, so moved on again. This quasi promotion didn't really change much on a day to day basis, nor as far as I can remember, on a financial one, but at least it was a step in the right direction.
Being one of the more junior employees, but at the same time the boss's son wasn't always an easy situation to be in. On the one hand you were one of the workers, but on the other you obviously had very close ties with the management, and as such you were treated with a certain amount of suspicion. How much of what was said would find its way back to dad? There were times when my 'special relationship' came in useful however, like when they wanted an increase in holiday allowance from two weeks to three. It was decided that I was in the best position to deliver 'our' request, and so we all congregated in the kitchen to put forward our case. Dad was genuinely taken aback by the request: what would we do with a whole three weeks off? Surely we would be bored to tears? He could see that everybody was quite resolute, and as three weeks had been the norm for quite some time, acquiesced.
By now I had given up on a career in motor sport, having been turned down by BRM in Bourne, although I was still at college, another prize leading dad to suggest I should at least complete the full course. I would soon be the most mechanically adept dog biscuit salesman in Lincolnshire! I managed to find an outlet for my motor sport aspirations in the form of East Elloe Motor Club, who organised road rallies and autotests. The now repaired Mini Cooper was kitted out with spot lights and a sump guard, and accompanied by Alice's brother in the hot seat; we would tear around the local lanes, having great fun. Another part of motor club life were the inter club quizzes, held throughout the region. I remember on one occasion the question came up 'What is the name of Eric Carlsons wife?' The answer he was looking for, of course, was Pat Moss, (less well known sister of racing legend, Sir Stirling Moss, and a keen competitor in her own right) but out of devilment, I gave the answer as Mrs Carlson! The quiz master pondered the answer for a few seconds, and then said, 'Well it's not the answer I

was looking for, but I suppose I will have to give it to you, if only for your cheek!'

We are not really what you would call a close family, and with the restricted social life already mentioned, there were several relatives, particularly the more distantly related ones, who I hadn't even met. One such I discovered when I went to be measured for my first 'adult' suit, at the local branch of Burtons. Having done all the usual tape measure stuff, (36'' inside leg, hence why the suit had to be made!) the chap asked me for my name, and upon hearing it he looked a little taken aback; had my reputation already spread as far as Spalding? Apparently not; his last customer had also been a Limming, but not the dwarf 6'3'' version he had before him now; this one was 6'7'' tall, and about twice as wide as me! Upon further investigation, this turned out to be Bob Limming, and our grandfathers were brothers. It would be some years later before we actually met, and we did then keep in touch. I will never forget the sight, many years later, of Bob standing next to Geoff Capes at his 50th birthday party: there are not too many people that fill more cubic feet than Geoff, but Bob does!

In the summer of 1974, dad rather surprisingly announced that he was thinking of selling up. He asked me where I saw my future, as by now I was an integral part of the business. I said I was happy for him to cash in his chips, and enjoy a well earned rest; it might even push me into getting a proper job. Although in his early sixties by now, I had always imagined he would carry on as long as he could; after all, the business was his life; what would he do with himself? It turned out he had been approached by one of our suppliers, who were looking for an acquisition, but the real motivation for giving up his baby wouldn't become clear until the next year, when events took a dramatic turn. (Oh; the suspense!).
By now I was of an age where I had my own opinions about where the business should be heading, and naturally they did not always accord with those of dad. Our differing opinions came to the fore

when a local flower grower had two of his boilers fail late in the November of '74, and he desperately needed new ones collected from the factory in Larkhall, Scotland. He asked dad if he would send our truck up to fetch them, with me as driver of course. He ran the idea of what he thought the job was worth by me, but I thought it was way too cheap; after all the man had glasshouses full of flowers, worth thousands of pounds, which would probably all be lost without heat, so that had to be worth a bit. I suggested a price of £40, which dad reckoned he would never pay. After a bit of a debate, dad decided the best idea was for me to take the job on, and he would hire me the truck for £10.00! I worked out that the round trip would be about 600 miles, say £7 for fuel, less a days lost pay, this would still leave me with about £20 profit; more than I would earn in a week normally.
I rang the grower, who was more than happy to accept my price of £40 for the job, and so off I set the next morning for Scotland, with the intention of loading up the boilers, and heading straight back. I duly arrived at the factory, only to be told that one of the boilers had failed its pressure test, and was having to be re-done. As time ticked by it was obvious that this was going to be a very long day. By late afternoon I was starting to get concerned, and went to enquire on progress. Even worse news; the boiler would not now be ready until tomorrow. This presented something of a problem, as I didn't have enough money to go to a B & B, having taken just enough with me for food and petrol, with very little in the way of a contingency fund.
I suddenly felt very alone, and a long way from home. I drove to a pub to find something to eat, and was soon picked out by the regulars as being a bit 'foreign'. A group of them befriended me, and by the end of the evening we were great mates, if only because they saw me as the chance of a lift home! After dropping my new best friends off, I returned to the factory to bed down for the night. Well I say bed down; trying to fit 75 inches of me across about 65 inches of Volkswagen seats was not conducive to a good night's sleep, but there again, I was so cold, with just a coat draped over

me, that the sound of my teeth chattering would probably have woken me up anyway! For somebody who despises the cold, this was not a happy situation. My humour was not improved the next morning, when the security man told me I could have used the bed in the sick room, had he have known my predicament.
Anyway, lunch time came and went, with still no sign of the boiler. The prospect of another night in chez VW did not appeal, so I thought I had better chivvy the job up a bit, and went off to seek some answers. The response that they would not have time to complete the job before home time was not the one I was looking for, but some impassioned dummy spitting persuaded them to work until the boiler was finished. So it was that I set off on a freezing November night, at 6.00pm, to head back south. Any idea of making rapid progress was thwarted by a sign saying simply 'roads not salted'. The truck was far from stable as it was, the boilers being both tall and heavy, so I was on tenterhooks; going as fast as I dare, without risking a visit to the scenery. As the miles ticked by, I noticed that there seemed to be a distinct lack of petrol stations, or at least ones which were open. As the needle on the fuel gauge sank further into the reserve section, I started to envisage another character building night spent shivering in the truck. Just as desperation was setting in, I spotted a sign pointing to 24 hour petrol, just off the A1. I had never been so pleased to part with money, as I fed my pound note into that machine!
The rest of the trip passed without incident, and I eventually crawled into the haven of my bed at about 1.00am. That bedroom of mine had never seemed so warm!
The profits from my haulage exploits, plus a wage increase to the princely sum of £20, meant I could start to consider a replacement for the Cooper. I rather fancied the idea of a Triumph GT6 Mk 2, a sort of a poor man's E Type Jaguar. After searching the adverts, a deal was eventually done with a chap from Yarmouth, for a white example, with black sunroof. The new acquisition proved less suitable for rallying than the Cooper, but was probably more to Alice's liking. As for the Cooper, it was sold on to Tony, Alice's

brother, who also rolled it, making me very grateful a proper job had been done on repairing it after the first inversion! For me the novelty of the GT6 soon wore off, and I started to hanker after an immaculate Mini Cooper 'S' Mk3, which was often parked in town. I knew this would be a good investment, and eventually persuaded the owner to part with it for £800. The GT6 was sold for £550, a profit of £50, which was a good result after just 5 months.

We were now selling quite a lot of solid fuel, and if you bought a twenty ton load, out of season, the price was much better. The trouble was, we didn't really have the space for that amount in the stores; or so we thought. Dad being dad, the small matter of having no where to put it would not stop him actually ordering it. So it was that a lorry duly turned up with 800 bags needing a new home. A human chain was formed, decanting bags firstly into the back room, and then, to the thin passages further forward. It was so dark and cramped down there in the cellar, that it felt like you were putting the coal back in the mine! This was in the days of 'Little Robert', a lad who stood not much over five feet tall, and weighed about the same as a bag of crisps. He tried manfully to do his bit, but if his predecessor in the chain dispatched the bag with a little too much oomph, he would receive it, and then continue on down the passage with it, unable to arrest its momentum. The next person along would then have to deal with both Robert and bag! We certainly didn't have to go to the gym, that's for sure.

Things had now reached the point where dad felt he could actually justify a holiday, and a trip back to the part of the world he had visited during his war years seemed like a good idea. I say he, as mum was not keen on boats, and certainly not ones that were going where this one did! You see, dad had decided on the Eagle, which was really more of a ferry to Tangiers. Part of the appeal was that the route included the Bay of Biscay, which was notoriously rough, something he loved. Sure enough, when they got to the Bay, conditions were perfect for him, and as most of the passengers took to their beds, he was there, having found a forward facing porthole, recording the whole event on his cine camera. Just looking at the footage afterwards was enough to make you queasy! Meal times were also a source of amusement for him. It would be fair to say the dining room was sparsely populated, and even a good proportion of the crew had been laid low. His take on the situation was to order soup, just for the entertainment value of seeing how much of it was left, once the waiter had zigzagged his way across the room with it.

Later that year, the ever increasing burden of bureaucracy, meant that we had to now have an approved person, in order to continue selling loose vegetable seeds. This involved completing a course at the Ministry of Agriculture in Cambridge. The exam process was pretty straight forward, although it amused me that when I asked why parsnips were not included in the germination tables, I was told it was because the rest of Europe does not recognise them as a vegetable; which is strange really, because they don't exactly look like a toothbrush! So, one of the most difficult seeds, from a germination point of view, had no standards attached to it, just because it wasn't grown in other parts of Europe. This was the start of the rot, as far as self governance was concerned! As I now held the lofty title of Approved Seed Sampler, dad wrote to the ministry to enquire if I was allowed to call myself an ASS! Unsurprisingly, no reply was forthcoming. As with all such things, this new system involved paperwork, and we now had to record each sale of vegetable seeds. This did not go down too well with the old boys, who had been coming for their 2 ounces of whatever for many years. (I maybe ought to explain that an 'old boy' is actually a man of post retirement age, as a lot of non locals get very confused by the term!) None of them was more damning in their criticism of the new system than Mr Frankish, who thought the whole thing ridiculous, which of course it was. Knowing his volatile nature, I just couldn't resist temptation the next time he came in; this time for a bag of salt. I went and fetched a bag from the shelf, and then, as I handed it to him, said "you will just have to sign the salt book

Mr Frankish.'' ''The salt book?'' he enquired. ''Yes'' I said, ''they have decided it can be dangerous, so you have to sign the salt book for it now.'' Well; he went off like a bottle of pop, and it was some time before I could squeeze sufficient words in to convince him it was a wind up! He did eventually see the funny side of it, but it was quite a while before his blood pressure returned to a safe level. One thing I find strange about seed customers, is how often they ask for enough seed for a row. Err, how long a row?! When you pose this question, many of them just look at you gone out, as though you should have an intimate knowledge of their garden and know just how long a row would be, and how much seed would be required for said row!

Ever since dad had mentioned selling up, there seemed to be something bothering him; he no longer seemed to have the enthusiasm for the business, and his whole demure was more serious and introverted. The reason for this became all too apparent in November '75, when he dismissed one member of staff for 'failing to correctly register amounts of money tendered by customers', and then very soon after, a long serving, and trusted member of staff tendered his resignation.
It transpired that a customer had noticed that when a certain member of staff served him, the full amount of the sale was not rung up on the till. He alerted dad to this, and once the suspicions had been confirmed he confronted the member of staff with his findings. To dad's amazement, he denied any wrong doing, and produced a note book, listing details of the other party's indiscretions! Obviously they both had to go, but, with what I think was a lack of judgement on his part, dad was persuaded not to involve the police, one of the miscreants claiming the shock would kill his mother if she knew what he had done. So, at a stroke we had lost two key members of staff, and the reason for dad's seeming personality change became crystal clear. The financial strain on the business over this period had been considerable, and it had pushed it to the brink of collapse. Dad never did recover from

this on a personal level. He felt he had been betrayed by people he trusted implicitly; the easy going, fun loving side of him had been destroyed. I also think the lack of closure; by not having brought a prosecution, meant the whole thing just kept playing on his mind. I decided after this experience, that if I was ever put in the same situation, I would make sure I pursued the perpetrators all the way to prison if possible.

Chapter 4 Rising Through The Ranks.

After the dust had settled from the clear out, dad was in need of a new shop manager. I may have been a bit young for the position, at 20 years old, but I had been around the business for a lot of years, and hopefully would also be trustworthy! I took up the position on December 1st 1975, and would now earn £30 clear a week! Dad still had his hand firmly on the tiller, but at least I could now have an influence on the day to day things, like which items we stocked. With the move into management came the need for more training. Another college spell was not an option, (I had eventually finished my other course by the way, emerging as a qualified Motor Technician.) so it was fortunate for me that a retail training course started on television around this time. Or at least that's what I thought it was! The programme was 'Open All Hours', staring Ronnie Barker, and apparently it was meant to be a comedy! Ronnie's portrayal of Arkwright, whilst being hilarious, also struck a chord with many a small business owner. Maximising the amount of money you relieve each customer of is something every shopkeeper strives for, and if you can sell them something they didn't even know they needed, then that is a real bonus. Arkwright may have taken the technique to extremes, but the whole thing was more real than many viewers may have thought!

I don't think any of us who were close to dad realised just how much the previous year's events had affected him. He was always quite difficult to read, keeping his emotions well under control, and not being one to unburden himself on others. We were graphically reminded of just how much stress he had been under; when in March '76 he suffered a heart attack. There is of course no proof whatever that what had happened the previous year caused it, but I would take a lot of convincing that it was not a significant contributory factor.
A spell in hospital was followed by a period of recuperation at

Mundesley, in Norfolk. I think this gave him time to reflect, and he realised that maybe he needed to plan for the future of both his son, and his business.
On my 21st birthday I paid him a visit, and to my surprise I learnt he had made me a director of the company. (We had gone limited, on the advice of our accountants, at the time of 'the troubles'.)
For mum and me, having dad incapacitated made us realise just how much of the business he carried in his head. We had what you might call a steep learning curve, and had to fumble our way along as best we could. As he started to feel better, dad became keen to get back into the swing of things, and returned to the fray late in May.
Upon his return he was greeted by many well wishers, as he walked about the town; one of which was the local undertaker. In typical style, Franks "good to see you about again Jack." elicited the retort, "Yes; better luck next time!" This pretty much summed up his whole attitude to what had happened, and once back in the fray; he certainly didn't do too much to help his recovery. The lifestyle

TONY & I, AFTER UNLOADING A LORRY FULL OF PEAT. NOT THE BEST BIT OF STACKING. I WILL ADMIT!

changes suggested by his doctor, including working less and giving up the foods he liked, met with the response that if that was the way he had to live his life, then he might as well be dead. As the place hadn't gone to rack and ruin during his absence, dad decided that maybe I wasn't completely reckless, and let me do a bit more decision making: one of which was to buy bales of peat in direct from the producer, instead of buying them in small quantities locally. This seemed a good idea, right up until the time they actually arrived; all two-hundred-and-twenty-five of them! Many of the 'old boys' who came in the shop were deformed and doubled up by a life spent humping sixteen stone (about 100 kilos) bags of wheat about, now we were about to get some idea of what that was like! The lorry driver would slide the bales down to you, and then you would have to stagger down the yard, and stack them six high. Depending on how wet they were, the payload could be anywhere between ten and twelve stone. Featherweight in 'old boy' terms, but heavy enough to give me problems in later life. The only consolation was that the more knackered you became, the nearer to the lorry the stack got. By the time we had finished, Tony and I had the appearance of someone who had gone a bit mad with the fake tan, and had to have a good soak in the bath, before we were fit to resume duties in the shop!
With each passing year there seemed to be yet more legislation and restriction, employment being a particular minefield. So when the opportunity came to attend a free (we liked that bit!) employment seminar, we thought we had better go and get genned up. Most of the content had you pinching yourself to keep awake, but the summing up was memorable. In the presenter's opinion, the prospective employee most likely to cause you grief was a single, pregnant, fifty-eight year old woman, with five children and from an ethnic minority! I really must keep my eye open for that one.
One of the main drawbacks with shop work for a young man with a social life was that it involved working Saturdays. The thing that most people take for granted: a weekend off, doesn't exist for most people working in retail, something which has become even worse

over the years, with Sunday working now regrettably the norm: to the assured detriment of family life. Despite his aversion to time off, dad realised that normal people might quite like the idea of an occasional weekend, so he devised a system where during the quieter winter months, instead of your normal half day off in the week, once a month you would work all of the week days and have the weekend off. Of course, once everybody had become used to this there was no going back, and we have had the luxury of a weekend off a month ever since.

When you were working a 'normal' week, the truncated weekend had to be maximised: which would sometimes mean finishing work at 6pm, grabbing a bite to eat, driving up to Grimsby to compete on an 'all nighter' rally until about 7am, another quick bite to eat, and then back home in time to organise an Autotest for the Motor Club, another bite, perhaps a quick wash and change, then off to the pub! You tended to be ready for your bed, come Sunday night!

One consequence of 'the troubles' was dad having to part with his beloved Triumph 2,000, for a Hillman Hunter, in order to cut costs. He was never happy with this gutless wonder of British engineering, and as soon as the company had recovered a bit he was on the lookout for another 2,000. An estate version duly arrived, resplendent in green and sporting the legend 'Cognito' on the panel just in front of the bonnet. As intended, this used to arouse peoples curiosity, and when they enquired as to its significance, he would just reply "Oh it's nothing really; I just like travelling in-cognito!" His sense of humour never did improve a lot!

Around the same time I also had a life changing car experience. It started with an ordinary Saturday night, which as often, meant a party at somebody's house: there was very little 'organised' entertainment out in the sticks, so we used to make our own. There was a friend who had moved away from the area, but who would turn up from time to time. This was one of those times, and when we all saw his new set of wheels the male fraternity took on a distinctly green hue, me more than most! There in the drive stood a

beautiful, red over white Lotus Elan Sprint Drop Head. It was as though fate had intervened again, they always seemed to keep cropping up in my life. Until now Lotus had just been something to admire from afar, unobtainable for someone like me, a fantasy, a pin up with wheels. But this was different, this was a mate, and that meant I could actually get to experience my fantasy; if only from the passenger seat! Poor old Pete had every man and his dog wanting a ride, (well, maybe not the dog!) but at last I got a chance. Unbelievable! The way it accelerated, the way it rode, the sound of the exhaust sans roof, but more than all this, the way it went around corners. Until now I had thought my Mini was a fairly handy bit of kit, but this was something else all together; a completely different league, like comparing a cart horse with a stallion. By the time we arrived back at the party I just knew I had to have an Elan. I had no idea how I was going to pay for it, but there was no way back now, I was hooked. From now on my already strict spending allowance would be cut even further, and any chance of overtime would be grabbed with both hands.
One event during this time did prompt the temporary suspension of my austerity drive: a fellow employee and I had the chance to go to a product launch at a swish hotel in Nottingham. Dad was very generous, and gave us £40.00 expenses money, with the instruction that as long as we turned up on time for work the next morning, he was not bothered how we chose to spend it. After the presentation we decided to retire to the hotel bar, where the surroundings were quite a bit different to what we were used to; as were the prices! Lager at £1.10 a pint came as a bit of a shock, as it was about four times what we were used to paying! Still, we were on expenses, so we invested in quite a few of them! Late into the evening we were even joined by Matt Monroe, after his performance at the local theatre. As night passed into early morning, it became clear that neither of us would be driving anywhere, and we decided to try and book a room for the night, even though we had no overnight gear with us. Looking back, it must have seemed strange to the reception staff that there were two men, who had obviously had a

couple of beers, wanting to get a room together, without so much as a sponge bag between them! If they did find us strange, we certainly didn't pick up on it, so perhaps this was just normal for a Tuesday night in Nottingham. After the previous night's indulgencies we were not too keen the next morning, and despite my best efforts behind the wheel, we didn't quite make it into work on time. Dad was really quite good about it, and not too many questions were asked!

After nearly four years together, Alice and I decided to go our own separate ways. The relationship had reached the stage where you either had to go to the next level, that is to say, get married; or call it a day. Neither of us was ready for the former, as Alice wanted to further her career in accountancy, and I felt there were still a lot of things I needed to get out of my system: I still hadn't been to the Monaco Grand Prix, nor owned that Elan I so wanted. We remained good friends, but at least for now, that was it. We parted on very good terms, and agreed that if we didn't find anyone we liked better, we could always find each other again, further into life's journey.

I think once you have had a relationship like Alice and I, which really works, it stands you in good stead for the future: you may still need time to know if a person could be right for you, but at least you can tell very quickly if they are not!

In July of the same year dad suffered a second heart attack. This was very worrying, as one may be just a warning, but two is getting a bit serious. This one really knocked the stuffing out of him, and he did slow down a lot afterwards, letting mum and I do a lot more of the day to day stuff. He was also conscious that he was nearing pension age, and he really wanted to get some of the money back he had paid in over all those years! There was even talk of retiring to Clacton, a place we had holidayed, pre shop! Dad's setback rather took the shine off another event, as after having been like a tight version of Scrooge, and managing to sell the Cooper S for a £65 profit, I actually achieved my ambition and bought a Lotus Elan Sprint! It may not have been the tidiest one I had ever seen, and the orange over white paint scheme definitely didn't do it any favours, but after much haggling the price came down to £1,300, and that just happened to be all the money I had! I was that thrilled with it that any little foibles were overlooked, and it has to be said that in its 'as bought' state, there were quite a few foibles!

MY FIRST LOTUS, AN ELAN SPRINT DHC, AFTER I HAD REPLACED THE ORIGINAL GARISH ORANGE PAINT SCHEME!

Still greater involvement in the business after dad's second 'do', meant I started taking a keener interest in the finances, which were not great, thanks to the drain put on them by events the previous year. One thing which came to my attention was that we were paying an enormous amount of water rates on the Park Hall warehouse. This seemed very strange, as there was no water connected: no toilets, (difficult without water!) and therefore no sewage to dispose of. I called in at the local water authority's offices, to enquire as to why the rates were so high, and was informed it was because they were disposing of our rain water. I said "OK., that's fine, but there were 214 dry days last year, (or some such figure, plucked out of thin air!) so I will need a rebate for those". Well; this sent the poor girl scurrying off to have a confab with her supervisor, where upon they decided that this wouldn't be possible. Not one to be dissuaded, I then suggested a compromise, where I would pay a reasonable amount for draining the rain water, but as they were only providing a partial service, with no water or sewerage, common sense dictated that I should only pay partial rates. I put forward a figure of about half, which I thought more than fair. This olive branch was also dismissed, and it became clear, that as with most large organisations, common sense was not going to get a look in. Still undeterred, and by now starting to feel the onset of the Harrison stubborn streak, I enquired what would be the scenario if I cut the drain pipes and installed water butts. This curved ball seemed to really throw them, but it was eventually decided that as there would then be no service at all being provided, there would be no rates at all to pay. At last we had arrived at a solution which seemed acceptable to both parties, so the water butts were duly installed, and that was the end of the saga.

As I was now unattached I decided to join the local Young Farmers club. This seemed like a good move, as not only was there an active social side to the club, there also seemed to be quite a good crop (well, it was a farmers club!) of girls, several of whom were also unattached. I was going to Donington Park circuit to watch some racing one Sunday, and asked one of the girls if she would like to accompany me for the day. She accepted the invitation, and obviously must have reported where she was going, and more importantly, with whom and in what, to her father. Obviously he was very protective towards his daughter, and was worried about her going with me in this fast car. As he knew my father, he decided to ring him for some reassurance as to the safety of his girl. Not a good idea! Dad immediately saw the opportunity for a wind-up, and offered comfort by explaining that we would complete the journey that quickly, there wouldn't be time to have an accident! Not quite what he wanted to hear. Anyway; we eventually set off, after a lecture from the girl's father about the perils of driving too fast, and duly arrived at Donington. We walked around to what I considered a good spot, at the top of the Craner Curves, and

awaited the start of the race. After quite a while I noticed there seemed to be very little enthusiasm for the on track action from my companion. I started to wonder if this had been such a good idea for a first date, (or indeed any date!) and enquired if she was enjoying the racing. She looked a bit sheepish and then said "Well actually, I can't see anything". Stupidly I had completely overlooked the fact that she was the best part of a foot shorter than me, and all she could see was the tops of the driver's helmets, as the cars sped by! Once we had found a vantage point where she could actually see over the safety wall, she became far more enthused, much to my relief. All was now well with my date, but I don't think I was quite such a hit with her father when we arrived home. The trouble is I have inherited a bit of dad's propensity for winding people up: and here was a prime candidate! As soon as we entered the house he was keen to point out an antique occasional table in the hall. Now, even somebody with my scant knowledge of antique furniture could see that this was a really nice quality piece, but the temptation was just too much when he went on to tell me how old it was. I kept as straight a face as I could, and in my best sympathetic voice, said "Never mind, I'm sure it will do until you can afford a new one". Not quite the confirmation of his good taste he was looking for I fear, but at least his wife saw the funny side!
November 13th 1977 was a day which would change my life completely; as dad's ticker finally gave up the fight, and he passed away peacefully in bed; aged just 64 years old. So; he never would get to collect that pension he was so looking forward to. I doubt he ever would fully have retired, as he was the business, and the business was him, but even so I thought it was a shame that he and mum would now never get the chance to actually enjoy a bit of time together away from the work environment.
I think it was the mark of the man that the church was packed at his funeral with all the friends he had made over the years, some of whom had travelled long distances to be there. Things would never be the same again. Suddenly it was just mum and me; and at just 22 years of age, that was a bit scary.

Chapter 5 At The Helm

Once we had come to terms with the loss of dad, mum and I took stock of our situation. I often think back to that time when people say "It's alright for you, you were handed this business on a plate." What I was actually handed was a bank account which was on its overdraft limit, a list of creditors, most of whom were well overdue for payment, as money was so tight, and a ledger full of debtors, some of whom thought we were a cheaper alternative for credit than the bank! My only attributes were that I was young, naive and had a Lotus habit to feed.

One of the first things we did was rationalise the way we invoiced goods, to cut down the amount of book work. Instead of issuing an invoice for every transaction, we just had one ticket, and added to it throughout the month, thus saving a lot of administration. The late payment situation also needed addressing, so I wrote to all the stragglers, explaining that we could no longer extend credit for the periods dad used to allow, and in future invoices would be due for payment in 30 days. Most customers realised that they had been on a good thing, and complied with the new payment regime, those that didn't would receive a couple of polite reminder letters, followed by a County Court Order. It's surprising how word gets around about that sort of thing, and although it may have offended a few people, the vast majority could see it was just sound business practice, and our debtor situation became a lot better.

I do find it strange that people assume being 'gifted' a business sets you on the path to certain success and riches. I have always maintained that if you were to give three people £100,000, and send them off into the world, three years later one would be a millionaire, another would still have the same amount as they had started with, while the third would have squandered the lot. Being given the tools to be successful is no guarantee you will actually achieving that goal.

It is also quite scary how many times that old adage about the first generation starting it, the second building it and the third loosing it

comes to fruition. Thankfully I am only the second generation; unless you count granddad Limming of course....Whoops!
Once the company was on a firm footing we set about expanding. At that time there were still a lot of flower growers in the area, who all needed packaging materials. We had always been in the market, but only in relatively small way. Fortunately for me there was a likeminded manager, Don Rudd, working for my flower box supplier, and he was instrumental in helping me grow this side of the business. He gave me the prices I needed to compete, and I did the leg work to secure the orders. Other alliances were formed with various suppliers, and before long we were a major player in the local horticultural sundries market.
As for the retail side of things it also grew, making the compromised layout of the premises more and more of a pain. A typical scenario would be a customer wanting a dog bed. You would have to go out of the front door of the shop, run up three flights of stairs, into number 19, select as many dog beds as you could manage, stagger back down those same three flights of stairs, back into the shop, and then present your offerings to the customer. They would then say "Oh, I'm not sure I want a wicker one now, have you got any plastic ones?" and so the whole process would be repeated, until hopefully, you found one the customer liked. On a busy Saturday you would make the trip more times than I would care to remember. For the time being that is how it had to be, but it was obvious that at some point things would have to change. As mentioned, dad had plans drawn up for a new shop in the early 70's, but he was never able to raise the finance to turn them into reality, so it would be a fitting tribute to create something of which he would have been proud.
In his will, dad had left me a bit of money. This presented me with several options: I could squirrel it away in a Building Society, buy some Premium Bonds, or even buy some shares. All very sensible. Unfortunately, not long before I received my bequest, I had been taken for a ride in local tuning firm Vegantune's demonstrator Elan, fitted with one of the engines they used in Prodsports racing.

This thing absolutely flew, and it became a foregone conclusion where my money was going to end up! Once equipped with its new motor my Elan was transformed; if I couldn't kill myself in this thing I just wasn't trying!
Not long after the new motor was run in, I had a chance to stretch its legs a bit. Alice's brother Tony and I were travelling back from an exhibition on the A1, (the exhibition wasn't on the A1 you understand, that was us and the car!) when we came upon a Jensen Interceptor, which like ourselves, was making good progress. The road was empty, and we both ended up travelling at a speed appropriate to the prevailing conditions, which judging by the way the Jensen started popping and spitting, was probably something it hadn't done for some considerable time. It sounded like it had indulged in a particularly vicious curry the previous night! Now, it is fair to say that the chap in the Jensen did not expect to still have my girl for company at the velocity he reached, bearing in mind he had 6.3 litres of V8 under the bonnet, and we had a puny 1.6 litre engine. As we approached traffic, he responsibly eased his pace considerably. We drew along side, lowered a window, as did our friend in the Jenson, and Tony nonchalantly said "right; everything is up to temperature now, so we can open her up a bit more." Our new friend just looked aghast, waved his hand dismissively, and off we went, leaving him to ponder what ever sort of roller skate he had just encountered.

As is the way of things, many of my gang of mates were now in quite serious relationships, all of which made it more difficult to organise the 'lads' days out' we used to go on. This came to a head one Sunday, when we were trying to assemble a group for a trip to a rally. Each phone call was met with some feeble excuse as to why they couldn't come; but the bottom line was that they were 'under the thumb' we decided. This was, admittedly, a bit of a chauvinistic attitude: but that was how it had always been, and we were a bit resistant to change!
Still reeling from our inability to lead our compatriots astray, we

hatched a plot to 'reward' the person who, in our opinion was most obviously under 'petticoat rule', with some sort of memento. As luck would have it, my co-conspirator's brother was a cabinet maker, so he soon turned a base up for us on his lathe, and I just happened to have a sawn off thumb kicking about, from the old stock of joke items. A bit of wire and plaster of Paris was all that was required to complete our masterpiece, which was duly emblazoned with the inscription 'The Golden Thumb Award'. A victim was selected, and a shield was engraved with their and the lucky girl's names on it. Obviously the presentation of such an auspicious award would have to take place in front of as big an audience as possible, so it was decided that the usual Friday night gathering in the White Hart would be the best choice. When the usual gang had all arrived, I stood on a chair, and requested the assembled throng's attention. To my surprise complete silence ensued, and so it was that the whole clientele of the pub got to hear the names of the lucky recipients, together with the details of how they came to be nominated for this most coveted award. Now; you know how at most awards ceremonies the recipients feign surprise, and then launch into a well rehearsed thank you speech? Well; this wasn't quite like that! The surprise was very genuine, and I can't

'THE GOLDEN THUMB AWARD'. LIKE THE OSCARS, ONLY WITHOUT THE SYCOPHANTIC SPEECHES

remember there being too many votes of thanks uttered. From that day on 'The Trophy', as it became known, was awarded on a quarterly basis, with anybody who thought they may be in line for it trying to avoid being in the pub around presentation time. Sometimes 'the committee' had to get really devious: I remember one likely candidate was adamant she was not going to receive it, not in public at any rate, and she would make herself scarce if she so much as suspected its presence. Our opportunity eventually came at a party, where a game of 'pass the parcel' happened to be organised. With some forward planning and deft work on the record player, the honour of removing the final layer of paper fell to our intended target. Not quite the Faberge Egg she was hoping for, but there you go! As 'The Trophy' gradually worked its way around the crowd of friends, it started to be received a bit more in the vein in which it was intended, and as the number of shields grew, and an additional base was added, it became a valuable memento of times past. It was eventually decided that whichever member of our group of friends was the last to get married would keep it for posterity. It is still in existence, all these years later, still waiting for that one final scalp to fall…!

As mum was now in her sixties, it was decided that she should start to ease back a bit. To this end I took on the job of opening up at 7am, an hour before the first of the staff arrived. Neither of us were over keen on early starts, (we still aren't, come to that!) so she was more than happy to relinquish the job. At that time of morning the customers were mostly land workers, who would drop in for their cigarettes and sweets, whilst waiting for the works transport to collect them. My body clock never did get comfortable with getting up half way through the night, when it was still very much set to sleep mode, and so I would rock one of the kitchen chairs back onto two legs, against the worktop, and then drop off to sleep, until the shop door bell roused me. I would then spring to my feet, walk through into the shop to serve the customer, and then return to my slumbers. I didn't even used to bother with breakfast in those days,

so on a quiet day I could probably fit another 45 minutes of kip into that first ungodly hour of the day.
Another benefit of mum taking things a bit easier, was the opportunity to stay with her long time friend Vera for extended periods. Not only did this enable me to hone my cooking skills, it also meant there was a good excuse for a party! The combination of a large circle of friends and a small, stock filled house was not ideal, so as much space as possible had to be created. This involved the removal of pretty well anything that wasn't screwed down, (all furniture, television, etc) and a few things that were; like the doors! It was a job to know quite how many people turned up at these events, but about 70 would be a good estimate. Our next door neighbour Ken Tabor was a really good sport on these occasions, and when he saw preparations being made during the day time, he would come around to complain about the noise in advance, as he reckoned there wouldn't be a cat in hells chance of getting himself heard once the party was in full swing!
I remember prior to one party some fragile goods had been delivered, packed in yellow polystyrene chips. I struck me how closely these resembled Quavers, a popular snack at the time. Unfortunately curiosity got the better of me: would it be possible to pass these off as the real thing? On the night of the party I filled two Pyrex bowls with these faux Quavers, sprinkled them liberally with salt and vinegar, and placed them with the other nibbles. At first there were not many takers, but there again, from what I remember of them, there may be wouldn't have been for the real thing either! I eventually confided in a girl friend, who thought it was a really good wheeze, and proceeded to circulate with a bowl of these delightful treats. She returned a short time later, bowl empty, and set off with the second one. Not one person reported anything odd about them, and several had second helpings. Although, with hindsight, it may not have been the most sensible thing to do, I still can't help but wonder how many people had serious trouble with 'floaters' the next day! I should add that I did enquire after peoples' well being after the event, and nobody

reported any ill effects; well not from the 'Quavers' at least!
Although living 'on the job' did have its drawbacks, there was an upside on February 15th 1979. Our part of the world does not generally suffer too badly with extremes of weather, but on this particular day we had so much snow that none of the staff were able to make it in, the only time in the firm's history that it has ever happened. Mum and I were kept busy supplying locals with paraffin, coal and other essentials, and a real community spirit was evident, with local farmers loading people from the outlying villages into their tractors and trailers, and once the roads had become passable, bringing them into town to buy their supplies.

ONE OF THE MANY VW TRUCKS WE HAVE OWNED. I DIDN'T BELIEVE IN TRAVELLING HALF EMPTY!

'The Gang of Lads' would go on holiday together most years and often we would meet up with some interesting people, particularly at Le Mans! On one trip, which also included Switzerland we met a German girl called Ute. We spent a pleasant evening with her and a friend, and as is often the case with these things, swapped names and addresses at the end of it. I thought, as was usual, that all would be forgotten on returning home, and that would be the end of it: how wrong I was, as we shall see later!
By now I was seeing a young lady called Jane, who was studying at Nottingham University, so this meant a fair amount of travelling, which was often done either after closing the shop, or very early in the morning, in order to open it. Whilst I loved the Elan, its somewhat temperamental nature, admittedly mostly caused by my

inability to afford to have it serviced properly, meant it wasn't the ideal car for my current circumstances. Thus it was that I ended up buying my first new car, in the form of a Mk2 Ford Escort RS2000. This turned out to be a marvellous car. It was driven everywhere flat out, including being rallied, and yet in 18 months and 27,000 miles the only non service items it had were a fan belt and a headlamp bulb. Although I was very sad to see the Elan go, as was Jane, the blow was softened a bit by over doubling my money on it, which effectively meant I had two years free motoring.

Back at our local in Spalding, something of a crisis had arisen: at Christmas time the previous year there had been a particularly boisterous night at the pub, during the course of which the Christmas tree somehow went missing. Now; although Dennis, the barman, had many qualities, he ran a tight ship, and was not too amused about the tree's disappearance, and so deemed that there would be no Christmas tree this year.
The regulars all thought this a bit mean spirited, and so we decided that something must be done to rescue the situation. It was decided that I would 'donate' any trees we had left over that year to the cause, and we would then take them up to the pub on our usual Christmas Eve get together. Now, as it turned out this had been a particularly bad year for tree sales, and at the close of play on the 24th, we still had 35 in stock. A quick phone call secured some back up transport, and so it was that our mobile forest arrived at the pub aboard two vans. Fortunately for us, the bar area was located at the rear of the pub, with the front sitting area facing on to the market place. This enabled us to decant our cargo into the pub through the front windows, without Dennis becoming aware of the contribution we were making to the decoration of the pub. As the trees ranged in size from 3' to 10', they had to be fitted into all sorts of nooks and crannies, the largest one ending up wedged in a beam and extending out horizontally across the room; all very artistic! All went well until a few fellow revellers thought it would be a good idea to add a bit of festive cheer to the bar area. The first couple of

trees managed to sneak through unnoticed, getting lost in the sea of bodies that was the White Hart on Christmas Eve, but as the bar slowly started to take on the appearance of Kielder Forest, Dennis sprung into action, to try and find the source of this invasion. I think 'not best pleased' would sum up his reaction, as he entered the front lounge and saw the full extent of our contribution to the decor. He was met with the sight of his clientele ensconced amongst our winter wonderland, the odd body or two just about visible from within the undergrowth! Everybody apart from Dennis seemed to take it all in good part, and at least there was a Christmas tree the next year, so I think our subtle hint did the trick. One amusing aside to the evening was a customer who was seen leaving late on in proceedings, armed with a nicely shaped 4' tree. He remarked to his companion: 'that's a bit of luck; I forgot to get a tree today, so this should get me out of trouble!' I felt like approaching him for payment, but perhaps owning up to being the supplier of the trees wouldn't have been the best plan just at that time: Dennis may have had his suspicions as to the 'benefactor', but couldn't be sure, and I was happy to keep it that way!

As the 80's dawned, our employees' expectations changed, and they decided that they were no longer happy with the traditional half day off in the week, and requested a change to a five day week. What dad would have said I don't know: it was beyond his understanding why anybody should want more than a week off a year, and as for needing two whole days off in the same week; what were they going to find to do with all that spare time! Anyway, a five day week was agreed upon, apart from the boss of course, who still did six eleven hour days in the shop, plus up to another five hours of book work at night. The increase in the wholesale side of the business had been very welcome, but it also meant a lot more invoicing. In a busy month there could easily be over a hundred invoices for the Holbeach Growers Group (a buying group, consisting of local growers, as the name suggests!), and at least as many again for our other customers; all priced and added up manually. There used to be some very late nights at month's end in strawberry season, but it was always a matter of pride that of the ten or so suppliers to the group, our invoices would always be the first to arrive, usually before noon on the first of the month, and would have the least number of errors, especially when compared with those suppliers who were computerised!

Even though we were now in our mid twenties, most of the 'gang' were still independent enough to get away for a 'lads' holiday. We decided on one such occasion that none of us had a suitable car for the planned 'grand tour' of Europe, and so one member of the group was tasked with sourcing a hire car. He eventually came up with a rather well worn Vauxhall Cavalier, sourced from a local garage. What we didn't know is that he hadn't been particularly descriptive to the garage owner as to where we were actually planning to take the car! Part of our trip included the Monaco Grand Prix, and by coincidence, or should that be fate, one of the garage owners employees was also attending the race. He could not believe his eyes when he saw their old Cavalier parked up in Monaco! He took a picture of it to show his boss, which gave our mate quite a bit of explaining to do when he returned the car the following week! The old girl really did us proud; she was driven flat out, with a full payload of bodies and luggage, over a distance of more than 2,000 miles, and apart from a good portion of the exhaust tail pipe burning away, owing to the merciless thrashing, she never missed a beat. As an aside, we could only afford the cheapest ticket to the Grand Prix, which involved perching up on the hillside, but even so, I doubt nowadays you would find any kind of ticket for the £7.00 we paid then!
The other big social event of the year was our first Beach Party; another of those schemes which get dreamt up in the pub after maybe one too many beers, and then have to be turned into reality!
It was decided that Hunstanton would be a good venue, and being a responsible bunch, we made enquires as to what was required for such an event. As it turned out, quite a lot! Not only did we have to

obtain permission from the land owners, (surprisingly the beach was privately owned), we also had to inform the police and coast guard. There were also time constraints: we could go onto the beach no earlier than 7pm, and had to have it cleaned up and vacated by 8am the following morning.
As our 'gang' had a reputation for not doing things by halves, the whole operation had to be planned with military precision! We parked our 'Task Force' in the Cliff Top Car Park, and at the stroke of 19.00 hours, we sprang into action. We had just one hour to carry a truck load of straw bales onto the beach for the seating, erect support poles for the lighting, install the generator and connect the lights and disco, assemble and stock the bar and construct and light the barbecue. To our relief all was up and running on time, and the party proved a huge success, which is more than can be said for the clearing up operation early the next morning, which was tackled with somewhat less enthusiasm, not to mention a hangover! We had only just judged our site right, as by morning the tide was mighty close!
Back at the shop, things were still moving on apace; in the September we set a new record for flower box sales, with 3,500 going out through the shop in one day, which may not mean much to you, dear reader, but to us that was a lot of boxes!
Another exciting event was the completion of the purchase of Park Hall, the warehouse we had rented for many years. This had not been without its trials and tribulations: all should have been plain sailing, as the owner, East Midlands Electricity Board, had instructed their agent to arrange a sale to myself, as the sitting tenant, for an agreed price. The only trouble was that the agent took things into their own hands, and offered the property on the open market. The first thing I knew about it was when another local trader asked if he could look around the property, as he was going to buy it! Fortunately the properties manager for the Board was an honourable man, and was furious that their agent had not acted according to his instructions. Not long after we spoke I had a call from a very crestfallen estate agent, with some lame excuse about

THE REAR OF PARK HALL, AS IT WAS WHEN I PURCHASED IT. THE OPEN SHED IN THE BACKGROUND WAS LATER ENCLOSED.

DEMOLISHING THE OLD PAPES SHOP, SHORTLY AFTER PURCHASING THE PARK HALL WAREHOUSE

trying to do the best for his client, (nothing to do with trying to make more money for his company of course!) and the sale proceeded without further incident.
Over a year had now passed since I parted with my beloved Elan, and in the words of the song, "you don't know what you've got 'till it's gone''. The financial side of the business was looking quite good by now, and this prompted me to start hankering after things Lotus.
I am a great believer in fate, which on this occasion presented itself in the form of a chance conversation with a Lotus dealer. I happened to mention that I had the afore mentioned hankering, preferably for an Esprit, and as luck (or fate) would have it, he knew of an absolutely beautiful one, which was only for sale as the elderly owner had just had a hip replacement, and could no longer

IMMACULATE LOTUS ESPRIT S2, BOUGHT IN 1980

insinuate himself into the car. I was pleased to hear however, that in an act of defiance, he had ordered a Lotus Sunbeam; maybe his physical limitations had put his Esprit out of bounds, but that wasn't going to stop him having a Lotus of some description. More

power to him I say! Anyway, I duly contacted the owner to arrange a viewing, and as soon as I saw the car I knew I had to have it. There she sat, her black paintwork gleaming, and not a mark on her, as well there shouldn't be, with only 2,418 miles on the clock, after two years! The deal was soon done, although I wasn't in a very strong negotiating position, as there were no faults on the car over which to haggle! So, that was my Christmas present to myself bought, and I couldn't have been happier with it; I had a proper car again. As is the way of things, this state of contentment only lasted about six months. I had agreed to take a party from the Motor Club on a visit to the Lotus factory in Norfolk, but as I had been before I stayed in the office area, which was one huge open plan area. (I should think Colin Chapman was just too tight to pay for all those walls and doors!) Eventually this chap took pity on me, and invited me to join him at his desk. It turned out he was the sales manager for Europe, and once he realised I was an owner, he asked if I had been in the new S3 Esprit, which I hadn't. The next thing I know he is on the phone requesting an S3 to be brought round to reception, and away we went onto the test track. (Lotus are based at the old WW2 US air force base at Hethel, and they have re-configured some of the old runways to make a test track.) This new version was so much better than my S2 that I glibly offered the opinion that there hardly seemed a need for the turbo charged version that had also been announced. Wrong! Oh so very wrong.
What followed was an experience I will never forget. This time I wasn't to be driven by my host, who modestly claimed he did not have the level of skill required to do the Turbo justice, but by a chap he referred to simply as Roger. Now; I didn't realise who this Roger was at the time, but as my knowledge of the 'Lotus Legends' grew, it transpired it was none other than Roger Becker. Never heard of him, you are probably thinking. Maybe so, but there is a good chance you've seen him perform! When they were filming the Bond epic 'The Spy Who Loved Me', which featured an S1 Esprit, the stunt driver just couldn't perform the spectacular manoeuvres the director wanted. Roger was only supposed to be there to look

after the car, but when he drove it up the mountain road they were using to film the action, ready for the hapless stunt driver to make yet another attempt, the director noticed Rogers's naturally flamboyant driving style, and proclaimed that that was what he wanted. So it was that Roger Becker, Lotus Engineer, became Roger Becker, stunt driver! Anyway, back to the (other) plot. Off we went on to the test track again, but this was a whole different ball game! Now; I had been driven by some quick drivers on race tracks before, but nothing quite like this. There was a corner on the track at the time called Windsock, (sadly no longer there in its original form) which was a long, nearly 90 degree turn. Anybody with even a fairly deficient sense of self preservation would probably consider 80mph to be about as quick as this should be tackled, so when Roger approached it with the speedo reading the wrong side of 100mph, I decided he was either imbued with more than his fair share of talent, or the throttle had stuck open. Fortunately for us both it turned out to be the former, and we drifted through the corner, with the car right on the limit of adhesion, as Roger calmly balanced its attitude with small adjustments of throttle and steering. If like me, you would love to be able to do something well, that you at best do adequately, it is aggravating in the extreme to sit next to someone to whom it seems second nature! Any way; the upshot of all this was that I came away from Lotus knowing I just had to have an Esprit Turbo: I guessed I was going to have to try even harder at the day job.

Around this same time, Brian, one of the 'gang', was courting (that's what you did in those days you know!) a nurse who was based in Oxford. She and her friends were a pretty mad bunch, and therefore proved a good match for our crowd. Every now and again an expedition would be arranged, and we would descend upon this campsite, just outside Oxford. The owner was justifiably suspicious of a group of noisy young hooligans, and kept us under very close supervision. Then, in between visits, he had to go into the Radcliffe Hospital for an operation, and was subsequently cared for by some of our usual camping party (poor fellow!). Obviously they made a favourable impression, as on our next visit we could do no wrong: it was like being given the freedom of the city! Anything his nurses wanted to do was alright by him; which was perhaps as well, as Ann's boyfriend Gary decided to join us on this occasion. Now Gary was a larger than life character, hailing from Birmingham, and at this particular time he was working in a camping shop. Well; he turned up with this tent, the likes of which I had never seen: you could have held a circus in it! Suffice to say it covered quite a bit more than his allotted pitch, and the rest of us ended up pitching our meagre two man tents inside it; still leaving enough space to hold a dance.

Having sorted out the accommodation, it was time to explore the delights of Oxford. Punting was a favourite pastime of the crowd, and something at which I am actually less bad than I am at most other things! As we sped along the waterways, Nurse Liz (as she was known) kept goading us with tales of this nudist camp, right on the water's edge. We assumed it was one of her wind ups, but she assured us that there was no catch. Surely there must be a fence around it we asked? No, it was all open to public gaze, we were assured.

Now; being young, testosterone filled lads, we had visions of nubile young ladies, frolicking by the water's edge, and so we decided to press on; just in case any were in need of assistance, you understand. We eventually reached this set of rollers, over which you could haul your punt up to the upper river, and sure enough, there was the sign, warning of the nudist area, just ahead.

Apologies duly made to Liz, we surged ahead, and as we entered the demarcated area, it was indeed populated by people 'dressed' as God intended.... and every one of them a bloke! When this glaringly obvious fact was pointed out to Liz, she nonchalantly replied: 'Oh, didn't I mention that?' She came mighty close to going overboard, I can tell you; not that she would have been a lot wetter, as our somewhat exuberant punting style had decanted a good portion of the river into the punt; something which didn't go unnoticed upon our return, earning us a fine from the rental company. We'll leave the story of Brian trying to dry his underwear afterwards... with a hot air hand drier... whilst still wearing said underwear, for another occasion I think!

By the end of the summer petrol was £1.70 per gallon, (that's just 37.5p per litre, just to make you feel even worse!) and the firm had recovered sufficiently from the purchase of Park Hall to finish off the shed around the back of the main building, which currently consisted of just a roof, with open sides and a dirt floor. Far more importantly, it also meant we could at last use a forklift, something which was not possible in the main building, as the floor was a suspended wooden affair, with a cellar below; definitely not the place for a 3 ton forklift! As things moved on, lorry drivers had become more reluctant to 'hand ball' loads, and so a forklift had really become a necessity; it also meant that unloading became a one man job, so shop staff no longer needed to be commandeered for the job. With the amount of flower boxes we were now selling, the extra storage space, and speed of unloading were a boon, although my thoughts were already turning towards what could be done with the retail side of the business. Although things were looking good at the moment, you could already see that the supermarkets were starting to move in on the flower job, and the traditional outlets for the growers, the wholesale markets, were already starting to feel the effect, with several stands going out of business. Allied to this was the 'shrinking' of the world: it was now possible to fly exotic flowers in from all parts of the globe, and with their cheap labour, and naturally warm climates, it was very difficult for the British growers to compete. Whereas before the consumer was happy to have daffodils and tulips at the start of the year, sweet williams, lilies and pinks in the summer, and then chrysanthemums to finish the season, now they could have virtually any flower they desired, at virtually any time of year.
Thinking of farming reminds me of one very dear friend, who was in that profession. He was different from the rest of us, in so far as

he had no real interest in cars: he did drive a BMW 1602, but that was only because they were robust and reliable. He thought servicing a car a complete waste of money: he had done it just the once, and thought the size of the bill outrageous, just for having oil which was a slightly different colour from that which they took out. It was therefore with some foreboding that he told us the car had got to go in to the garage, as it had been getting slower and slower, and now accelerated with all the alacrity of one of his tractors. The next week in the pub I enquired as to the diagnosis, expecting his lack of care and attention to have caught up with him at last. "What was wrong with the BM then Beano?" I enquired. "Oh nothing really," came the surprising reply. "They just chiselled all the mud away from behind the accelerator pedal, and it was absolutely fine". To this day he still runs his cars in exactly the same manner.

I never was that taken with night clubs, but occasionally a group of us would make the 20 or so mile trek to civilisation to experience one. Sometimes it would just be a group of lads who happened to be 'single' at the time, as was the case on this particular night. Often our night out would conclude at my place, especially if mum was away. After a drink or two, talk turned to the new season's fireworks, which had just arrived. I had been particularly impressed by some of the rockets this year, and fetched one of the largest ones to show the lads. Given the reputations of those present, with hind sight it was perhaps not the most sensible thing to do; but anyway, they were suitably impressed, and naturally talk then turned as to how it was likely to perform. Before you could say A & E we were out in the garden, rocket and matches in hand! What we didn't have was a launching tube, which for a missile like this you really ought to have. Undaunted, it was decided that the ground was soft enough to just push the rocket in. (Health and Safety warning: DO NOT TRY THIS AT HOME). This may have been fine, had Taff not pushed it in holding the rocket itself, and not the stick. Unbeknown to him, the stick had only gone in a short distance; the rest of the movement had been the rocket sliding down it. Nobody noticed the surplus bit of wood, protruding above the rocket, and so the touch paper was lit, and we retired to what we considered a safe distance. The rocket did a fair impression of a Saturn 5 on the launch pad, and then took off like a rocket: as I suppose it would! Now, rockets have a certain length of stick for a very good reason; namely balance, and if you alter that balance, by say sliding the rocket down the stick, it is not going to perform as expected. This fact dawned on us about three seconds after launch, as the projectile did a 180 degree turn, and started to return earthwards, still under full thrust. Panic set in about one second after this, as we tried to second guess the likely impact zone. As it turned out it missed us, but probably worse, it instead unleashed the full splendour of its display just above street level, right outside Cyril Tabor's bedroom window. Now if you think a large rocket makes a spectacular display a few hundred feet up, you should see one at 20 feet! The reason its choice of Cyril's was not the best was that he happened to be a Special Constable, and an Inspector at that. We decided that the best plan would be to return inside, and hope that nobody had noticed. This unlikely scenario was soon disproved, as a commotion from a couple of doors up ensued. It was our local plumber neighbour, who had been rudely awakened from his slumbers, and assumed that an explosion such as he had just heard could only be caused by a gas leak, so he was shepherding his family out into the open, in case there was another one! As expected, Cyril came over to see me the next morning, and he was quite rightly not best pleased. He said he couldn't prove anything, but he was pretty certain who the perpetrator of last night's pyrotechnic display had been, and if I ever pulled a stunt like that again, there would be repercussions. Believe me; I had no intention of doing so!

I always think that if you are going to take financial advice, it's best if the person giving it has made a few bob themselves, that way it stands a reasonable chance of being sound. One such piece of advice had come from a local character and very good customer called Roy Munton. Roy was a bachelor, who had started with very little, but made a small fortune, much of it from growing gladioli. His speciality was growing them very late into the year, which is how we came to supply him. Previously he had bought his flower boxes from our main competitor, who was in a much bigger way than us. Roy had rang them late in the year to order more boxes, only to be told that the gladioli season had finished, and they had no more stock. Telling Roy the season was finished, when he still had acres of flowers still to crop, was probably not their brightest move, and so it was that he came to us in desperation. Roy didn't suffer fools, but he was dead straight, and he promised that if we got him out of this fix, he would use us the next year. He was as good as his word, and the competitor never sold him another flower box as long as he lived.

Anyway, his pearls of wisdom were this: if you are going to borrow money for a project, never borrow more than half of the cost of it, and only ever borrow half of what you can afford to. That way, if things don't go quite to plan, you leave yourself a bit of leeway. I have always tried to conduct my financial affairs on this basis, and have also added my own little footnote; which is never be beholden to a bank. By that I mean, never get yourself so committed to them that you can't still call the shots: once a bank has you in their grip life can be very difficult indeed, if things don't go quite as well as they would like.

So, with regard to the afore mentioned, I felt the company was now in a position to start thinking about developing our existing site. It had become obvious that only being able to display about 10% of our stock in the shop, with the remainder being hidden away in the nooks and crannies of the old houses next door, was a less than efficient way of operating. Allied to this was the fact that the shop was now in need of some TLC, with the wooden floor rotting through in places. The prospect of a dozen customers disappearing down into the cellar one busy Saturday was not one I relished! It was time to think about taking the plunge, (before they did!) and investing some serious money in the future.

These were still the days when a provincial bank would have a proper manager, who was empowered to make decisions regarding a sizable business loan, without recourse to some faceless regional overlord, who knew nothing about the characters involved, or the intimate workings of the business. As such I duly wandered along to see my friendly manager, and told him my plan, and the likely cost of the building work, together with the approximate amount of money I would be looking to borrow. He was well aware that the firm's bank account had been building up a healthy surplus, and that the amount I proposed to borrow would be more than covered by my assets, and so just told me to let him know when I required the money and he would arrange it. Now the planning could begin in earnest, and I began to get excited about the prospect of realising dad's dream of building a proper shop, of which he would have been proud.

One thing about running a shop in a small town in those days was that you knew nearly everybody who came through the door; and if somebody new came into the area, it was not long before you knew about them as well: we are a nosey lot around Holbeach, and we like to vet any 'incomers'! One such was Ivan Pambakian, who eventually became a well liked 'Honorary Local'. Ivan was even more interesting than usual: he was not merely non local, he was properly foreign, hailing from a country I hadn't even heard of called Albania. (Geography was not something which interested me at school: I always thought it was something you needed to go and see, rather than read about!). He had bought a small holding locally, and needed a flame thrower to burn off some of the rubbish. He had been told we hired them out, and came in to ask if he could have it for the day. Now; it's at times like this that a little inner daemon seems to take control of my oratory functions, and instead of the intended reply of "yes sir, I will just go and fetch it for you", what actually came out was: "yes sir you can hire it, I will just need to see your flame thrower licence first". Not surprisingly the poor chap knew nothing about this licence, and enquired how he might obtain one. Still under the spell of 'the daemon', I told him he could get one from the police station, this being in the days when our police station actually had a police man in it! Thus enlightened, he toddled the few yards to the cop shop, and asked the officer for a flame thrower licence. Guessing that the poor chap had been set up, he enquired who had told him he needed such a thing. As soon as my name was mentioned the officer said something to the effect of ‘that figures’, and sent him back, with the reassurance that he did not need the licence. Ivan took it all in good part, and he became one of our friends come customers, often calling in just to tell one of his ‘Moldavians jokes’, which were very similar to the type we might tell about the Irish!

As the year drew to a close, that fate thing cropped up again. The car magazine I regularly read happened to run a competition to win….a Turbo Esprit, and not only that, the question involved predicting what speed a Lotus Esprit Turbo, driven by Roger Becker would reach by the end of the main straight on the Lotus test track. Been there, done that! Just one slight snag: I had taken note of the speed at which we exited Windsock corner, but not of our terminal speed at the end of the following straight! I spent hours trying to work this out with a scale map of the circuit and acceleration graphs for the car. I eventually arrived at a figure, and off went my entry. After an agonising wait, the results were published, and I had come so, so, close to the correct answer; but as they say, no cigar (or in this case car!).
The middle of December saw very heavy snow falls, which was good for fuel sales, but not so good if you happened to have tickets to see ELO at the NEC! (That’s a pop group and an arena by the way). In those days the route to Birmingham involved some fairly exposed, lightly trafficked roads, so I phoned the police for their view on the chances of getting through. The chap who took the call was very helpful, but said several of the roads we needed to traverse were virtually impassable, and unless the journey was essential, and we had a 4 x 4, it was best not to risk it. I said it was a shame, as we had tickets for ELO. That changed things

completely: "I'd definitely give it a go in that case!" was his revised assessment of the situation. Jane and I set off in good time, and all went well until we reached a particularly exposed and windswept piece of road. The snow was just about manageable in most places, but where there was a gap in the hedge it was about two feet deep. Now, the Esprit may not be a 4 x 4, but its flat underside makes it a pretty good toboggan: so I would go as fast as I dare on the better bits, and then hope that the momentum would allow us to slide across those bits where the snow was too deep to get any drive. To our great relief we leapfrogged our way to the main road, and the further west we went, the better conditions became. By the time we reached the NEC there was hardly any sign of snow, and we noticed that people were staring and pointing at the car: it always did draw a bit of attention, but not usually this amount. As soon as we got out it was obvious what had been causing the interest: the radiator duct and wheels were just packed solid with snow, it must have looked like we had driven straight from the North Pole!

Early in '82 the trauma of missing that Turbo Esprit prize became too much for me, and I succumbed to a limited edition Essex Turbo Esprit. Its blue red and silver paint scheme was maybe a little on the garish side, but it was the right price and went like stink; and that was what mattered to me! This car proved to be an asset in a way I hadn't considered, as Mark Thatcher had one identical to it at the time. Now; when he wasn't busy getting lost in the desert, he used to do a bit of motor racing, and on one occasion he was competing at a Silverstone meeting that I was going to attend as a spectator.

As usual I had to work on the Saturday, so I blasted off to Silverstone as soon after closing the shop as possible. Before the days of water tight security, it was always a bit of a challenge to see how far into the circuit you could get before one of the officials turned you back. Sometimes you may get no further than one of the outer car parks, another you may make it as far as the outer perim-

LOTUS ESPRIT ESSEX TURBO. FLASH BUT FAST!

eter of the circuit itself.
On this occasion I was really perplexed: as I approached each 'check point' I was just waved through. This went on until not only was I in the circuit itself, I had been waved straight passed the pay kiosks, and allowed over the bridge in to the inner sanctum that is the paddock! Not wanting to cause a fuss, I thought I had better just pitch my tent, and make myself at home. Later I went for a wander around the paddock and all became clear: there parked next to one of the transporters was my car's doppelganger. As Essex Esprits were as rare as German comedians, the officials had obviously assumed I was Mark Thatcher returning after a trip out, and didn't feel the need to stop 'him' and inspect 'his' pass.
As expected with such an extrovert car, news soon spread through the town about my latest acquisition, only this time the perpetrators of tittle-tattle had even more to occupy them, as I still had the previous Esprit! The trade in offer on it had not met my expectations, so I decided to sell it privately. This naturally meant taking people for test drives, so one day I would be seen in 'The Essex', the next in the S2.

All this speculation eventually came to a head when one customer, unable to contain her curiosity any longer, asked me if it was true I now owned three Lotuses', as she had been assured I also still had my Elan! By this time the S2 had gone, so I was able to reassure her that I was now down to just the one.

Remember Ute, the German girl from all those years ago? Well, one day at the shop, a member of staff called me to the phone, as there was a girl asking for me. Now in those days this was not unheard of, so I took the call. I was greeted by this heavily accented voice: "Hello Patrick. This is Ute, I have come to see you." It turned out she was on Spalding station, and wanted me to collect her and as it turned out, accommodate her! Poor old mum didn't know what to make of it all. This German girl, who I had never even mentioned, turns up out of the blue, expecting lodgings, for a non specified amount of time. I could hardly leave the poor girl stranded, and so went to collect her. Luckily she and mum hit it off, so she stayed for a while, and then just wandered off again. Several more years past, still with no contact, and then exactly the same thing happened again; just substituting Peterborough station and Alice! Fortunately for me Alice was also very understanding, and after a few days she was gone again (Ute, not Alice). Although we have had no further visits, a letter or email may turn up every three or four years. Strange girl; but likeable with it.

As we were now selling some serious quantities of packaging materials, over six million tulip wraps a year by now for example, (that is enough for over 30 million tulips!), I decided to start looking for the best source to buy from. Compared to Holland, Britain was only a small producer of flowers, and so I decided to look at some of the big suppliers over there, to see if it would be worthwhile importing flower sleeves. I arranged some meetings and then set off for Holland, with Brian along for the ride. To see how their flower auctions operated was really an eye opener. The one we visited at Aalsmeer, is the biggest in the world, covering

nearly a million square meters, and trading about twenty million flowers a day! The flowers come into the various bidding rooms on automated trolleys and bidding is done against a clock which shows a descending price. You have the choice of either getting in an early bid, paying a higher price, and making sure you secure the flowers you want, or holding out until the price drops, and hoping somebody else doesn't beat you to them. It seems to work really well, and to make sure there is never a glut of unsold stock to depress prices the following day, any unsold produce is destroyed.
As business is done early in the morning, and all the sundries suppliers are clustered around the market, it was not a long job to get the deals done for the flower sleeves I needed. It turned out I could not only buy them cheaper, but they could also offer quicker delivery than in the UK.
All this speedy dealing meant that I had concluded my business by 10.30 am. I asked Brian if he fancied a trip to the Mosel for the couple of days we had left, as I had been before, and enjoyed it. It also happened to involve a lot of German Autobahn, and not a lot of speed limits. This was the sort of trip the Esprit was made for, and we managed to do the 350 miles in less than 3½ hours, an average of just over 100mph. We may mock the Germans about their adherence to rules and regulations, but when applied to driving it makes for much better safety and progress. Even though we were cruising at between 120 and 145 mph, the other road users were aware of us, and would usually pull over so as not to impede the faster car, even if they themselves were overtaking a string of slower vehicles. We could certainly learn a lot about lane discipline from them.
One of our major garden suppliers came up with the idea of holding an annual conference, with various expert speakers in attendance. To make these a more enticing proposition, they were held somewhere warm and sunny; and I don't mean Cardiff! There was a catch of course, and this came in the form of having to earn points towards the trip, by purchasing products from them: so there may be a promotion on spades, for example, where if you bought

ten, you would earn 100 points towards the next conference. It was at one such event, in Tenerife, that a speaker giving ideas about the best way to lay a shop out, started me thinking seriously about what to do about our premises. Sure, we met his turnover and profit figures per square foot recommendations, and easily beat his target of 4 times stock turn, (This means that if you have £50,000 of stock, you should have a turnover of at least £200,000 per year.) but it was obvious that there was far more potential to be unlocked.
One idea I did like was to have a staffed central kiosk area, where customers could go to ask for help and advice, and from where the staff could get a good view of the shop, and so see if any customers looked as though they might need assistance: it is amazing how many times a customer will come in, you greet them by asking if they would like any help, and they refuse; only to approach you five minutes later asking where they might find a particular item. It is almost as though they don't want to bother you, when actually the main part of your job is to offer help and advice. Customers are not an interruption of your work; they are the purpose of it!
I drew out a rough layout of how I thought the new shop should be, and then had the first meeting with our designer in September 1982. By November the drawings were ready to be submitted to the planning committee, just right for a spring start I thought: how wrong was I!
While all this had been going on, things had moved on a pace in my personal life. After several fun filled years, Jane had a lucky escape and I was back on the shelf, and some would say getting past my best before date! Although Alice and I had parted some years ago, we had bumped into each other on an infrequent basis, largely through my continuing friendship with her brother, Tony. As we had both been 'free agents' for a while, we started to see each other a bit, and then a bit more, and then …. I proposed to her, late one night, beside the Serpentine Lake in Hyde Park! As we had done all the preliminary stuff first time around, we saw no point in a long engagement, and so the date was set for August Bank Holiday the next year. As her brother Tony was also getting

JUST SOME OF THE MANY, MANY DESIGN PROPOSALS THAT WERE SUBMITTED BEFORE WE WERE ABLE TO SATISFY THE COUNCIL'S CONSULTANT.

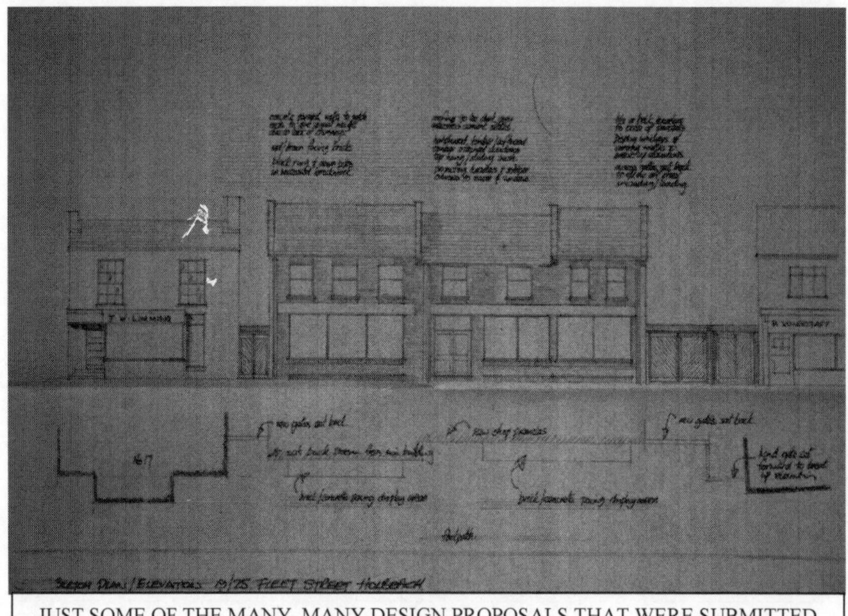

JUST SOME OF THE MANY, MANY DESIGN PROPOSALS THAT WERE SUBMITTED BEFORE WE WERE ABLE TO SATISFY THE COUNCIL'S CONSULTANT.

married to Louise that year, it was decided to ruin the whole of the Bank Holiday, and have their wedding on the Saturday! This meant that the Dutch contingent only had to come over once, (Alice & Tony's parents were originally from Holland) and I didn't have to close the shop; so a result all round.
We would need somewhere to live of course, and I had just the place in mind: my father's sister had married a farmer, Les Hammond, and we had spent many a happy time at their house in Whaplode Fen. This very house had been empty for over a year, as Les had retired, and he and May had moved to Spalding. We both agreed that it was ideal for us: quiet and secluded, and importantly for me, three miles from the shop. Having experienced all the disturbed meal times when living at home, I knew the one place I wasn't going to be living was the shop! Buying the house would mean making one huge sacrifice: the Esprit would have to go. At the time mortgage rates were 10% and climbing, and to have nearly half the cost of the house sitting there on four wheels made no sense at all. It was replaced with a second hand RS2000, and so the Lotus era came to an end....for now.

The plans for the new shop went before committee in the January of '83, and were to my amazement, rejected. This was the first time I had seen the planning process in action, and it did not imbue me with a great deal of confidence! There was one committee member who was most insistent that one design was acceptable to him, but he would not countenance the other. After he had bumbled on at some length, another committee member had to whisper in his ear that the two drawings were actually of the same design; it was just that one was shown as a front elevation, and the other in perspective. It was good to see the future of my project was in safe hands!
Whilst this set back was bad enough, it soon became clear that the biggest problem wasn't going to be getting permission to put the new building up, but being allowed to knock the old ones down. There are various organisations which busy themselves with the

preservation of Georgian buildings; fine for some splendid stately pile, but not quite the same for our dilapidated eyesores.
It appeared however that they did not differentiate: if it was Georgian, they would oppose its demolition, even if, as in this case, they had not even seen the building. To make matters worse, they had an ally in the local conservation officer, a man called Freakley, (although I soon found other names by which to refer to him!), who was a lover of Georgian buildings himself. It was with Mr Freakley that we were told to liaise, to find a design which would not upset his sensibilities. It soon became clear that he was going to do anything but help us, and when asked what sort of design he would like to see, all he would offer is that we must come up with something which 'blended with rhythms and sub rhythms of the surrounding buildings'.
Neither me, nor my designers had a clue what he was talking about, especially as the buildings around us encompassed a whole range of very different styles and periods.
By the May planning meeting we had at least got permission in principal for the demolition, but Freakley was still making life as difficult as possible for us. Fortunately the chairman of the Planning Committee was himself a businessman, and he could see that all the delays were costing me time and money.
I think he also had an inkling of what was going on behind the scenes, and decided that the only way forward was to have a meeting between me, my representatives, and Freakley, which he would chair.
As you are not allowed to speak in Committee, this would be our first chance to put our case across, and we took full advantage of it. Once he heard of the lack of cooperation we had received, and the ridiculous 'guidance' we had been given, he made it very clear that the conservation officer was to work with us to find a design which was acceptable to both parties, as once the proposal had been approved by him, then the rest of the process should be plain sailing.
I will never forget the now chastened Freakleys visit to our shop, a

few days after the meeting: he strode up the stairs to the top floor of the building, looked around him, and then in one sweeping statement, declared that the whole building could be restored for £50,000. No survey, no structural report, not even a builder's estimate. Unbelievable!
Having received very clear 'guidance' from the Committee Chairman, finally, in October, Freakley approved our plans. The goings on of the last nine months were made all the more galling by the fact that ultimately he only requested we change some very small brick work detailing around the area of the guttering on the design!

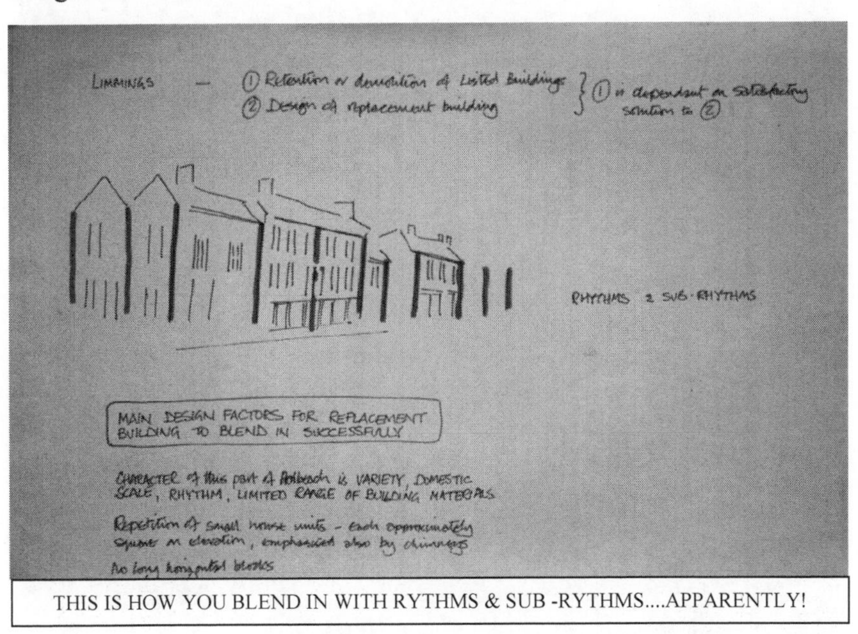

THIS IS HOW YOU BLEND IN WITH RYTHMS & SUB -RYTHMS....APPARENTLY!

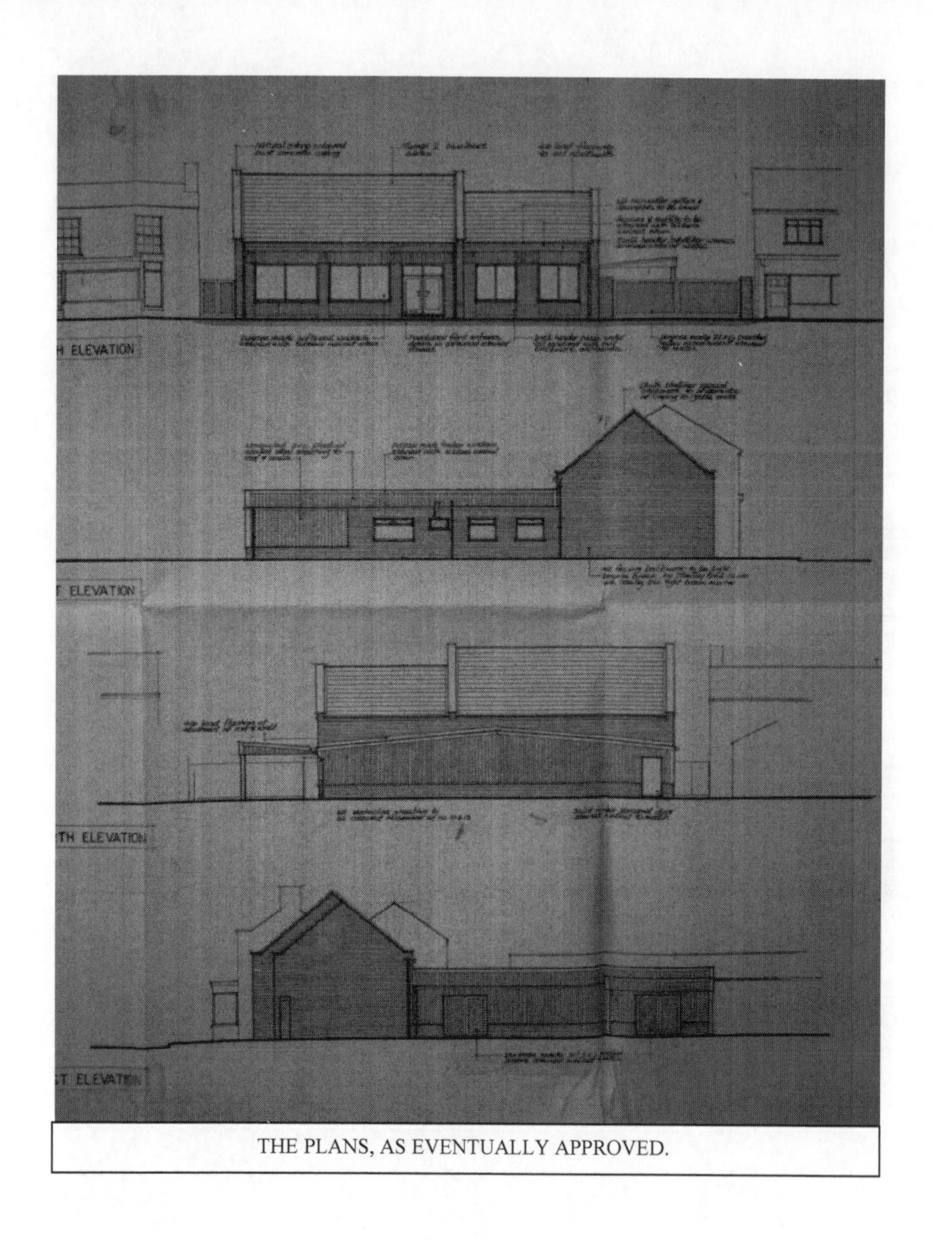

THE PLANS, AS EVENTUALLY APPROVED.

Chapter 6 No Longer A Bachelor

In the middle of all the aggravation over the building of the new shop, Alice and I had married and moved into Bridge Farm. Unlike a lot of newlyweds today, we didn't have an instant 'show home'. The carpets had been left by Uncle Les, and were far from new; the furniture was all second hand (or worse), with the exception of that in the bedroom, which had been paid for by selling Alice's Triumph Spitfire. We did have a television of sorts; a tiny black & white portable from Alice's flat, which was kept in a cupboard, and only brought out on the rare occasions there was something worth watching!

The wedding itself was, of (financial) necessity, a low key affair, although there was one amusing aside. Some time earlier, Alice and I had been guests of Lin Pac and Don Rudd, at a horse racing meeting. At the time Alice was reading a book, one of the ladies in which drank Krug Champagne. So it was that when Don asked Alice if she would like a drink, she enquired as to what was available. He rather sweepingly replied she could have anything she wanted; they had everything. "In that case I will have a glass of Krug Champagne, thank you", she replied. Needless to say, Don returned empty handed, requesting a second choice! This event must have stuck in Don's mind, for when he wanted to buy something to mark our marriage; he went with a work colleague to seek out a bottle of Krug champagne, assuming it to be Alice's usual tipple, when in fact not a drop had ever passed her lips! The tale of the purchase was related by his colleague thus: Sales assistant, "Krug Champagne, indeed sir; vintage or non vintage?" Don, "Which is the best?" Assistant: "Vintage sir". Don, "Right; vintage then, thank you". Off the assistant went, doubtless rubbing his hands at the prospect of such a good sale. Of course, up to this point, the thorny issue of money had not been approached. Don being a pint of bitter sort of guy, probably had no idea that bubbles can be very expensive, especially if they happen to be vintage ones. Apparently, when the cost of his purchase was finally broken to him it was touch and go as to whether Don would require medical assistance! He felt he couldn't now renege on the deal, and handed over a substantial sum of money, although the person relating the story was discreet enough to withhold just how substantial. Don was now convinced that Alice and I lived this hedonistic life style, quaffing bottles of vintage Krug Champagne! We did eventually find an occasion to justify opening the bottle, and very nice it was too.

This tumultuous year had one more 'happening': Tink came to work for us. Now over the years many staff have come and gone, although we are fortunate in that our 'turnover' is less than many places, but there are some who leave an indelible impression, and Tink is one of them. She was, in fact still is, a larger than life character, (and in Tink's case, that is already fairly large!) who exudes this great torrent of energy which by the end of a day spent in her company leaves you exhausted. The 'old boys' used to love her outgoing character, knowing they would always get as good as they gave. I truly believe, that had she had the inclination, Tink could have rivalled Holbeach's other famous field sport's star, Geoff Capes. As evidence I will offer the occasion when she stood there with a sack in her arms, while she casually posed the question, "Patrick, is this batch of Lime in four stones or hundredweights?" "Hundredweights, I replied". Tink just said "I thought it felt a bit heavier", and carried on to the customer's car with it, as if carrying a pillow from her bed! I fully realise there are supposed to be weight limits for female members of staff, (by which I mean as to the weight they are supposed to lift, not the staff themselves, I hasten to add!) but to try and restrict Tink to these would have been futile, she would have taken it as an insult, and trust me, the one thing you wouldn't want to do is upset Tink; I've seen the results first hand, and it is quite scary! The occasion was a New Year party, held at our house. Now for all her bravado, Tink is actually well mannered, and would not wish to cause offence. Her then boyfriend, (now husband) Richard, is of necessity, a much more subdued character….until he has had a drink that is, then he becomes far more brave, which can be a tad fool hardy. On this particular night, Richard had consumed what Tink considered to be sufficient beer. She advised him of this fact, and probably proving her correct, he begged to differ. Now Tink did not want to be shown up in front of her still new boss, and took him aside to the dining room to offer some advice. The layout of the house was such that the kitchen, where the rest of us were, had a view down a hall, with the dining room to the right, and the sitting room directly opposite on the left. Obviously Tink's counselling did not received the hoped for response, as the next thing we knew, Richard flew backwards out of the dining room, his legs vainly trying to arrest his progress, while his arms did a fair impression of a windmill in a force nine gale. Next there came a thud, as all that kinetic energy imparted by Tink was absorbed by the sofa! A short while later, in an act of defiance/recklessness Richard emerged from the sitting room, walked calmly into the kitchen, and as if nothing had happened, poured himself another pint!

As '84 dawned the planning permission issue still progressed at a glacial pace. Now a man was sent from the Department Of The Environment, to assess the merit of our application for demolition. As someone who was used to getting things done, this was all getting a bit tedious, so I decided to contact my MP, Richard Body, to see if he could bring any pressure to bear. This proved to be a really good move, as he was very supportive, and took the matter to the House of Commons, demanding a decision on the matter from the D of E. That decision turned out to be that a Public Inquiry would be held. This was really bad news, as now we could be in for some serious expense. Depending on how far the various societies wanted to take the matter, they could do anything from not turn up at all, to arriving armed to the teeth with barristers and the like. It seemed unjust that the opposition could get away with just the price of a stamp and a piece of paper (alright, and an envelope!) to oppose my application, not even being obliged to attend the hearing, and yet I would have to stump up all my costs, even if the hearing found in my favour. My dilemma now was how much fire power would be required. How serious were these guys; just a letter serious, or barrister serious? A meeting with my solicitor soon confirmed that a barrister was out of the question, at £1,000 for the first day, and £750 per day thereafter; and this was in 1984 remember! It was decided that George Hastings himself would put our case, and so the evidence gathering began!

Fortunately business was still going well, Lin Pac, our flower box supplier, had decided to divest itself of any non core business, and this meant that the strawberry punnets had to go. Now these may have been a mere distraction for a giant like Lin Pac, but to us the three million a year they sold was very worthwhile. An agreement was reached, and their client list was handed over. Suddenly we were almost international, with customers in such far flung places as North Wheatley and Hayton, they were even in a different county for Pete's sake!
The strawberry season is short but intense, and trying to service all these new customers with the same staff meant some fairly long days. We used to hire a lorry in to deliver the initial orders, but once the season was under way lead times could be very short, as the supermarkets might decide at the drop of a hat that they wanted the fruit in pound punnets instead of halves, so you would have to respond. It was not uncommon to get a phone call at 4pm from one of the growers, requesting a delivery any time before 5am the next day. This would mean closing the shop at 6pm, loading the truck to the gunnels and then driving up to Yorkshire. With a bit of luck you would be unloaded in time to catch a local pub which was still serving food, before arriving home about 11pm. What didn't get done in the week had to be cleared up on a Sunday, so that put paid to my rule about not working on the day of rest. Still, there was a new shop to pay for, so I was grateful of any business I could get, even if it did mean some 100 hour weeks.
As part of our evidence gathering, we had a visit from a structural engineer, to assess the full extent of the dilapidation of numbers 19

and 21. He did a thorough survey, and concluded that the buildings were far from structurally sound, and amongst other things, would need underpinning. His estimate for the structural work alone was £50,000; coincidentally the same amount as Freakley seemed to think the building could be fully restored for!
As the Public Inquiry was now looming, I thought I had better formalise the loan agreement with the bank. Unfortunately my long standing manager had now retired, and as no replacement had yet been appointed, I had to deal with somebody from Peterborough. He was a completely different kettle of fish, and mythered on about gearings and other such things! Where we really fell out, however, was on the subject of the level of security he wanted. Not only did he require a charge on the new shop, he also wanted Park Hall and our house as security. I pointed out that the shop and stores alone were over double the value of the amount I wished to borrow, and there was no way he was getting our house as well. He then really upset me by suggesting that without my house at stake, I could just go bust and drop the bank in, without any personal loss: giving no consideration to the fact that I would have lost my livelihood, and all the money I had invested in the business. If I was upset, my accountant, who had accompanied me at the meeting, was fit to be tied! He stormed out of the bank after the meeting, muttering about what a good 'risk' I was, and that we could go to any bank and get a loan, no problem. For the time being however, we seemed to have reached something of an impasse.

On July 5th the big day dawned, and the public enquiry began. Would the opposition turn out in force; would the adjudicator be sympathetic to our cause? All was about to be revealed. A quick scan of the opposition's side of the council chambers showed there to be no wig wearers, nor indeed my friend Mr Freakley, so that seemed like a good start! The problem for the planning department was that as none of the factions, who were supposedly so against the demolition, had bothered to turn up, they would have to put their case for them. As the planning department had actually been

supportive of our application, this seemed a little unfair; and seemed even more so, once George Hastings got started on them! It was a real education for me, seeing George ply his trade: it was *nearly* worth his fee, just to see him in action.
His opening gambit was brilliant, and immediately wrong footed the 'opposition'. He stood up, and addressing the adjudicator, said. "Purely as a point of law, I don't think Mr Limming even needs to re-apply for demolition permission, as his father did so just under ten years ago, when the East Elloe Rural District Council was still in existence, and at that time permission lasted for ten years." (It was now three) "As you cannot legislate retrospectively, it is my contention that the demolition permission is still actually current." Boy; did this cause some consternation on the other side of the room! After some frantic whispering amongst themselves, someone was dispatched to the records office to check the validity of George's claim. As no counter claim was forthcoming, it is fair to assume that he was correct in his assertion.
Next in the firing line was the poor old council employee, who had been elected to take the stand and answer George's questions. Firstly he was asked how they had arrived at their figure for the restoration costs. Well, he couldn't say guess work, but that's what it was, and with no documentation to support their figure, the adjudicator was not too impressed. As he did throughout the hearing, George then presented him with a copy of our report, and moved on to what could be done with the buildings, once restored. The suggestion that they would make excellent offices played right into George's hands, as the council had just demolished the old East Elloe Rural District Council offices, just up the road from our buildings, in order to sell the land for house building. This was pointed out in George's usual eloquent way, and that was another small victory won. He really hadn't missed a trick, and every time the adjudicator looked towards the opposition side of the room, to ask if they had a particular piece of documentation, only to be met with blank stares, George would approach him with the requested information, having pre-empted what he would require.

Such was the efficiency of George's presentation that by lunch time he had completely demolished the case against demolition, so to speak! All that remained was for the adjudicator to inspect the buildings, and write his report; and for me to pick up the tab for the whole show of course! It left a bitter taste that I was now £6,000 poorer, merely because a couple of organisations had written a letter as a matter of principal. Were it that they had to pay the costs if they 'lost', I feel there would be a few less letters written.
After a further agonising three months, we finally had our decision: the buildings could go. Now all we needed was planning permission for the new one, now surely just a formality, and the money to build it. Fortunately for me we now had a new, young bank manager at the Holbeach branch, and he was far more affable than his colleague. He asked me why I wanted to build the new shop, and I told him that I really wanted another Lotus, and could not see that happening unless I increased the retail turnover of the business, which would require larger premises. He thought that seemed like a good enough incentive as any to succeed, and granted the loan; as simple as that!

DOMOLITION UNDER WAY. 23 AND 25 ALREADY GONE, 19 AND 21 NEXT!

So; we now had the money, planning was just a case of waiting for the 'rubber stamp', all that remained was to find a builder and work out how we were going to operate while the rebuilding took place. I also had a bit of luck in the shape of a large homewares shop going broke in Boston. All the shop fittings were to be auctioned off, and as there was not too much interest, I managed to buy most of what I would need for the new shop for just £200. The hardest bit was that they had to be cleared that night, so I had the job of carrying everything down a long flight of stairs, and out to the truck. I was well and truly cream crackered by the time I had finished!
As there was now nothing to stop us demolishing 19-25, I started to look for suitable candidates. I knew that quite a lot of the materials would be recyclable, and so didn't expect to have to pay much to get the job done; I didn't however expect to get paid for the privilege, but in the end that is what happened; to the tune of £1,400.
On July 10th 1985 the plans were finally passed, two years and seven months after that first planning meeting, what a rave that had been! A couple of weeks later demolition started, with stock having

PARK HALL, PRESSED INTO SERVICE AS A TEMPORARY SHOP.

to be moved out just in time to allow that part of the buildings to be taken apart. As 19-21 and 23-25 were separate entities, it at least meant we could operate fairly normally whilst the first of the units was dismantled, once they started on 19-21 however, everything had to be transferred to Park Hall, with the shop having to be 'topped up' from there. We also had to staff Park Hall, as any items too large to keep at the shop would have to be collected from there. I must say our customers were very supportive during this period, and the growers in particular soon got the hang of going straight to Park Hall for all their sundries; it just meant they could no longer grab a bar of chocolate while they were at it, as many of them like to do!
It was during this period that an interesting character set up shop in Holbeach, just down the road from our stores. I first met him when he wandered into the shop to introduce himself, and suggest that I should sell up, as he was going to be 'doing the job properly', which would inevitably lead to me going out of business, and as he would hate to see that happen, he was giving me fair warning, so that I could sell up! I said I was willing to take my chances, and would see how things panned out. I have to admit that he did promote himself very well, and certainly didn't do us any favours for a while, but fortunately he also didn't have much of a clue about running a retail business. In common with a lot of people, he seemed to think you bought an item for ten pounds, sold it for fifteen pounds, and therefore had five pounds to spend. Nice in theory, but it doesn't quite work like that! In reality, if you buy, for example, a case of twelve items, the first eight you sell cover the cost of buying the stock, the next three and a three quarters cover wages, rates, utility bills, vehicle expenses, accountants fees, etc. etc. and if you are really lucky, once you have sold that twelfth item, a quarter of the sale price might be yours to spend! A little simplistic maybe, but that's how it works: 'your bit' doesn't come until the end, so you can't spend it until everybody else has had their bit. Anyway, as the realities of running a business began to dawn on our new friend, he became far keener to work together; to

the point where he thought it would be a good idea to buy his pet products from us, seeing as how our warehouse was just up the road. Obviously alarm bells went off and I agreed on the condition that payment would be in cash. This all went well until he caught my van driver at the store one day. Although he knew it was supposed to be cash only, 'W' managed to convince him that a cheque would be just as good, and predictably it bounced. I was not best pleased, as I knew the chances of getting recompensed would be slim. There was only one thing for it: I would have to go shopping. I waited until 'W' was not about, and then paid a visit, filling my trolley with goods to the value of the rubber cheque. When it came to paying I simply took the cheque out, backed it, (in those days you could transfer a cheque made out to you to a third party by signing it on the back, hence the expression) and handed it over. That was the last I really heard of 'W', as a short while after the business folded.

By September we had a clear site, and the tenders for construction of the shop and stores started to come in. These varied by about 20%, the cheapest coming from Godfrey Construction, a company just started by the son of a long established local builder, in fact it would be his first job, if he secured it. After careful consideration we decided to go with the new boy, and informed the other hopefuls of our decision. To my amazement I then had a visit from the secretary of one of the other builders, with an offer to match the Godfrey price and give me a substantial 'cash incentive' as well. I told her that I didn't conduct my business in that manner, and had they wanted the job, they should have put in a lower price in the first place. I thought that would be the end of the matter, but no: the next day she was back, with an even more generous offer! I had to be a little less ambiguous in my rebuttal this time, and the message finally sank in.

After all the shenanigans building work finally started on November 1st 1985, with a six month build schedule. I had been advised to engage a quantity surveyor, and although this seemed like a bit of an extravagance, Eddie Humphries turned out to be worth his weight in gold. All he asked of me that was I didn't 'stick my nose in' when it came to making decisions about the build, and as time went by I could see why. It would have been easy for the builders to ask me if it was OK to do this or that, and then when Eddie came to pull them up on it later, they would be able to say I had given my blessing, which would have undermined him somewhat; and I have to say, he didn't miss a trick! One example was the flooring, which had been quoted for the whole shop area: but as Eddie pointed out, there were pillars and various other intrusions, which reduced the actual area to be tiled, so he measured the exact square footage, and that is all he would sanction for payment. It was the same when they asked for an extension on the build time, owing to bad weather. Eddie reminded them they had started the job in November, so there was a fair chance there would be bad weather at some time during the build, and they should have allowed for it. As such the agreed penalty clause would still apply. Despite his tough stance relations between Eddie and Paul remained amicable, and the shop was indeed completed on time and to budget. When I asked Paul what he had thought of Eddie's approach, he opined that I had not paid for one screw nor nail more than I should have done, but that he had been absolutely fair; so that was good enough for me!

You would think being in business, you would soon learn to treat people with suspicion, but I think country people are generally pretty trusting, even though this can bite you on occasion. One such was when our moss supplier came to me with a story of how he couldn't get to where he harvested his moss as his van had broken down. You may think 'why would you want to buy moss, isn't that something you try to eradicate from your lawn?' Well, it can be, but it's also used to make holly wreaths, and we used to supply bags of it. Although I was aware that many of the characters involved in moss gathering were of a somewhat shady disposition, our chap seemed pretty straight, even being quite happy to issue receipts: something most were reluctant to do! So, as the only way I could see of getting my moss that day was to lend the chap our

truck, this is what I did. Bad idea! The first phone call was from Norfolk Police, telling me a vehicle registered to me had been seen in the woods, where the driver was illegally harvesting moss. The next call was to inform me that our truck had just filled up with fuel, and driven off without paying! Besides all this, I was now getting concerned, as it was now dark, and still no sign of our truck. (I had already gathered I wouldn't be seeing any moss!). I eventually found it abandoned in the pub yard across the road, and fortunately the Police believed my story, so I was able to offer to pay for the petrol, and that was the end of the matter. Needless to say our erstwhile moss supplier had disappeared into thin air!
I suppose I always should have been suspicious of a chap called Jagger: after all, a rolling stone gathers no moss!

Chapter 7 A New Beginning

The 'Grand Opening' was set for May 6th '86, my 31st birthday. I was conscious of the fact that to build a new shop had been dad's

DAD WOULDN'T HAVE LIKED THIS SHOW OF SENTIMENTALITY!

dream, and acknowledged such by having a stone plaque built into the brick work, with the inscription 'This Shop Is Dedicated To John W. Limming. The Realisation of His dream. May 6th 1986'. Hopefully he would not be offended by such sentimentality!

We had to put in some silly hours to get the place ready, bearing in mind we still had to run the 'old shop' during the day, and there were times when I thought we would never be ready in time, but a few hours before the allotted time we finally had the last piece of racking assembled and the last bit of stock on the shelves. Of course, this was a big event for Holbeach, and the place was packed on opening night. It was a rare old party, and even though we were all exhausted, we were a very happy crew.

I know the great, and now regrettably late, Colin Chapman always

used to say you make your own luck, but looking back now, I have to say that I was at the very least fortunate to open the new shop when I did. House prices were on the rise, and banks were trying to lend people as much money as they could talk them into. With all this equity in their property, and banks more than willing to turn it into cash, house owners could go on a spending spree, thinking the bubble would never burst, and that's what a lot of them did, which was very fortunate for us!
We couldn't believe the difference our new environment made: no longer did we have to run up and down three flights of stairs every time somebody wanted a dog basket; now we merely walked through to the neat and tidy store room and picked it off its neat

DAD'S DREAM BECOMES REALITY IN MAY 1986.

and tidy shelf. Also, growing from a sales area of 256 Sq. Ft. to one of 1,500 Sq. Ft., plus a warehouse the same size, meant we could display nearly all of our retail stock, which opened up the possibility of impulse sales. Before a customer would come in, ask for their packet of Weedol, be served with it and leave. Now they would come in, wander around the shop, spot a lawn roller, and leave with that and the packet of Weedol! I must admit the browsing element did take a bit of getting used to: in the old shop, if somebody came through the door it meant they wanted to buy; with all the stock in the place there was hardly space to turn round, let alone browse. Now customers would sometimes just want to look around the shop, and the old approach of asking people if you could get them something could offend if all they wanted to do was browse. It is difficult to find the right balance between being attentive and yet not bothering people. Some people want you to serve them as soon as they walk through the door, where the same approach with others will put them off, and make them feel like you are pressurising them. The safest 'middle ground' seems to be to acknowledge them, and then ask if they are happy browsing, or whether they would like help; most people seem comfortable with this approach.

With all the expense of the shop, my car ambitions had to take a bit of a back seat, but a Capri 2.8i, quick and fun, but with brakes that faded faster than a fake tan, had come and gone, replaced by a Peugeot 205 GTI, nimble and nippy, but liable to put you through a hedge backwards quicker than you could say 'lift off over steer', if you took liberties with it.

Another departee was our most colourful member of staff; Tink. She had a week off, and on her return I enquired as to what she and Richard had done. She related all the detail about various places they had visited, and then as a foot note added, "Oh and we got married". Typical Tink: matter of fact, no fuss, just do it! I did feel a bit sorry for her mother, having been deprived of all the pomp and ceremony, although on the plus side, it did spare her Tink's likely choice of wedding attire; which most certainly wouldn't have been conventional. As Richard was in the RAF, it was not possible for her to stay with us, so sadly she left, and a long forgotten calm once more descended upon the shop.

As the void left by Tink would be difficult for one personality to fill, we took on two new members of staff. One somehow ended up with the title of 'Naughty Netty', stood upright and was normal in respect of height and hair. The other was short, hairy, walked on all fours and answered to the name of Walt, or Walter to give him his full title. Fortunately Walt was a Chocolate Labrador, so the short and hairy bit was not a worry! Alice and I had wanted a dog for some time, but would not take on the responsibility until we were sure we could dedicate the time necessary to look after one properly: and properly to us meant walking him twice a day, for a total of at least three miles, and being able to take him to work with me, so he wasn't shut up at home during the day. Surprisingly for someone with a vested interest in people owning a dog, I spend more time trying to talk people out of having one, if they are not able, or prepared, to dedicate the required amount of time to them, than I do talking them into it! Walt made an immediate impact, and soon had his own fan club. Although it was not the intention, he also turned out to be an excellent sales man: people would want to know what I fed him on, as he was a good looking lad, even though I say so myself, and would want the same food for their dog. He would also demonstrate dog beds, if the customer had a dog of a similar size, although he somehow seemed to think he deserved a dog chew for performing this service. You only need to do something once with a Labrador before it becomes a routine, especially if it involves food! The only trouble was that meant he wanted to demonstrate every dog bed, so you put a bed down on the shop floor at your peril, as before you knew it you would have 45 kilos of Labrador adorning it, even if it was Jack Russell sized!

Thinking of things dog related, it has always fascinated me what happens to people when they order a dog identity tag. I engrave these, admittedly not perfectly, with a hand held machine my father bought many years ago. I usually do them late on a Friday, ready for collection the following day.

It became apparent that the container in which they are kept was getting ever fuller, so the decision was taken to request payment at the time of order, to ensure people collected them. The fascinating bit is that it has made no difference whatever to the non collection rate: we still get left with about a quarter of all the discs I engrave; so what happens to all these dogs I have no idea: surely they can't all die.

January '87 saw some of the worst snow for many years; it was so bad that even our trusty VW Truck ended up wedged in a snow drift, not far into my journey. I had to walk the rest of the way up to the main road, and then managed to get a lift into work. I didn't fancy the four mile walk home at night, so ended up staying in Holbeach the night; the only time I have ever had to do so.
As mum was now 71, it was decided that she should maybe ease back a bit more; her idea of this being to start taking Mondays off. Things were still going well in the shop, so much so that serving and doing deliveries would keep all five of us busy, so I would often stay behind at night to fill shelves, or price up stock. We were also able to buy the firm's first new truck, which was quite a milestone. What I hadn't forgotten was my reason for wanting the new shop in the first place: to feed my Lotus habit! Right from the start I had a three year countdown chart in my office, as that is how long I had given myself to be able to afford another one, and it was looking like I was ahead of schedule.
Despite the reservations of the original bank manager, two years down the line I had cleared a large proportion of our ten year loan, and now felt in a position to order another Lotus, and this time a new one; what I didn't do was tell Alice, as I thought it would be a nice surprise for her; the only trouble was, that meant I was going to have to not let anything slip for over four months!
A couple of years prior to this I had been approached by a chap, who asked if I could let him have some storage space in Park Hall. We didn't need the space on the balcony, (which had been the projection room, in its former life) so I let him have that. What turned up was this jumble of military stuff; it turned out my new storage tenant had been in the Foreign Legion, and now dealt in articles with a military theme. He always paid his rent, and was no bother, but then one day he just disappeared, and never did return! After a couple of years I approached the police as to what I should do with all this stuff and they saw no reason why I shouldn't dispose of it as I saw fit. I eventually sorted out a few bits and pieces that may come in for fancy dress parties, and took the rest to

an army surplus shop. To this day I have not seen hide or hair of my former tenant: mysterious!
It was at about this time that the gradual decline in the horticultural supplies part of the business started. The supply of packaging had always been a very cut throat affair, but now a new competitor had entered the arena, backed by an investor with a shed load of money to throw at the job, and a manufacturer wanting to break in to the horticultural market. They employed a very clever tactic, by telling our customers that they could cut the prices and still make a reasonable profit for themselves, implying that we had been 'ripping them off'. The fact of the matter was that we supplied the 'direct delivery' flower boxes (that was deliveries of over 2,500, which went direct from the factory to the customer), at virtually cost price, in order to buy the volumes necessary to get a low enough price to be competitive: the profit, such as it was, was made on the smaller quantities we sold through the shop. Naturally the growers came to us, wanting the same prices as they had been quoted by the new boys on the block. As this would have meant us selling at a considerable loss, we let the business go. I did approach our manufacturer, but they were not willing to get involved in a price war. With hind sight, the amount it would have cost them to see the opposition off, before they could get established, would have been a fraction of what they subsequently lost, but by this time I was dealing direct with the factory, not through my ally Don, so I had no support from within the company.
On the subject of getting rid of opposition, I have always wondered just how ruthless the big companies would be. This thought was prompted by something which happened to an acquaintance of mine. He was in a fairly senior position at a well established produce company, which was doing well. They then 'head hunted' a new MD, who came with a very high reputation within this field. From day one she seemed to do everything she could to upset their customers, going out of her way to alienate them. They lost some very large accounts, and as hard as the sales force tried to repair the damage, she just kept on shedding customers. The staff could see

the writing on the wall, and those that knew they would be welcome elsewhere left, so weakening the company even more. Within a remarkably short time the company had gone bust. What has always bothered me is how somebody who had previously been outstanding at their job could suddenly be a disaster. Then I got to thinking; what if a rival company 'let her go' so that she could infiltrate the opposition, and remove them: surely far cheaper than competing in the normal way, and of course you would have the necessary information to pick up the pieces. All a bit 'cloak and dagger' I know; but I just can't think of any other rational reason for such a drastic change in her supposed ability.

As mum's 72nd birthday loomed, we at last managed to persuade her to move out of the old family home at No17, into a bungalow at the other end of town. Not only did this provide her with a more comfortable environment, it also meant she was now far enough away from the shop to ease a bit further into semi-retirement.

She probably felt I could be trusted to run the place now without winding up too many customers, although I must confess to the occasional lapse: sometimes an opportunity was just too good to miss; like the lady with the fish bowl for example. It all started off innocently enough, with the common scenario of the child having won a goldfish at the fair, and requiring a bowl to keep it in. By now the traditional round glass bowls had been replaced by plastic items, which were prone to damage if wedged into each other too tightly. To prevent this there was a piece of polystyrene placed between each one. On this particular occasion I brought the bowl through, complete with polystyrene. When I presented it to the lady, she wanted to know what the polystyrene was for. What should have come out as 'Oh, that's just a packing piece', somehow transformed into, 'Oh, that's to test your water with'. Naturally she wanted to know more, so I explained how you needed to be sure your water was suitable for the fish to float in, so you just placed the polystyrene in a sample of the water, and if it floated, then your water would be suitable for the fish. Without so much as a query she took her bowl, complete with free water tester, and toddled off home to put it to the test. I suppose I was a bit slow really: I should have sold here a bottle of 'water buoyancy aid', just in case it didn't float!

It was not long now before Alice would be put out of her misery; or more to the point, suffering my misery! She reckoned that I had been 'like a bear with a sore head' since I had parted with my Lotus, but at last the arrival of my new Esprit was imminent. As befitted such an event I had arranged for it to be delivered on April 1st, but not to our house: I thought a nice hotel would be far more in keeping, then it could just happen to be in the car park the next

MY FIRST NEW LOTUS AND MY THIRD ESPRIT.

morning. The first Alice knew of it was a letter in the bread bin that morning, telling her to be ready by seven that night. I gave her no clue as to where we were going, but knew she would need a 'posh frock', so I had bought her a complete new outfit, and delivered it to the hotel a couple of days previously. I had rather disingenuously given her the idea that the place we would be staying at was rather more casual than was actually the case, and so when we arrived at this posh hotel, she was a bit concerned that her attire would be unsuitable. This was all part of the plan of course: I let her 'stew'

until she started to unpack, and then said, "Why don't you have a look in the wardrobe: you never know your luck, maybe someone has left something behind." No doubt the rational side of her brain was saying 'he's really lost it this time', but fortunately the bit she uses to tolerate me said 'better humour him, and go and have a look.' Now she was really confused: not only had someone left a dress, but also shoes and tights; Oh, and a new dinner suit for me! By now I had been well and truly rumbled; at least about the clothes, however, the biggest surprise was yet to come.
Once Alice recovered from the shock of me spending some money on clothes, something for which I am not renowned, the evening went really well. The hardest bit for me was containing my excitement, knowing what was coming the next morning. As we walked down the stairs that next morning, Alice's suspicions began to be aroused; as there in front of the hotel sat this stunning shiny red sports car. It was not however the car that did it, it was my lack of reaction to it! Usually I can spot an interesting car at 200 paces… in the dark… through a brick wall! As this was a brand new model, Alice thought it was a Ferrari, but in any case, she knew it would warrant my attention under normal circumstances. Her suspicions grew further when she spotted two 'wide boys' (her description!) loitering in the reception area: she thought they looked out of place in this setting, which in fairness, they did. When said 'wide boys' accompanied us outside to our new Esprit, she just couldn't believe it, and still wouldn't until about two days later, after I had finally convinced her that I hadn't just hired it!
Holbeach being a typical small town, it was a given that word about my new car would spread like Marmite fired from a cannon. (Sorry to interrupt the flow, but that has just reminded me of dad's comment when told that our local vicar had been made a Canon. His only to be expected response was, "I suppose they'll fire him now then", followed by his usual appreciation of his own joke: but as he used to say; he hadn't heard it before either!). Anyway, as I was saying, I had to brace myself for the obligatory comments about my prices going up, how I must be charging too much etc.

Fortunately for me, an insurance company had just published the cost of bringing up a child from birth to the age of sixteen, coming up with a figure of £168,000. Alice and I had sorted out before we decided to marry that we would not, baring disasters, be pursuing that particular option, so when tackled, about the car my response would be, "Yes I know; we are still wondering what to spend the other £137,000 on". This would really get them going, thinking I had a windfall of some sort. When they tired of trying to guess the source of this new found wealth, I would enlighten them as to the findings of the insurance company, and as they most likely had children themselves, there would usually be sigh of resignation, and at least a tacit admission that I had a point.
It has always amused me how people tackle the subject of you being a childless couple: some don't like to mention it in case… you know…there are problems in that department! Others try to enlighten you as to the errors of your ways, and convince you of what you are missing, while others warn of the major regrets you will have later in life. All may be true; although if it is the former it would have saved a lot of 'organisation' had we known in the first place! The people I find most confusing are those who say; 'well, what if your parents hadn't have had you?' Not a problem. I wouldn't have known anything about it, so it was hardly likely to cause me any concern! Now; had they let me get to about fifteen, and then decide they didn't want me, that may have been a little more awkward! I fully realise it is not 'normal' to have no desire to add to the population, but for me there was never a decision to be made, it was just something which I always knew, in the same way as I never had to make a conscious decision about not wanting to hammer a nail through my hand; it was just something I knew I didn't want to do: I suppose in the same way that a Moto GP rider has a malfunction in the 'self preservation' department of the brain, mine is in the 'go forth and multiply' section. Either way, 30 years down the road, Alice and I are still very happy with our non decision, and at least now we are in our fifties the enquiries as to when we are going to start a family have receded.

Thinking of the above reminds me of a customer who had moved into the area fairly recently, and was intrigued by the dedication stone to my father on the shop. She enquired as to the story behind it, and then asked the usual question as to whether I had any family to carry on the business. When I told her I was pleased to say I hadn't, she seemed a little bemused, but before she had a chance to interrogate me further I confided in her how worried I was, as several of my contemporaries now had grand children, and as they seemed even more expensive than their progenitors I was fearful in case I suffered the same fate! The poor lady was now completely perplexed: she couldn't decide whether I had no grasp whatever of the way succession actually came about or if I was just plain crackers!

Back in the real world, I was brought back to earth when I knocked some bottles of flower dye off the shelves in the stores. As it hit the floor the bottles shattered, and there was dye everywhere, including just about every bit of exposed skin I had. This product was used by the flower growers to colour flowers which were naturally white, such as esther reeds, and it tends to stay where it's put! Soap and water wouldn't even touch it, so drastic action was called for: a trip across the road to the hair dressers. Once they had brought their fits of laughter under control, they set about me with all manner of potions. As I sat there receiving the attentions of three attractive young ladies, it occurred to me that maybe this hadn't been such a disaster after all. Eventually they did manage to lessen the effect, but on the brighter side, at least I could act as a mobile colour chart for our range of dyes until they faded completely!

We had a bit of good fortune at the beginning of September, when the local mill decided to stop selling animal feeds to the general public, to concentrate on their core business activities. We were only too pleased to take the job on; the only problem being where to store it all. The most cost effective solution seemed to be a 40 foot shipping container, which we had room for at the rear of the shop. What we didn't have was any access to get it there! After much debate and head scratching, it was decided that the only way would be to hire a crane, and with the blessing of our neighbour, hoist it over the bungalow behind us, and drop it into place: simple. The one small drawback to this plan was that the crane driver would have no vision whatever of the 'drop zone'. When the day arrived the crane driver seemed totally unfazed by the challenge we had set him, and just picked the container up, and with guidance from his 'eyes on the ground', dropped it in to place as easily as one might drop a new pat of butter into a butter dish. Quite amazing.

As the sun started to set on 1988, although we didn't know it at the time, it was also going down on the boom times for the shop. The base rate was now 13%, and the reality of all that seemingly easy money was starting to hit home. House prices were no longer on the rise, so there was no more collateral to be sucked from that source. The only bright spot was that those with savings were doing quite well, so they maybe had a few bob to spend.

With mum now slipping gracefully into retirement we needed another member of staff. As we are a six day a week operation, days off have to be staggered throughout the week, which means a lot of days you are a member of staff down, plus with five of us there was often someone on holiday, which also left you short staffed, so we really needed someone else to ensure we always had cover. After all the upset dad had, I vowed that if anybody ever stole from me, I would pursue them all the way to the courts, and preferably to prison. I always made this crystal clear when a new member of staff started, as was the case in this instance. After you have been around a shop as long as I had by now, you develop a sort of sixth sense for how things should be; you know what sort of a day it has been, and know roughly what to expect to find in the tills at close of play. A while after our new girl started I began to get this feeling that something wasn't quite right: I didn't have any evidence of wrong doing, just a gut feeling. As there had only been one change to the line up, suspicion naturally fell in that direction, but obviously everybody else would have to be eliminated before I could be sure it was her.

At the beginning of '89 an event occurred which gave me the perfect opportunity to issue a 'Gypsy's warning' to any member of staff who may be confused about what belonged to them. Two young lads came into the shop, wanting to know where they may be able to get a bike puncture mended. They seemed quite worried, and it transpired that they had biked all the way from Orton Malborne, about 20 miles away. As the local bike shop had closed some time ago, I couldn't think of anywhere that would be able to do the job, and remembering the epic bike rides Richard and I used to undertake when we were their age, I could relate to their situation. I told them to load their bikes on the truck, and I would take them back to my house, where I had a puncture repair outfit, and I would mend it for them. They seemed very relieved at the offer, and we set off to Whaplode. I soon had the puncture repaired and showed them the best route back home from my house, before setting off back to the shop, with a glow of satisfaction in having got them out of their predicament. The glow didn't last too long, as when I returned home that night I noticed the shed door where I had carried out the repair was not properly closed. On further investigation I could see that the lock had been forced, and my bike was missing. The identity of the likely perpetrators was pretty obvious, but it just didn't make sense to me, as they could only ride one bike at once, so how were they going to get mine back to Orton Malborne? A quick reconnoitre of the boundary soon answered that question, for hidden around the back of the hedge was one of the boy's bikes. I was absolutely incensed, and went up to the Whaplode Police house to report the crime. (This was in those halcyon days when we had local Bobbies, who knew the local people). As the old way of policing was still in operation at this time, instead of issuing me with a crime number and telling me to claim on my insurance, he decided this was a despicable act, that needed investigating. Of course, all we had to go on was that they were two lads in their early teens, who we could assume, as they had told me before they planned the crime, came from Orton Malborne. It hadn't occurred to me, but this was not school holiday time, so the first thing the officer did was to visit the school which they would most likely attend and ask if they had any absentees on that day. Sure enough two lads had been missing without explanation. His next stop was the local police station, and a bike shop opposite to alert them to the situation. It was at the bike shop that the reason for taking my bike became clear. Unbeknown to me I had a rare and sought after model, as it had been made at the time when Raleigh had just taken over Carlton, and as such was a bit of a hybrid, and now quite valuable. I may have been ignorant to the fact, but the two lads obviously weren't. The shop owner promised to keep an eye out for it, in case the lads tried to sell it on, and assured the officer that he would recognise that model as soon as he saw it: and see it he did! It was that fate thing again, as the very next day what should be leant up against a shop front nearby but a Carlton Pro-Am bike, just like mine. The shop owner shot across to the police station, and as the miscreant came out of the shop, there was a police officer waiting for him: I would have loved to see his face! Never in a million years did he think he would be tracked down; he was so shocked and admitted to the theft. So, two days after it had disappeared, and with virtually nothing for the officer to go on, I had my bike back: well most of it anyway! The little toerag was obviously not too repentant, as he had tried to hang on to some of the accessories that had been on the bike. I told the officer it didn't matter; I was just pleased to have my bike back, but he was now really hacked off with this lad, and it became a matter of principal, so after another visit the lad handed the missing items over. This had been proper police work, and I did write to the Chief Constable commending the officer concerned on his excellent work.

I don't doubt those in favour of 'modern policing' would say that recovering my bike was not cost effective, but that is a very short sighted attitude. Had things stopped at the issue of a crime number, that lad would have got away with his crime, decided that crime does pay and very likely have gone on to bigger and better things. As it was he was caught and prosecuted for a crime he thought

undetectable, and hopefully that gave him a big enough jolt to make him think very hard before trying it again; potentially saving other people grief and money and the police time and money.
So it was that I recounted this story at work, reiterating how I would bring the full force of the law to bear on anybody who stole from me. Unfortunately the warning went unheeded, as the money still continued to disappear. The culprit was being very clever, as they made sure that they only stole on days when everybody was at work, so making it difficult to establish a pattern. Even so, by now I was all but certain who the perpetrator was, and also knew the money was going from the till at the pet counter. Apparently if a person steals money they generally want to get it to a safe place as soon as possible. With this in mind, I thought our girl's best window of opportunity would be just before she went for lunch. This way the till would have enough in it for the missing notes not to be noticed, and while others were at lunch she would have the opportunity to 'under record' amounts spent by customers, in order to make the till balance: she certainly knew how to cover her tracks.
Once I was sure of my facts, I marked up some notes and then took them to the police station, for them to verify the markings. The notes were placed in the till just before lunch time, from where I was pretty sure they would disappear. A quick check just before our girl was due to go for lunch confirmed my suspicions, and the 'sting' was put into action. As our girl went to get her belongings to go for lunch the police officer challenged her, and asked to see the contents of her purse. Sure enough there were the marked notes. Initially she denied all knowledge of how they had come to be there, but the officer just looked her in the eye and said "Look, I deal with cleverer people than you every day of the week", and with that she just broke down and admitted to the whole thing, so bringing to an end what had been a very distasteful and costly time.
As I had made crystal clear from the start I would; I pressed charges, which prompted a visit from the girl's parents. I was given the full emotional blackmail treatment on how I would ruin their

daughter's life if I pursued the matter, along with myriad excuses. Unfortunately for them my father's experience had taught me that this was the only acceptable course of action, and I would not be swayed. Harsh maybe, but it was not me who would 'ruin her life', she did that herself the first time she put her hand in the till.
On a more positive note, by April of that year I had paid off the final portion of the loan on the shop, just three years after opening it, so that was a great relief; especially as the base rate was now heading towards 15%. I have never liked borrowing money, and always try to pay it back as soon as I can, although that doesn't seem to stop me having mad ideas which necessitate borrowing it all over again!
We also dragged ourselves into the twentieth century by purchasing a fax machine; a £800 investment in those days; that's 2.5% of a Lotus! At this time they were still quite novel, (well they were in Holbeach anyway) and at last it meant an end to confusion over orders. Previously we would place orders by phone, and when an item didn't arrive, or was wrong, there was always the excuse that we hadn't ordered it, or had asked for the wrong thing. Now there was nowhere to hide and it did improve things for a while. With ubiquity however came new excuses, usually that the fax had not been received.
At the end of the year, Pat Thomas, who has always looked after my Lotus's since I have been able to afford to run them properly, phoned to say he had one of the new SE Esprits at his place, if I would like to take it for a spin. Like a lamb to the slaughter I took him up on his invitation, and predictably was blown away by it. By today's standards its 264 BHP was not a lot, but with there not being a lot of weight to shift either it was a seriously quick car! Whilst I put forward all the reasons to myself why I didn't need a faster Lotus, I knew I had been seduced, and it would only be a matter of time and money.
On the subject of money, the firm actually had some again, and this prompted me to resolve something which had been niggling away at me ever since we built the shop. At the time the bank had a

financial interest in it, and naturally wanted to make sure their part of the asset was insured. This I understood, and was happy to supply a photo copy of the insurance details; but no; this was not good enough, they must have the originals. Now quite why they thought I would be stupid enough to risk my own money, as well as theirs, by not insuring the property I don't know; but it did upset me to think that after all these years they did not trust me even to that extent. As they say, what goes around, comes around, so when our deposit account had reached a reasonable amount I wandered into the bank one day and said that as they now had quite a substantial amount of my money in their care I would like to see their insurance certificates. This was obviously not a request the girl at the counter received on a regular basis, and so off she went to ask the manager, who by now was of the non empowered variety, neutered by the unrelenting shift towards centralisation. He explained that they did not keep such things, but was sure a copy could be obtained for me. "Oh no, a copy won't do" I explained, "it will have to be the original". This caused real consternation, as I suspect the procedure for such requests was definitely not in the manual! By now I thought my point had been made, and so I just said, "It's alright; I'll trust you have got the place insured, but wouldn't it have been nice if you could have done the same when I had your money". No doubt they thought 'awkward old sod', but I felt better for it.

By now Walt was three years old, and had wormed his way in to most of the customer's affections, managing to con a good proportion of them into buying him a treat when they came in. Good for trade, but not for Walt's waist line, (if dogs have such a thing!). He was from the larger strain of the breed; this is not just an excuse for his over indulgence, he genuinely was a big lad, with a massive head, (bigger even than my own!) and a really powerful physique; all 45 kilos of it. This 'brick outhouse' stature stood him in good stead one day when he did something totally out of character. Alice and I had put a lot of time and effort into training in the early days, reasoning that if the dog knows what is expected of it, life will be easier for all concerned. He therefore knew that he had to go to the side of the road and sit if a car came when he was on his walk, failure to do so resulting in him having to have his lead on for a period, something he hated, as it limited his 'sniffing' potential: this 'punishment' ensured transgressions were rare. Similarly, but more importantly, he knew that he was not allowed out of the shop door unless he had his lead on. Unfortunately, on the fateful day, the lure of a rather attractive Labrador bitch on the other side of the road proved too strong, and he attempted to get a closer look. What he actually got a look at was the front end of a Ford Orion! My heart sank as I heard the screech of tyres, followed

WALT WAS A VALUABLE & MUCH LOVED MEMBER OF THE TEAM.

by a sickening thud: I just knew something had happened to Walt. I reached the door just in time to see him running, adrenalin fuelled, towards the passage way along the street from the shop. When I caught up with him he lay there shaking, not knowing what had hit him. (I'm afraid he wasn't too hot on his car recognition!)

I rushed him to the vets, dreading the diagnosis, as by now I had seen the car, or at least what was left of it; and it didn't bode well for Walt's chances. After a thorough examination the vet concluded that apart from a torn dew claw he was in one piece, although likely to be heavily bruised. Bruised! He'd just done £600 worth's of damage to a car, how could he be just bruised? Anyway, she gave him a strong sedative, and advised that he would probably sleep most of the time until the next morning. We assumed this would be the first night since he was old enough that there would be no walk. Wrong. As far as he was concerned we always went for a walk when we got home, and he saw no reason to change that now. So off we went, and by the next morning there was only the repair bill to remind us that anything had ever happened: unbelievable, and very lucky.

Not only did Walt train the customers, he also did a comprehensive job on Ivor, the local butcher. Initially I would leave Walt outside while I went in to get my meat, but Ivor reckoned he was cleaner than some of his customers, and as such invited him in to sit at the back of the tiny shop. Whilst accepting that this may not have been strictly correct, Walt was such a well loved character about town that nobody seemed to object; why we could nearly have been French, such was our disregard for abiding by the absolute letter of the law! Naturally Walt would avail himself of a supply of bones whilst there, and try as Ivor might to trick him into taking the smaller of the two on offer; he would always pick each up in turn and then depart with the heaviest. Ivors other downfall was to offer him a piece of whatever meat he had on his slab at the time. One day this just happened to be a piece of fillet steak, and Ivor noticed how, instead of his usual technique of trying to prevent the meat making contact with his insides on the way down, Walt just took it reverently, and then savoured it. "Do you think he could tell that was fillet?" Ivor enquired. "Well, I'll put it this way" I replied, "you know he has a better sense of smell than us, his hearing is better and so is his eye sight; so what makes you think his sense of taste isn't better as well?" "Oh so you think he appreciates a bit of

fillet even more than us then?" Ivor enquired. "Very likely" I replied. Ever after that Ivor always had an off cut of fillet waiting for Walt on his 'butcher days', and boy did he know which days they were. Lovely old boy Ivor, whatever the rights or wrongs of his 'dog's policy'.
One last thought on dogs in general. If their sense of smell is really up to 1,000 times stronger than ours, then how come they can expel something so putrid it would clear a concert hall, and yet still lay there as if nothing had happened? I never have worked that one out!

Tony, my right hand man of many years, has always had a soft spot for Jaguars; of both the four wheeled and four legged variety, and so it seemed a good idea to do something in that vein for his 40th birthday. As it may have been a little difficult to arrange to hire a four legged one, I decided on the car. I did a deal with his wife Sue that if she arranged a weekend away, I would sort out the Jag. Rather than just announce our plan to him, I thought a surprise would be more fun; so a Barbecue for all the staff was arranged at our house and the Jag was hidden in the old barn. We blindfolded Tony, and led him into the barn. We then placed his hand on the front wing and set him guessing. He soon identified it as a car, but the instant he opened the door he just exclaimed "It's a Jaguar!" which makes you realise just how special they do smell.
They had a lovely weekend away, and apart from how special the car was to drive, the other thing which left an indelible impression was how differently people treat you when you roll up in a Jag, instead of his usual Escort. It shouldn't be that way I know, but it is a fact of life that people are influenced by such things.

A rather sadder event was the demise of our old Gross mechanical till. This had done sterling service for many years, and had been put into semi-retirement when we moved shops, by being consigned to the pet counter. It really was a marvel of engineering, with all those wheels and cogs churning away. Its replacement was about a

quarter of its weight, and had probably 90% less parts, but such is progress.
For my birthday, mum had paid for a couple of flying lessons. I think she was aware that I was getting disenchanted with the lack of opportunity to use the Esprit properly, as the 'Nanny State' continued to tighten its grip, and she thought flying might offer a less restrictive outlet. I did enjoy the taking off and landing, even though I wasn't at the controls for that bit, but once up there it just didn't give me a buzz, so the Esprit was safe for a little longer at least! Talking of the Esprit; it had landed me in hot water, not with the police, but the tax man!
Alice and I had gone over to Holland to see her sister, and whilst there took part in a Dutch Lotus Club event: a hill climb would you believe! I did ask Alice what they were doing with a hill in Holland, but she reckoned it was a bit they pinched from a neighbouring country at some point in the past! Anyway, things went quite well, and we came away with a couple of trophies, and as Pat, who serviced the car, was also there, he asked if I would mind him putting a picture of the car and trophies in the local paper, as a bit of publicity. I saw no reason why not; but didn't reckon on the eagle eyed tax inspector, always on the lookout for prey!
Before I knew it I had a request to supply the tax office with full details of how my motor racing activities were funded! Fortunately they accepted my explanation that this had been a one off 'social' event, which I was able to show, had been funded with my own, tax paid, money.

Ninety One started off badly with the Gulf War flaring up. Dad had always said that the next war would start in the Middle East, and would be over oil, so he was not too far wrong really. It also saw Alice and my plan to extend our house gather pace. This was something which had been on the 'back burner' for some time, but we wanted to save enough to apply my 50% rule, which meant it had to wait. A twist of fate then brought our plan very much onto the 'front burner'. A plot of land came up for sale, and we decided it would probably be better in the long run to build from scratch, and sell Bridge Farm; much as we loved its location. We asked a local estate agent to value the house, and he immediately saw a snag: the house had subsided, so making it un-saleable. In the meantime it had been made clear that we would not get permission to build the house we wished to on the other plot, and so plan B came into operation.

I approached the insurance company with the proposal to have a cash settlement for our house, so that we could then demolish it and build what we wanted. They were amenable to this solution, and said they would pay us the lowest amount of four quotes for the necessary repairs. Strangely enough, three of the quotes were within a very small percentage of each other, whilst the fourth was way, way lower. There then followed a lot of negotiation, with the insurance assessor not keen to move very far at all. Things finally came to a head one night, when I received a phone call with yet another derisory offer: I decided it was time for a bit of brinkmanship, and so told him that the amount on offer was not enough for us to be able to re-build, so they had better get on with the repair work; which of course they would be able to do for the amount originally offered! Suddenly we were talking sensibly; and I gained more money in the next ten minutes than I am ever likely to again, bar winning the Lottery. Quite what I would have done if they had decided to go ahead with the repair I don't know, but I was fairly confident that I could push pretty close to the amount of the other three quotes before that would be the case.

Amidst all this I had succumbed to the temptation of that SE Esprit, so there was another child we would have to not have! I had pondered long and hard over whether I could justify this latest extravagance, but as a good friend said to me; can you afford it? If the answer is yes, then you don't have to justify it! As I have only ever bought my cars for cash, I thought this was fair comment: I have always regarded them as an indulgence, and as such could never justify borrowing money to fund them, that way if money

ESPRIT NUMBER FOUR. LIKE THE LAST ONE, ONLY FASTER; MUCH FASTER!

does get tight; at least you can 'cash them in'.
What we were going to have to borrow money for was the new house, and so we started looking around for a good mortgage deal. This was the time when endowment mortgages were all the rage, and we were steered very enthusiastically in that direction. The trouble was it all seemed too good to be true to me. We were going to pay over this money for twenty years, and then at the end of it, we would have not only a house, but also a big wad of cash. Any possible pit falls were glossed over, and questions as to whether we could pay chunks off, as we had in the past, were neatly side stepped. Being cautious types Alice and I were really bothered about all this, so in the end I arranged another meeting with the advisor, and told him that the only answer he could give to my questions was yes or no: no reassurances; no explanations; just yes or no!
My first question was "Is there any possibility at all that the endowment will not clear the mortgage?" Reluctantly he had to answer yes. My second question, "could we pay off lump sums?" No! That was all we needed to know: we would be having a repayment mortgage; but what an effort it had been to get some straight answers!

As far as our part of the world was concerned, we were now at the start of a gradual downturn. Initially it was the weaker businesses which failed, but the still high interest rates meant anybody heavily indebted to the bank would struggle, as falling demand, and ever increasing competition from abroad started to take its toll. We saw the loss of several growers, which reflected on our business of course; halving our profits in '92.

We had already cut back on shop staff. When Naughty Netty left, to take up a career in motherhood, we decided as a group, that instead of replacing her, we would all work a six day week when somebody was on holiday, and the rest of the time would manage with just three shop staff.

We also had tragedy on a personal level, when a young female member of staff was killed in a road accident; just a week before she was due to leave for another part of the country. Her replacement, Sal, was very much a local girl, and had some unique sayings, mostly passed down from her father, who was a bit of a local character himself! Somebody like me, for example, who may be some way short of reckless with their money, would be described thus: 'He would skin a fart for a shilling, and ruin a two bob pocket knife doing it.' A whole different language, I can tell you.

Actually, having a reputation for being a bit 'tight' is no bad thing when you are in business; it makes people less likely to ask for discount! Such discouragement can be reinforced with comments like: 'That will be three pounds twenty, or anywhere upwards', or 'We only state a minimum price, you are welcome to give more.' When giving change, (something on which most of our customers seem to insist!) I also tend to say 'And you get all that change', just to make them feel they have done really well!

Most of our regulars love the banter of course, and will often come out with something like 'I would love to be a quid behind you' to which I usually reply: 'Well, if you gave me about a half a million from your pile, you probably would be!' That usually sends them off chuntering!

Another saying I really like is 'He who counts the cost of everything, knows the value of nothing'. I think this is a really good criterion by which to judge things, especially when trying to justify a new Lotus!

Another thing customers seem to expect is for you to have a sale in January. No matter how many times I explain there are only two places for sails: windmills and sailing ships, they still keep asking! I have even explained that a sale is just an admission that you got your buying wrong in the first place, but they still insist, even though I tell them our prices are that good, it's like a permanent sale!

I do sometimes wonder what a 'newcomer' must think if they happen to make their first (only?) visit when one of our regulars and I are giving each other a verbal going over: it must be like they have wandered into that Monty Python sketch about paying for an argument!

Our area has seen a lot of 'incomers' over recent years, as people from the south realise they can sell their house for far more than they pay here, and so leave themselves with a nice pot of cash to make their retirement more comfortable. Some find it difficult to adapt to the slower pace of life, and relative isolation of our area, and return to whence they came, but the majority really embrace the quality of life a rural area can offer, and after a bit of readjustment fit in just fine!

Having mostly come from an urban environment, served only by faceless multiples, they initially find it difficult to grasp the concept of dealing on trust. In a small town like Holbeach, if you do somebody down, word will soon get around: you trade on your reputation; simple as that. I remember one 'new arrival' who came in to order a water butt, and paid in cash. I took his details and told him it would be delivered on Friday. I thought I had concluded the sale, but he just stood there. When I asked him if there was anything else I could help him with he said he was waiting for a receipt for his cash. I apologised, and explained I had forgotten he wasn't a local. I said he was welcome to have a receipt, but usually in Holbeach you paid your money and you received your goods, no receipts needed. He was amazed by this and said where he came from if you handed over cash without getting a receipt for it you were highly unlikely to see the goods or your cash again.

Another strange one was a young girl who wanted to buy a barbecue, but only had a credit card with her. At that time we did not dabble in such things: all that money flying about in the ether, it just wasn't right somehow! Anyway, I said it wasn't a problem; I could assemble the barbecue, deliver it and give her a bill. "What's a bill?" she enquired. I explained how I would record the amount in a book, and give her a copy; she could then come in and pay the amount at a later date. She was now warming to the idea, and enquired as to when she would have to pay. I explained that the usual time was up to 30 days, but we were not rigid on this, and she would know if she had been too long paying, as we would come and throw a brick through her window, with a reminder attached! She was suitably impressed with this new innovation in credit provision, and went off clutching her bill, returning exactly 30 days later to pay.

Cheque writing etiquette was another thing which got me into hot water with non locals. When the 'old boys' came in to buy their supplies, they would expect you to take their cheque book and make the cheque out for them, including filling in the stub. They would have liked you to have signed it as well, if they thought they could get away with it. This procedure was so ingrained, that when a customer came in one day and wished to pay by cheque, I just automatically took their cheque book and started to write out the cheque. They went off like a bottle of Champagne, (I think they were too well to do for it to have been pop!) and it took an awful lot of explanation and apologising to calm them down.

Chapter 8 Another New Beginning!

We started off '93 by moving into our new house. This wasn't exactly a Pickfords job, as we had been living in the old one whilst the other was built, so it was just a case of carrying everything across the yard. Once installed, the old house was demolished to make way for a garden store shed. I was determined that the garage would be for cars, and not filled with all the rubbish we seem to accumulate with our modern lives, and so another dumping site had to be provided for it!

One of the reasons we decided to rebuild on the original site, rather than elsewhere, was our neighbours. We are very lucky to be surrounded by people who are friends as well as neighbours. In Holt and Lizzi's case they were actually friends before they were neighbours! I suppose the friendship really started when we had not long moved into the original house, and wanted to do some major work in the garden; as in bulldozer sized work. As is the way locally I asked around as to where I might borrow one, and Holts name came up. Ever helpful, he arranged to deliver the machine the next Saturday. Being a bit unsure of my likely aptitude for bulldozer driving, I asked Holt to back it off the trailer for me. Sensing my apprehension he enquired as to if I had actually driven a bulldozer before. I confessed to being a 'dozer virgin', but assured him I was a quick learner. Holts reply was that you don't learn to drive a bulldozer in a garden, and with that he set about the task for me! I will not attempt to relate the whole saga here, but suffice to say that two days, most of Holts farm equipment and many tons of imported soil later, we had formed a lasting friendship. Probably one of the reasons we hit it off was our shared penchant for a good wind up! April 1st seems as good a time as any to instigate such activities, and your next door neighbour is as good a victim as any.

The catalyst for our first attempt on Holt and Lizzi was the construction of their tennis court. It seemed that they now had the perfect venue for a country club, so why not open one for them? A

quick rifle through the photo albums came up with a shot of Holt in drag and Lizzi stood next to a fast car, so all we needed was a photo of the tennis court and we, or rather they, were in business. So it was that a batch of posters were printed announcing the opening of this new facility, hosted by 'Madam Holt' and offering driving courses with the resident 'Fast Lady'.
Showing remarkable dedication to the cause, I was up before day break on the first, and by shop opening time there were posters in Spalding, Holbeach and every village in between. Thanks to my efforts the new venture was a great success, with applications flooding in from all quarters! Naturally, once the ball had been set in motion, there were plenty of people willing to help it along: a pseudo letter from the planning office, pointing out the lack of planning permission being just one example. I fully realised there would be repercussions at some point, so all the more reason to savour the moment!

Although mum was by now officially retired, she would usually still walk up to the shop on a Saturday, and help out behind the pet counter; just to keep her hand in. She was now 77 years old, and our longer standing customers would always be pleased to see her, proffering such comments as 'I see you're still keeping your eye on him then'. On one such occasion the customer went on to confirm to me how well he thought she was looking: "Yes, no chance of my inheritance just yet, by the looks of things." Was my provocative reply, but quick as a flash mum came back with, "And what makes you think I am going to go first?" Twenty years on I am starting to think she has a point!
The retail side of the business may have slowed down quite drastically, but at least the remaining growers still had to buy packaging, with strawberry punnet sales holding up particularly well.
By now I had spent over 20 years lugging heavy stuff about, and the strain was beginning to show on the old chassis, with my shoulder in particular giving me a fair bit of discomfort. As men

tend to I ignored it, assuming things would sort themselves out in due course.
Back with the neighbours, one of them had a milestone birthday approaching, and her husband for some reason, assumed I would have something planned to mark the occasion. Although I hadn't, it didn't take much provocation to alter my stance, and a deal was struck whereby he would hire a Gorilla costume, if I would 'do the deed'. Birthday celebrations were to take the form of two dinner parties, held outside, under a very grand giant parasol, for want of a better description. As we were booked in for the 'Saturday sitting', I had to perform on the Friday. Aware of the crowd I was dealing with, Alice secured the various sections of the costume with safety pins, to prevent any 'unauthorised removal', a wise precaution, as it turned out. I had let my good mate Taff in on the plan, and so he decided to come along as my 'wing man', in case I needed emergency back up! We set off to our target, equipped with peanuts and bananas as props. Having secreted ourselves in the garden, where the party was now in full swing, we launched the first salvo: a hand full of peanuts. These rattled on the canopy above the revellers, causing immediate silence. Various theories were put forward as to the source of this intrusion, a nearby apple tree eventually being deemed the culprit. (It was too dark for them to see the missiles on the grass) We allowed proceedings to re-commence, and then let go with another wave of peanuts, followed by a banana. Now we had really got their attention! At this point I loomed out of the undergrowth, being mindful to keep a Neanderthal stance, so as to disguise my height, which would have been a fair clue as to the identity of their attacker. Emitting as Gorilla like grunts as I could muster, I circled the table, making sure not to get within grabbing distance. A cry of 'let's have him' from one of the girls was incentive enough to make good my escape. They did manage to get hold of me, but Alice's safety pins were up to the task, and throwing the envelope I had been carrying into the air distracted them just enough for me to leg it down the drive to safety. I was walking down the road back towards home,

feeling pretty pleased with the way things had gone, and oblivious to the fact that to the rest of the world I was still a six foot three inch tall Gorilla. I may have been unconcerned about my appearance, but the poor old dear who was reversing out of her drive certainly was not! As she swung the car around, there I was, caught like a rabbit in her headlights. Whether she then had a David Attenborough moment, or was just mortified with shock, I don't know, but the car just sat there motionless. I just continued on my way, thinking it best not to stop and offer an explanation, for fear of sending her over the edge altogether! Stranger things have happened in Whaplode Fen I am sure, but not to that poor lady I feel, I just hope that when she related the story they didn't commit her!

Occasionally you do get asked for some strange things, one of the better ones being liquid Derris Dust: I didn't like to ask if they wanted to spray it or puff it! Another was a request for something to revive a dead rubber plant with. I have only known one successful attempt at that particular trick, and he was far better connected than I am. On a similar vein, I remember when I was first told about the attributes of a then new weed killer, called Roundup. The salesman was expounding its many attributes, including its relative safety, given that the whole purpose was to kill things. When asked to expand further on his claims, he said "Oh, you could drink the stuff; you'd just have to be very careful where you p****d afterwards!"
Things were not any better trade wise by year's end: growers continued to either go bust or just abandon the job, and no new blood was coming into the growing game. The younger generation could do far better getting a proper job, free from the vagaries of the wholesale markets and demands of the ever more powerful supermarkets. The growing trade was gradually polarising into small one man bands, which could just about make a living, without all the overheads employing staff brings, and bigger growers, who had the economies of scale to make the job pay.

By now even I had to admit that time wasn't going to fix my shoulder problem: the pain was now sufficient for even me to part with money. I say part with money, as the pain killer and rest route suggested by my doctor was not really an option in my job. I visited various practitioners of the black science of tweaking, but although they pulled me about and cracked various bits there was no discernable improvement in my condition. Finally I ended up at a proper Chiropractic Clinic, and immediately I was filled with confidence. As soon as she saw my skewed torso Kim said, "You did a lot of heavy lifting when you were younger didn't you?" This I confirmed, and she then enquired as to whether I was aware that the left side of my chest was far more prominent than the right. As you are likely to see more appealing specimens than me crawling out of cheese, I don't tend to spend too much time studying my physique in the mirror, but now it had been brought to my attention, she was absolutely right. To her it was simple: a man's spine is not 'set' until he is in his mid twenties apparently, and all the lifting had compressed my vertebrae, so causing my spine to twist. This in turn had twisted my rib cage, so causing it to rub against my shoulder blade, which showed its displeasure by giving me serious aggravation.

She warned me at the outset that as things had become so set in their positions it would be a long job to fix me; but such was my faith in her diagnosis that I stuck with the treatment, even though, as before there was no immediate relief: the difference this time was that I knew the right bits were being tweaked!

It took over four months, but eventually the breakthrough 'crack' reverberated through my abused bones, and the pain was gone. What a rewarding job to have; seeing a face drawn and full of pain walk in and then watching that same face, now relieved and smiling walk out. Just like being a shopkeeper really!

One part of the year I never did look forward to was February, and the Springfields Horticultural Exhibition. This was a combined forced flower show and trade exhibition, which any one supplying the flower growing industry really had to exhibit at. The forced flower show really was magnificent, with large displays of beautifully scented flowers bringing some much needed cheer to this drab, grey winter month. In its hey-day this show drew massive crowds, with many of the bulb salesmen coming over from Holland to do business, and socialise with friends. It really was a gathering of the clans, and the bar area was always a lively place, later on in the evening. I used to share a stand with Lin-Pac, but as I was a local, most of the growers knew me anyway, so from my point of view it was more a case of being seen, and keeping an eye on the opposition. The problem I had with the show was that I am not particularly fond of making small talk, when I could be doing something more productive back at base, and the draughty old halls in which it was held were *unbelievably* cold, when you were just stood about. The cold would work insidiously up from your feet; numbing your knees by noon, and your nether by night! For someone who hates the cold at the best of times, this was sheer purgatory.

THE STAND WE USED TO SHARE WITH LIN-PAC, AT THE ANNUAL SHE EXHIBITION.

You may think this a negative attitude and what about all those potential customers from further afield. Well, in my experience, if somebody has travelled from out of the area to buy packaging, there is usually some reason other than your super keen prices. I remember one year this chap came on the stand with a very convincing story about how he had taken redundancy from the mines, and bought a small holding. He reckoned he couldn't get the type of packaging we supplied locally, in the West Country from whence he came, and was quite happy to pay any transport costs. Pre-empting my suspicions, he name dropped another local firm, who he claimed he had been dealing with for some time now. A quick check with his referee confirmed that they had indeed been supplying him, and he was an exemplary payer. It seemed that for once my prejudices were unfounded, and we duly shipped a load of cauliflower crates off to him.
A couple of months later no payment had been forth coming, so I had another word with my fellow supplier, who had given him the all clear. Surprise, surprise, their payments had stopped too. A quick call up on the grape vine confirmed my worst fears. We were dealing with one very clever and deceitful customer. He obviously knew business was still done very much on trust and recommendation in our area, and so he had cultured a reputation as a reliable prospect, some months before the show, so that he could then hit us all in one fell swoop. He caught a lot of people for a lot of money, and naturally when we tried to seek redress through the courts, he didn't own a thing; it was all in his mother's name. I suppose it was one way of getting a new business up and running at very little cost, but it was a really low trick. I hope his cauliflowers were ravaged by greenfly!
The reason I bring all this up now is that '94 was the first year I didn't bother to exhibit at the show. Lin-Pac was no longer interested, and a lot of our smaller growers had disappeared, so it made no sense. The show was now a shadow of its former self, and gradually other exhibitors followed suit, until the show just petered out; a bit like the flower industry itself unfortunately.

It is sad to think that an area once a mass of colour in the spring, with hundreds of acres of daffodils and tulips providing a magnificent spectacle, was now just like any other agricultural area, nothing but 'tates and caulis. The previously mentioned polarisation of the industry had moved the two sectors even further apart, with massive concerns now dealing mainly with the supermarkets, and the one man bands, who without labour costs, and often with a lot of help from their other halves, could still just about make a living.
The bulb industry is the main reason why we have such close ties with the Dutch (except in my case of course!), but they were also the main source of expertise behind the draining of the fens, and coming from a similar landscape they somehow seem comfortable in our area, which is even called 'Holland Lincolnshire', so many of them have settled, to ply their trade as flower and bulb growers.
It's strange really; we tend to call their homeland Holland, but actually that is akin to calling the whole of Great Britain, England; something which I don't think would sit well with our Celtic neighbours!
Although most of the bulb growing fraternity do come from Holland, the actual country is Nederland. (The Netherlands to us English). Award yourself three points and a chocolate biscuit if you can name any of the other regions that make up Nederland….and two biscuits if you can pronounce them correctly without choking on your own phlegm. Conditions apply!

As growers started to become an endangered species, some of the suppliers dropped by the wayside, but one of our main competitors, Nursery Supplies, chose an ultimately fatal strategy for increasing turnover: they opened up on the door step of Avoncrop, a supplier from the West Country. Predictably this did not go down too well, and the other party reciprocated by moving in on our patch. We now had outright war, and it was obvious from the start that this would be a fight to the death; who ever had the deepest pockets being the likely victor. One thing was for sure, we couldn't afford

to get involved, being a mere minnow in comparison to the other two. The only winners, at least in the short term, were the growers. They soon learnt how to play one combatant off against the other, and prices just tumbled, sometimes to well below cost.
Eventually this had repercussions right throughout the trade, as other suppliers questioned the manufacturers as to how their product was being sold to growers at less than they could buy it as a wholesaler. One producer even threatened to withdraw supplies from the two trouble makers, unless they started acting more responsibly.
Inevitably we were caught in the crossfire: match the prices and go bust, or let the trade go, and hopefully be there to pick up the pieces, once the other two had sorted themselves out.
Fortunately we did have some loyal customers, who were savvy enough to know that the current situation was unsustainable, so they helped us weather the storm. This proved to be a testing period, for although I had always had a policy of keeping a bit of wool on the firms back, sales to the Holbeach Growers buying group were down 50%, and that sort of hit takes a bit of coping with.

As April 1st loomed I braced myself for the inevitable backlash from the previous year. My indifference towards children has already been noted of course, but that can be misunderstood. It is not that I don't like them; on the contrary, I even went to school with them, and have since spent many happy hours in the company of well behaved kids (and their parents of course!). What I am less keen on is large groups of them, which tend to be both noisy and unruly.
Holt's intended plan was to encourage a plague of children to descend on the shop, by advertising a free crèche service. This would have been a great wind-up, apart from one small flaw in the plan: April the first just happened to be on Good Friday this particular year, and we don't open on Bank Holidays! Best laid plans, and all that. I realised this was only a temporary respite, but

at least I had another year's grace. Although activities were not confined to April Fool's Day, it had become something of a tradition, a bit like buying people presents on their birthday I suppose.
Later in the year I received a request from an acquaintance to take his brother in law for a ride in the Esprit. The prospective passenger was a pilot in the German Air Force, flying Tornados, who rather than supporting the 'home team' of Porsche, had a real liking for Lotus. As I see myself as some sort of unofficial ambassador for the mark, I didn't see how I could refuse. I generally try to take into account that some people are not good passengers, in fact I count myself amongst them, but I figured that as this chap's day job involved travelling at the speed of sound, I wasn't likely to bother him with the Esprit. Our starting point was not far from a favourite piece of road, so it wasn't long before the Esprit was doing what a Lotus does best: going around corners quickly. All was quiet in the other seat, so I assumed my passenger was just sitting back and enjoying the ride. We completed the circuit, and I asked my charge if he had enjoyed the experience. He said he was doing now, but had been completely petrified at the time! When I asked what had bothered him, he said he just couldn't believe that it was possible for a car to negotiate the corners at the speeds we had, and he was sure we were going to go straight into whatever obstacle happened to be in our path. I apologised for the scare, and explained how I thought any car would seem slow after his fighter plane. He explained that where he does his speed there is nothing to hit, and so it isn't a worry, but to see these telegraph poles and trees rushing towards you, only for the car to do the impossible, just as it seemed inevitable you were going to get rather too intimate with them, was something else. I suppose if he was to take me up in his plane, and put it through its paces, I would be similarly petrified, and probably sick into the bargain!
Ninety five saw the arrival of our first front wheel drive VW truck. We had Volkswagens right from the early days, but this was the first with a more conventional layout. The original trucks had the

engine in the back, which allowed for an under floor locker, where you could store ropes and sheets; or alternatively, four mates! This came in handy one year when we went to the 24 hour race at Snetterton. We needed the truck to transport the assorted paraphernalia necessary to survive this marathon event: tents, barbecue and most importantly the barrel of Lager. Two of us travelled in the VW, with another four in the 'support vehicle'. It is with some remorse that I admit to supporting a plan to lessen the financial impact of the weekend by making two tickets accommodate six people. So it was that I found myself holding open the locker door, as four bodies somehow intertwined themselves into the metal cave. Once inside the circuit I pulled over to disgorge my elicit cargo, but no sooner had I turned the key in the locker door than bodies spewed out like lave from a volcano! Sensing that this was not a controlled exit, I enquired what was wrong. Once sufficiently composed to speak, a lone voice uttered two words: Fred's farted! I suppose that was what they call Karma!

April first saw many of Holt and Lizzi's friends receive an invitation in the post to attend an auction, arranged by that well respected firm, Mires & Halt. Lots included vehicles and clothes but the star attraction was Lizzi herself; or the 'heiress production unit' as the particulars described her; in deference to the selection of daughters she and Holt had produced! I seemed to have escaped for yet another year, but I had the feeling I was on borrowed time.
I had promised Alice, and myself, that once I reached 40, I would start working a five day week, when possible. With an acre of garden to try and keep on top of, it had meant that summer consisted of six days work in the shop, followed by the seventh busting a gut gardening, a pass time I don't even enjoy! The theory was that I would have a day off in the week to sort the garden, leaving Sundays free for a bit of recreation. It has sort of worked, although as I get older I now need two days to do what used to take one, so I am nearly back to square one!

I marked the big four O with a serious party, held in a marquee in the garden, complete with a live band, which went on well in to the following day. Unfortunately my good friend Don was unable to make the party, but turned up the next day, with....a bottle of Krug Champagne, which I thought was a lovely gesture.
Another highlight was a drive in an acquaintance's Ferrari 355. What a revelation! It was just so good, and even I had to concede that it made my Esprit look very out dated; bringing into focus the difference between a successful company, able to invest in new product, and one constantly fighting for its very survival. I had already decided that my current Esprit would be my last, but this had served to confirm that decision. Luckily for me, Lotus was already well advanced with the answer to my dilemma, all I had to do was get them to admit it, and let me order one. Despite their previous denials of its existence, they finally accepted my deposit for an Elise in September, although I had to wait until the Motor Show in October to see if I could actually fit in it. With a feeling of foreboding I lowered myself down into its spartan cockpit, but I needn't have worried: it fitted like a glove.
The Esprit was sold, a BMW M3 was ordered to partner the Elise, and all I had to do was contain my excitement until my new toys arrived.
In the meantime we had an anniversary to celebrate, a uniquely Dutch type of anniversary. For reasons best known to themselves, the Dutch celebrate twelve and a half years of marriage. I have asked the question why, but nobody seems to have a logical answer, other than it's half of twenty five years. When asked if they also celebrate six and a quarter years, they look at me gone out, so presumably they give that one a miss!
We were now round to that time of year again, and my luck had finally run out. The first I knew of Holt's dastardly deed was a phone call from a chap in London. By now so many gushing reviews had been written about the forthcoming Elise that a two year waiting list had formed: places in the queue were being sold for upwards of £5,000. Holt had kindly offered my place, right near

the front of the queue, for sale in The Times, and this chap was responding to that advert. Try as I might to explain that he was the victim of a prank, he wouldn't be deflected from his quest to buy my deposit, and was most displeased when I finally convinced him my place was not for sale. There were also other repercussions, as Lotus had noticed the advert, and were somewhat bemused, as my car had been advertised as being for July delivery, and yet no firm delivery dates had yet been given, partly because Lotus didn't even really know if they would stay in business long enough to produce the car at that time!
Another problem was that when I had written to Lotus, setting out all the reasons why I should get one of the first cars, I had given an assurance that I would not sell the car to make a fast buck. Now here I was supposedly doing just that! Luckily they found the explanation amusing, and I did indeed get one of the first cars, albeit not until September!
When the Esprit was sold, it fetched far more than the Elise was going to cost, leaving us with a nice little nest egg. We had always been very careful with money, doing the 'sensible thing' which in this case would have been to pay off a chunk of the mortgage. Quite what happened to my sensible pants I don't know, but before I could help myself I had suggested to Alice that instead of doing the sensible thing, we should blow the lot on flying out to New York on Concorde, and sailing back on the QE2! Once Alice had satisfied herself I was neither an impostor nor under the influence of drugs, she packed me off to the travel agents to get the trip booked. I ended up booking four tickets, as the neighbours liked the idea that much they asked if they could tag along!
I love most things that involve engineering or technology, but Concorde has always been the pinnacle for me. I will not bore you with all the details, you've already suffered enough with my cars, but suffice to say that we flew from London to New York in 3 hours 16 minutes, whilst drinking Champagne, eating sumptuous food and flying at twice the speed of sound. If that isn't technological genius I don't know what is! Seeing the beautiful

hues in the sky, the curvature of the earth, looking down on other aircraft; seemingly going backwards, as you sped by five miles above them; all of this just made me so proud to be British. Naturally I went and knocked on the flight deck door, to see if I could wangle an audience with the crew. They were marvellous, and even more proud to be piloting and engineering such an icon as I was to be a passenger. New York and QE2 were pretty good as well, but Concorde….If ever one doubted the 'he who counts the cost' etc dictum, this was indelible proof of its validity.

I always find it strange when people say it must be nice being your own boss, able to have time off whenever you like. To me that shows a complete lack of understanding of what being 'your own boss' entails. It's a bit like those people who want to 'retire' and run a pub! I think I put some hours in, but I am a part timer compared to the hours it takes to run a pub properly. I suppose in the same way that people assume I just stand behind a counter and serve people, the perception of a landlord is that they stand behind the bar and socialise. That is just the bit we punters see; there is another complete job to go with that bit of course.

To me every customer is my boss, and I am usually the one who has to sacrifice their time off, if something happens which would leave us short staffed. Sometimes this can be a bitter pill to swallow; especially if it is a day you had something special planned for. I well remember having been invited to Donnington Park by BMW, to drive their M3 model around the circuit. For a petrol head like me this was as good as a day out gets, but a couple of weeks before the event a member of staff handed in their notice. I asked if he would stay until the Saturday, knowing that I had this very special day planned, but he was adamant he was going to finish on the Friday, so I had to cancel my day: the shop rules you, not the other way around; more's the pity.

At least my Elise finally arrived in the September, living up to every superlative that had been written about it. The only trouble was it made other cars seem so obese and dim witted, to the point

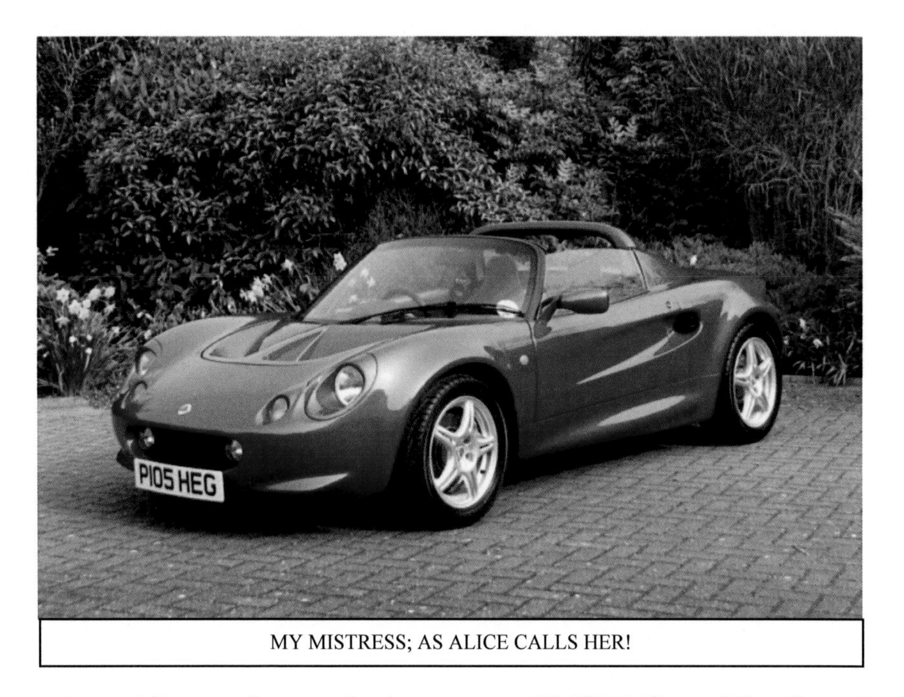

MY MISTRESS; AS ALICE CALLS HER!

where Alice took to referring to our BMW M3 as 'The Lorry'. Harsh maybe, but I could see her point.

In common with many others, Holbeach traders were finding it tough competing against the bigger retailers and out of town shopping centres, or 'sheds' as they are affectionately known. A group of us decided to launch a 'Saver Scheme', where customers would save stamps on a card, which when full would have a monetary value to be spent in participating businesses. This took quite a bit of setting up, but once implemented it proved popular with customers, giving them a real incentive to support their local shops.

Sometimes it takes tough times to spur you into action: when things are going well you tend to focus all of your attention on the day to day things, and maybe aren't as efficient as you could be. Well, things were certainly tough now, and we needed to have a long hard look at what we were doing, to see what could be changed for the better. One thing I did was to stop selling sweets: not

everybody realises that shops have to pay for change and at this time a bag of 20 pound coins was 32 pence, so if a customer bought a Kit-Kat and paid with a five pound note, the four pound coins you subsequently handed back would have cost 6.4 pence; more than the profit on the sale! Also, with less growers coming in and making an impulse purchase, a lot of the slower moving lines were going out of date, so sweets were no longer viable for us. Another action was to start accepting credit and debit cards. I always said that when I thought we were losing sales by not accepting them, I would reluctantly join the 20th century; and so I did, just before everybody else moved on to the 21st! My reluctance had some logic to it, as there was a cost involved. Banks like to perpetuate the myth of free banking, but there is no such thing of course. Not only do we have to pay a monthly fee for the card terminal, there is a fixed charge for debit cards, and a percentage for credit cards. Free for the consumer maybe, but most definitely not for the retailer. Even with the associated costs, it was a good move, as people would now buy bigger items, which previously they may not have. Being able to use their credit card meant they could delay payment until the next salary cheque had arrived, whereas had they needed to pay by cash or cheque, they would have to wait, or would have gone elsewhere of course.
In May '97 Labour came into power. Whatever the perception of a businessman's political leanings, I tend to be concerned only about what the incumbents will do to help or hinder my cause, and historically Labour has not been good news for people in my position. With hind sight I maybe should have taken my chances when one of the smaller supermarket chains wanted to buy the shop, but at the time things were still not bad enough to consider jumping ship.
We certainly had a trying time with staff for a year or so leading up to this time, as we struggled to find a driver/store man who would settle; with them variously finding the job too physical, or just not settling in for some reason. Fortunately we found a bit of stability when Mark joined us, and he soon jelled as one of the team.

I have always considered my staff to work with me, rather than for me, and once they know the ropes like to leave them to organise themselves as much as possible. I feel it more pleasant for all concerned if people are left to use their initiative and common sense, rather than have someone 'ordering them about' the whole time. For that reason, when interviewing to fill a vacancy I will more likely go for someone who seems to possess the aforementioned qualities, than someone who comes armed with a fist full of qualifications.
Unfortunately the gradual decline of the town continued with the town's electrical & toy shop Pledgers closing, and Walt's best mate Ivor deciding he was going to call it a day in the New Year. In my mind the start of the rot was when Graham Coley decided to re-locate to Norfolk, a county less infested with supermarkets than most, in the late 80's. He did sell the business on, but the new incumbents didn't keep the same standards, and the business soon failed. Every town needs its 'drawing shops', that is to say those which offer something unique, that people are willing to travel for. Coley's range of cooked meats and other delicacies were legendry, and people travelled from as far as Peterborough to shop there, so when he left that was one less reason for people to visit Holbeach. Our loss, Norfolk's gain I suppose.
At the beginning of '98 Cath, my long suffering secretary, decided to retire. I immediately spoilt her successor Eileen by treating her to a word processor, to replace the typewriter my dad had bought second hand from Noah.
This new piece of technology was also a boon for me, as previously I had to hand write any price lists etc, for Cath to then type out a stencil; which was an art in itself; before trying to fit it on to the duplicating machine without tearing it, and finally crank the handle to produce the copies. As the word processor allowed mistakes to be rectified without penalty, I could now use my very rudimentary typing skills to produce my own work.
The year was still young when C & P, the company who had muscled in on our customers a few years ago, became the first

casualty of the Nursery Supplies/Avoncrop war. This in part vindicated my decision to not get involved, and I could at least derive some pleasure in suggesting to customers that maybe our prices hadn't been so far out after all. Mind you I had nothing to gloat about, as the company made its first loss since I had taken over running it 20 years ago.

With the horticultural supplies part of the business effectively in limbo until the other two idiots sorted themselves out, and the retail side a victim of the recession, there seemed very little I could do except try and ride out the storm, and make economies where possible. To this end I decided to have what I termed 'a day of action'. When you are so wrapped up in the day to day running of a business, there is not enough time for strategic decision making, and so I decided to take a day out and sort out some of the things I had been mithering about for some time. As we were not going to be making money for a while, I thought I had better try and save some!

Bank charges were something which had been steadily creeping up, to the point where they were costing us about £500 per quarter, which seemed plenty to me. Although we obviously could not operate without a bank, as most of the charges were for paying in cash and cheques, I decided to open an account with the Building Society, where deposits were free. This also meant I was allowed to write six cheques per month, without charge; so I would pay five of my larger bills from the Building Society account, and then use the sixth cheque to transfer money from there to the bank account, from which I would pay the remaining bills. This move alone saved us about £1,800 a year, as our bank charges now dropped to about £60 to £70 per quarter.

The other action I took was to have a water meter fitted. Although our usage was very light, at that time the water rates were directly linked to the business rates, so we were paying about £600 per year. Having a meter immediately brought that down to £60 per year, so that was another good chunk saved.

On a happier note, Alice indulged my interest in things aeronautical by arranging for us to go up in a hot air balloon on my birthday. I found this absolutely fascinating, especially the fact that you could hear people below talking as clearly as if they were in the basket with you. Also interesting was the way in which the pilot managed to sense where the air currents were; to the extent that he managed to 'hover' for quite some time, by adjusting the balloons altitude, whilst the ground crew caught up to bring some extra maps. He then just dropped the balloon down, took the maps on board, and then re-gained height to find the air current once more. Knowing just where these bits of wind are must be like trying to catch a fart in a butterfly net!

Another highlight of the year was being invited by Chris Knight, the then MD of Lotus, to evaluate a new model they were going to launch sometime in the future. To me this was the equivalent of a football fan being asked to go along and help choose the England squad for the World Cup, so I felt well chuffed, not to mention honoured.

Needless to say I was in my element, and had a fabulous day, although sadly I can tell you no more, as I had to sign a 25 year confidentiality agreement!

If my day at Lotus was the highlight of my year, it was more than offset by a couple of low points: having the shop broken into; twice. The blighters took cigarettes and fireworks on their first visit, and Maglite torches, batteries etc on their second. Not only did they stoop so low as to break into the charity boxes, they even sorted through the contents, discarding all the coppers! This event made my mind up to stop selling cigarettes; the hassle just wasn't worth the small rewards.

In between the break-ins we acquired some new neighbours, across the road from us. When the window company who had previously occupied the premises decided to call it a day, we all speculated as to who or what our new neighbours would be. When they did eventually turn up, it became clear we would not also benefit from the patronage of their customers, as we had hoped: they were

undertakers! It transpired that one of the partners was local character and erstwhile shop keeper Derek Morriss, so when the local paper contacted me to see if I would take a support advert in the feature they were going to run about his new joint venture, I was happy to oblige.
I duly sent off my copy, only to have it rejected: apparently they did not think 'Congratulations to Morriss and Haynes on their new venture. You can't miss us we're dead opposite,' appropriate. Undaunted I rattled off version two, 'Congratulations etc….We are sure their competitors will find them stiff opposition'. Nope; they didn't like that one either! Third time lucky maybe? Apparently not: 'Congratulations….We hope they do more trade with us than we do with them,' didn't make the cut either. I eventually had to settle for something really boring, no sense of humour these advertising types!
We did prove to be of use on one occasion: they had a 'client' who was a little on the large size, and far too weighty for their standard trolley. I flippantly suggested that what they needed was one of the trolleys we use for our displays at the shop. We had these built especially by my good friend Taff, and if Taff builds something it tends to be well over spec for the job. Next thing I know they have come to see if they could take one for a 'test run', suitably ballasted of course! It proved just the job, and apparently performed faultlessly on the day!
Luckily, if that is the right word, the police had made some progress with their investigation into our burglary. They had raided a couple of houses, not a million miles away, and found goods fitting the description of those we had lost. From the positioning and shape of the marks left where the price labels had been peeled off, I was fairly certain they were ours. There were also other clues to suggest they had not been acquired by legal means. It looked like there was enough evidence to bring a case, so I was hopeful of at least some satisfaction.
The final year of the millennium started badly, when we lost Walt after a short illness. This absolutely tore me apart. I had spent more

hours of the day with him, over the twelve and a half years he was with us, than I had with Alice, and losing him was every bit as devastating as losing a human member of the family. Having to make the decision to say goodbye was the worst thing I have ever had to do, and I vowed then that I would never put myself in that position again. So; much as I loved Walt, no more dogs for us. What made matters worse of course, was that virtually every customer who came in the shop afterwards would ask where Walt was, as they all expected to see him in his usual place by the door, so there were these constant reminders for weeks afterwards, until word had spread. In the first few days I found it impossible to keep my composure, even though I am not given to outward displays of emotion as a rule, but gradually I came to terms with his loss, although 14 years later, as I write, my position regarding a 'replacement' has not changed.

Well, I don't know about you, but I need a bit of cheering up after that, so I will relate a story told by a customer, which well stands repeating! The person in question lives in a semi-detached house, on one of the many smallholdings in the area: a smallholding being a mini farm in effect. He was due to attend a wedding, and so went to the wardrobe, in order to bring his best suit out of hibernation from its customary resting place right at the back. He was somewhat bemused when he could not locate it: had it been whisked off to some charity shop by his wife; or was it languishing forlornly on some dry cleaners rail, having been taken for a spruce up some time previously? Consulting his wife eliminated these options, and so he decided to investigate further. As he scoured the wardrobe he noticed this nubbled up heap at the bottom of it. He pulled it out, and there was his suit; or what was left of it, for as he opened out the jacket, there was this gaping hole, ripped right through the back of it. How on earth was that possible, what could have dragged his suit off its coat hanger and then inflicted such mortal damage? Not mice that was for sure. He ventured further into the wardrobe, seeking answers, and suddenly found himself

peering into his neighbour's bedroom!
The owners of the adjoining property were newly married, and had recently moved in. Our man decided to pay them a visit, and informed them that if they needed guidance on the bedroom activities front, they were welcome to come round, and didn't need to resort to drilling spy holes in the wall! Somewhat embarrassed, they explained the 'hole' thing. It transpired that they had been having central heating fitted, and forgetting he was in a semi-detached house, the plumber had used a long drill bit, inadvertently drilling straight through the back of the wardrobe and best suit! It's the best excuse I have heard yet for not getting dressed up for a wedding.
Thinking of dressing for weddings, I never have liked the idea of wearing some rented, ill fitting clothes in which to get married; I have plenty of my own! For our wedding I wore my venerable velvet jacket, much to the chagrin of Alice's father. This garment went on to see service at many functions, to the extent that on one particular night at the Spalding Gentlemen's Club, it had a toast proposed to it. Ever after that I made sure that if I was to be in the company of this particular group of people, 'The Jacket' would always make an appearance at some stage of the proceedings. So it was that we had arranged to give Holt and Lizzi a lift to just such a function, and I duly had 'The Jacket' in the boot, ready to make a guest appearance at some point in the evening. Now, Holt and Lizzi tend to run to 'Myers Time', which is generally about 15 to 30 minutes behind the rest of the world, so when we arrived, we had time to loiter in the entrance hall. As you know, the Devil finds work for idle hands, and I happened to notice a suit cover hanging on the coat hook. Thinking it might contain Holt's dinner jacket for that evenings do, I had a peek inside, and sure enough there was a dinner jacket. It would of course been a criminal waste of a wind up not to substitute this jacket with 'The Jacket'! Assuming Holt would discover the impostor when he came down, I thought it would give everybody a bit of a laugh. My plan started to go slightly awry when Holt appeared complete with dinner jacket

already in place. Oh well; I wouldn't now be there when the substitute jacket was discovered, but it would still be a good ruse, even if it meant its non appearance on this particular evening. Just how good I had no idea. Apparently the dinner jacket was there as the cleaners had returned the wrong jacket by mistake, and Holt had an appointment with their manager to demonstrate that the jacket he now had didn't even fit him. It appears his outburst, when he unzipped the cover to reveal 'The Jacket', may have contained some not very polite references to me. As usual he took it in good part, and I was eventually reunited with my style icon. I am sure fashion will catch up with it again one day.

Anyway, back to business. This year saw my first attempt at public speaking when I was asked to give a talk to the Whaplode Gardening Club on the various pesticides and such like. It is a good job the talk wasn't now, or it would have been a very brief affair, most of the products we had sold for years now having been banned! It seemed to go quite well, as nobody nodded off or heckled me.

April 1st, rather appropriately, saw the introduction of the National Minimum Wage, set at £3.60 per hour. Now, at the risk of making myself as popular as Jeremy Clarkson at the Caravan Club Christmas Party, this is something with which I feel I must take issue. We are all entitled to our opinions, and yours is no less valid than mine; so if you disagree with what I say, you are just as right as I am, you merely have a different opinion, to which you are just as entitled. However, as I see it, purely in business terms, labour is a commodity; in just the same way as electricity or any other 'item' the business needs to purchase in order to function. Now, back in 1964 Resale Price Maintenance was abolished. This was a system where the price of certain items was 'fixed', so enabling a minnow like me to sell at the same price as the big boys. Rightly or wrongly it was decided that this was not the way things should be done, and we were all going to have to compete in a truly free market economy. Fair enough; but how can you have a true free market economy when the two biggest expenses most businesses have: the

wage bill and the Business Rates are fixed, with no opportunity for market forces to apply. Of course you don't want to see people exploited, but when times were supposedly good, the minimum wage was increased by three times inflation for three years running and then still continued to rise by well above inflation for several years afterwards. This is all very well while businesses are able to stand it; but what when you get to the situation where they no longer can? Whereas before you could have sat down with your staff and given them the option of working for a wage the business could afford, or closing down, now you just close down, even if all parties concerned would rather the alternative. Sorry, but that is not a real free market economy. As for the rates issue; I will not even get started on that one! A case in point is a friend who grows strawberries. Traditionally the pickers were always paid piece work, so the quicker you worked the more you earned. Now, of course you have to pay the minimum hourly rate, irrespective of how many punnets the picker fills. This nonsense now means that some of the 'old girls' (similar to an 'old boy', but the other gender!) who used to like to come and work at their own pace, combining earning a few bob with a good gossip with some of their co-workers, can no longer be employed. So a system which worked for both parties, and has done for years, has now effectively been outlawed, unless the grower wants to pay way more than is viable to get his strawberries picked.
On a similar vein, I remember a young nurse once challenging me about being able to afford my Esprit; her view being that if I was taxed more heavily, then she could be paid more. I said the only trouble with that theory was that the only reason I worked the hours I did, and took the risks I did, was to be able to have my cars. If that incentive was to be denied me, then I would no longer consider being self employed worthwhile, and would go and get a proper job. The trouble is if I and the thousands like me all do this, then there would no longer be all the money we do pay in tax, and not only would she not get her pay rise, she may not get paid at all. To her credit, she thought about this, and decided that maybe it wasn't

such a good idea after all.
A pleasant surprise during the summer was a phone call from the new owner of my old Essex Esprit. He had bought it to go with his other acquisition, the ex Nigel Mansell Lotus Formula One car. It was a good match, as Mansell used to race as number 12, and my Essex Esprit was also the number 12 car. I later went to see the two together at Donington Park, but unfortunately for me Mike had decided to bring yet another acquisition; the number 13 Essex Esprit, which was apparently in better condition than my old car. At least I knew she was in good hands, although our paths have still not crossed unfortunately.

Things were not getting any better at the shop, and the wholesale side of the business was also under even more pressure, from a direction I had not anticipated. This is not the forum in which to air my views on the supermarkets; all I will suggest is you read *Shopped* by *Joanna Blythman*, which will give you an insight as to their methods and lust for complete dominance of the market place. What I will relate is how this ruthlessness affected my business. Not content with trying to destroy anybody who dares to sell against them, they had decided to turn their attention to the supply chain, specifically the packaging used by the growers who supplied them. As I explained earlier, our growers expected an almost instant response to their order requests, and were very happy with the prices and lead times we were able to offer; it was therefore a big shock when I had a phone call from my biggest punnet customer, to break the news that he wouldn't be buying from me the next season. It transpired it certainly was not his own choice, but he had been told by the supermarket he supplied he would in future have to buy his punnets from their designated supplier; who also just happened to be my supplier! Of course the supermarket knew how to walk that fine line, and instead of, let's say the number 6 punnet he had been using, he would now be required to use a 6A; the only difference being the A in its type designation! This was bad news for both of us, as he would now have to order the total number of punnets he thought he might need for the season in advance, and would of course have to cover himself for both the sizes used, as he could never predict which size the supermarket would demand. As he also pointed out, if the supermarket was offered a bigger 'incentive' by a different manufacturer the following year, he would be left with a load of obsolete stock. To make matters worse, the prices he would be paying were no cheaper! Naturally I tackled the manufacturer about this, and asked if they would supply me with this 'new' 6A punnet; which they would, but at exactly the same price as my ex customer would be paying. They were obviously sympathetic, but explained that as it was the supermarkets punnet, they had set the price for it, and there was nothing they could do to help me. When I spoke to the rep he was really upset about the situation, and admitted that the supermarket was also getting a 5% 'incentive' from them. So, at a stroke the supermarket had taken my profit margin, plus another 5%, for doing nothing more than adding an 'A'; they didn't even so much as touch a punnet, let alone carry any stock! Of course, it made perfect sense from their point of view; they would make the best part of £2,000 for no effort whatever, but for me it was a bitter blow, and of course the other growers were forced to follow suit, so in one fell swoop 90% of my punnet business was gone, with no way for me to 'compete' to regain it.

There was no opportunity to take the slack up elsewhere, as flower growers were still dropping like flies, again largely due to the supermarkets, and my other supplier friends were still playing silly beggars, although one in particular was starting to feel the strain!

By September the burglary case had finally come to court, and I was summoned to give evidence. Although a little nervous at the prospect, I psyched myself up; determined not to let some silver tongued defence lawyer bamboozle me. When the time came I actually ended up quite enjoying the experience, as we had some quite interesting exchanges, and every time the defence tried to throw doubt onto what I had said, I would counter with more facts to support my claims. The Judge was very supportive, probably because he had a pretty good idea I was the one telling the truth: he also had the defendant's previous record to guide him of course! This does seem strange to me that the previous convictions are not allowed to be mentioned until after the verdict. I know all about the reasoning behind it, but this guy had, I think, 26 previous convictions, and given that he probably only got caught every tenth job, then that means there are potentially 260 people who had suffered aggravation and financial loss because of him. Courts are supposed to deal in facts, and if it is a fact that there are 26 previous misdemeanours, then that should be admissible. Either way a guilty verdict was reached on this occasion, so at least that was some consolation.

Chapter 9 Into A New Century (And 'Kev World')

40th BIRTHDAY PROMOTIONS BOOKLET.

A New Century dawns, and everybody's computer didn't crash! Especially not mine, as I still was managing to run my affairs without one, and the more I saw of those firms who were computerised, the less inclined I was to go that route. The problem is it seems to remove some of the thought process. When you actually write something down you tend to think as you write, where as if you are just pressing a few keys, and entering a code number, it can become a bit too automatic, or at least I assume that's what it is; all I know is that I often have to contact firms to tell them I have received 30 of something when I only wanted 3, or we receive dog leads, when we actually wanted cat litter, all because the wrong key was pressed.

It was also amusing on the run up to the millennium, as all these questionnaires kept arriving; asking for details of our strategy for ensuring our accounts system was prepared for the big event. I just used to put that I would get a rubber, rub out 1999, and write in 2000. Simple! It seemed to satisfy most of them, although I doubt

they quite knew what to make of my reply.
Of course we now all had to go metric, to fit in with our European neighbours, so we had our scales converted, at great expense, on pain of draconian penalties if we did not, only to be told a few years later that we could carry on with the old imperial system after all!

STAFF PRESANT & PAST AT FIRMS 40th BIRTHDAY PARTY. STANDING : 'NAUGHTY NETTY', ME, SAL & NEAL
SITTING: 'DENNIS THE MENACE' & TINK.

We also had a birthday to celebrate, with the firm reaching the big four O on February 23rd. It was decided to do some really special offers for this event, and a promotions booklet was published, which would run for the whole year. It also contained useful tips, along with a different offer for each month. For the birthday month itself we offered to deduct the full amount of the cost of lawn food from the price of a top quality spreader. This really caught people's imaginations, as in effect they only had to buy a couple of bags of lawn food to get the spreader for nothing. It did not take long to sell out, and although we made hardly anything on the deal, it was really good PR. The only fly in the ointment was that somebody had to deliver the booklets; all 6,000 of them. So it was that on the run up to the event Alice and I spent every day off, including Sundays trekking around the locality. Still, it kept us fit, and to this day it is the best promotion we have ever done.

The birthday week culminated with Alice and I hosting a party at home for as many current and past staff as we could think of (apart from the ones who had robbed us of course!). This was a really good gathering, and it was gratifying to think that so many previous employees still had fond memories of their time with us.

As the firm turned 40, so later in the year Tony reached 50, and it was fantastic to see that ten years after enjoying his temporary Jaguar so much, he now had his own. I don't think he could believe it himself; after all those years of waiting he now had a brand new S Type sat in his garage; and very nice it was too! Although Tony was still firmly entrenched, Mark had decided to move on, and so the search for a replacement was on once again .We did the usual round of interviews, but one candidate stood out as being a perfect fit for our dysfunctional crew! His name was Kevin, and he came across as straightforward and easy going, but the clincher was his reply to my question regarding his marital status (I am never sure, with all the absurdities of political correctness, what you are allowed to ask people, and what you are not; but I always assume if there is something they don't wish to tell you, they can soon say so!). Anyway, in reply to my question, Kev just said, "I have had a few girl friends, but; well; they don't buy a round, do they?" The way he just came out with it really tickled me, and I thought if nothing else, he was liable to keep the rest of us amused throughout the working day. You could say that again…. These last twelve years he has had us in hysterics on many occasions, and his story about his one day as a long distance delivery van driver, told at our Christmas party one year, literally had the tears rolling down our cheeks! I will not try and relate it here, because a large part of the appeal is the self depreciating way in which Kev tells the story, but

suffice to say his day did not go well!
As Kev will feature quite a bit from now on, I ought to try and explain, if it is even remotely possible, a bit about his psyche. It is no coincidence that both we work colleagues and his friends coined the phrase 'Kev World', to describe the place in which he exists. Kev is not 'thick' as he sometimes disparagingly refers to himself: ask him about most sports, or gambling odds, and he is a mine of information; but ask him to apply logical thought, and he sometimes seems of another world: Kev world in fact.

There are times when try as you might, you just cannot help a customer. One such occasion was when an elderly lady came in looking for a Christmas present for an even more elderly lady: her mother. It seemed we were her last resort, as she had scoured the whole town and still failed to be inspired by anything she had seen. I realised pretty quickly that we wouldn't be looking at chain saws and such like, and tried to steer her in the direction of kneeling stools or gardening gloves. It gradually emerged that although the original brief was that her mother liked gardening, she no longer actually did any; so our present quest became even more difficult. By the time we had eliminated pretty well every item in the shop, I had sussed that the lady had a good sense of humour, so looking suitably exasperated, I pointed across the road to the undertakers, and told her that I was pretty sure they did gift vouchers, and that may well be her best option. Fortunately she took the advice in good part, and had a little chuckle. I didn't notice her cross the road however, so I assume she decided that particular gift may not have been too well received!
That sort of thing reminds me of when customers come in who have moved from away, and ask if I have lived in Holbeach my whole life. I usually answer honestly, and say 'not yet'!
Alice often says that when she tells people she is Patrick Limming's wife she gets pitying looks: I suppose they may have heard me doing my marriage counselling bit in the shop! I often tell couples a man should never marry a woman who can't afford them,

and never have a garden bigger than the wife can manage. That usually gets the female party going. Another good one, if a wife enquires if her husband would like her to pay, is to interject with: 'Of course. He would have stayed single and happy if he had wanted to pay his own bills'. You then have to see how brave the man in question is of course, by looking pointedly at him and asking: 'Wouldn't you?' As often as not this enquiry is met with a stony silence!

Some also see my penchant for practical presents something to pity her for. These have ranged from a frying pan with a dent in it, (I was really proud of that one, as I bought it half price off the display in John Lewis. The poor young lad who served me just couldn't believe it was a Christmas present for my wife!) to an outside light, a generator and a tooth repair! Although I like to portray this image of being tight and ultra practical with my present choices, there is usually a 'proper' gift to accompany the headline item, but I always like to give something weird, if only to get people going when Alice tells them what I have bought her for Christmas. The frying pan was probably the best, with the general consensus from the ladies being that if I had given them it, there would have been more than the one dent. Funnily enough, Alice was genuinely pleased with it.

Talking of presents, for my 45th birthday, Alice booked me onto a driving course at Lotus. I suppose she thought that if I was going to keep having the things I might at least try and learn how to drive one properly. This was a brilliant day, with instruction on skid control, high speed avoidance, extreme braking and a slalom. We then got to put our new found skills to the test with a few laps of the test track. I picked up some really useful tips that day, and would urge anyone thinking of spending money on making their car faster to spend it on a similar course instead. You will find more speed and smoothness within yourself, and be a safer driver into the bargain.

As the punnet season rolled around again it became obvious that all but our smallest customers had been collared by the supermarkets,

and we only took two deliveries to our old stomping ground 'up north'. Things were not much better on the high street, with C & A closing all their British shops, and even 'the other' pet shop in Holbeach closing. This had been something of a recurring theme, as one would open up, only to realise that the town is not really big enough to support two pet shops and a year or so later it would be gone again. This was all very well, but whilst trading they would inevitably impinge on our customer base, and then after they closed, things would just get back to normal, and another one would pop up, and start the whole cycle again. I think this happened about six times in about as many years!
One innovation was the introduction of a Farmers Market to the town. This started off well, but unfortunately a lot of the locals seemed to think that 'Farmers Market' was a metaphor for 'cheap food' as opposed to 'good food', and support quickly dwindled, as did the market, so we were back to the usual four or five stalls that constitute a market as far as Holbeach is concerned.
Another blow was that we had to call it a day with the 'Holbeach Saver Scheme'. Unfortunately somebody had put their hand in the till for a lot of money, and although they were successfully prosecuted, it was felt too much damage had been done to the creditability of the scheme. It was a great pity really, as a lot of the local community had really embraced it, and anything which encourages people to use their local shops has got to be good.
A really sad event for me personally was the accident which put an end to Concorde's career. Although her demise is insignificant compared to the terrible loss of life which occurred, it still saddened me to think that the most daring technological gamble in history would now not end her days with an unblemished record, not withstanding that the accident wasn't actually her fault, as eventually confirmed by the somewhat protracted enquiry. I knew she couldn't keep going for ever, which is why I was so keen to fly on her before she retired, but it would have been nice for her to have just bowed out gracefully.

Back on the front line, the long running battle between Nursery Supplies and Avoncrop had finally reached a head. Knowing that they were mortally wounded, Nursery Supplies had sold out to Gibbs Palmer, a company who funnily enough had supplied us for many years. I don't think Gibbs had any idea what they were getting themselves into. They may have thought the businesses would be a good fit, as Nursery Supplies had quite a presence in the garden supplies market, but their main stay was still in horticultural supplies, an arena where the profit margins are wafer thin; all the more so if you sell stuff for less than you paid for it of course! Sadly Nursery Supplies pulled Gibbs down with them, and the whole enterprise went bust. Now of course would start the process of trying to return prices to a sustainable level. At least the players who remained were not likely to go looking for trouble, so Avoncrop could now be the dominant force, and hopefully the rest of us could just make a reasonable living.
When I say the margins are small in this sector, you probably don't realise just how small. I remember getting in trouble with the VAT office once, as our declared profits did not fit their template for a garden centre; which is what they had us listed under. When they came to visit I pulled out the purchase invoice for 2,500 flower boxes, together with the corresponding sales invoice. When she saw the difference was only £5.00, on a sale of nearly £1,000, the officer wanted to know what percentage of our business turnover this type of sale represented. When I put the estimate at between 25% and 30%, she was immediately placated. All she did was re-classify us, and all was well.

My new year got off to a good start with a visit from the Health and Safety officer. It transpired he had spotted us using the forklift to put up the Christmas decorations outside the shop, and had come to inspect our forklift licences. These guys are not renowned for their sense of humour, so when I told him he would have a bit of a job, as we didn't posses such a thing, he was not a happy chappy.

The fact that I had been using one without incident for more years than I cared to remember didn't cut any ice, and we were told to get ourselves trained PDQ. I have to say the subsequent course turned out to be quite good fun, although I was maybe expecting rather more from the written test than was the case. I thought the answer to the question 'how much tilt should you use when transporting a liquid' would require some complicated formula to be applied, of which I had no knowledge. Turns out the answer they were looking for was 'the correct amount'. Luckily Kev and I both managed to scrape through, and I am sure we are now far more competent operators!

More welcome was a cheque from our home electricity supplier. The back end of the previous year had seen some severe storms, and we were off power long enough to cause losses. Knowing how in such cases getting compensation can be difficult, I thought a pre-emptive approach was probably the best plan of attack; so I set out the details of our losses, and then inserted the following caveat: 'Now I know it is customary in these cases to blame an act of God; so I took the liberty of consulting with the much maligned deity Himself, and He assured me that although He does get blamed for many things, He has no jurisdiction whatever over the supply of electricity to Whaplode Fen, and as such absolves Himself of all responsibility for our loss of power.' Now whether the person who dealt with my claim really thought I did have friends in high places, or just liked my unusual approach, I don't know; but either way they paid up, and that was all I wanted.

Not far into the year foot and mouth disease struck the farming community. Although we are not a big livestock area, there was still enough slaughter locally to make you feel really sick about the whole affair: the sight of all those carcasses burning in the fields; that waste of such a precious commodity. I never forget how privileged we are in this country to have the abundance of riches we do, and to see thousands of animals just being squandered, when so many are starving, just seemed a travesty. How the farmers coped, seeing their livelihoods literally going up in stinking

smoke before them I don't know. I don't think I could have handled it.
Unfortunately we had our own 'devastating disease' with the arrival in the town of Tesco. This is something we knew was inevitable, as the 'incentives' they offered to the council were far too tempting to resist, and in fairness, if you were not a trader in the town, you would probably welcome their arrival anyway. The problem is they do not want to be in the town of course; they make sure they are just outside of it. They even managed to get the sequencing of the one set of traffic lights Holbeach possesses altered, to make the flow of traffic to Tesco better. As expected the effect of their arrival was immediate, with the pet side of the business seeing a 25% downturn overnight, and the footfall in the town generally decreasing. Part of me does have to admire the absolutely ruthless way in which they go about business; the re-phasing of the traffic lights, for example, had made it a real pain to get from Tesco's into the town itself, and customers even admitted that they just couldn't be bothered with the hassle of it any more, buying their dog food at Tesco, rather than coming into town for it, as they had previously. The same applied to the butcher, baker etc. of course, and so it was that the gradual decline of the town was set in motion. It is uncanny just how precisely Holbeach has followed the pattern of events set out by Joanna Blythman in her book, as no doubt have many other once thriving towns. It would of course be inaccurate and naive to blame all of Holbeach's problems on Tesco, but they sure haven't helped the cause of the independent traders.
On the car front, the BMW was due for a change, and having downgraded from an M3 to a 328 the last time, I was trying to find a way of justifying another M3. In the end it was not too difficult, as although the M3 appeared to be £10,000 more expensive, by the time you had put the 'essential' extras on a 328, which came as standard on the M3, the gap shrunk to £4,000. Then factor in that come trade in time, the extras on the 328 would add no value, whereas the M3 would always have a much higher residual value,

and overall the M3 becomes the more sensible choice! I am not sure Alice was wholly convinced by my reasoning, but a test drive pretty well sealed the deal really, I just needed to rationalise it to myself, with times not being as good as they once were.
I suppose one justification was that we were once again debt free, having paid off the mortgage on our house. Alice wasn't aware of this, as I had been squirreling some money away so that I could surprise her. I arranged a night away in a nice hotel in Norfolk, taking the chilled Don Rudd Krug Champagne with me. Once Alice was safely out of the way, in the bath, I brought the Champagne out of hiding, and took a glass through to her, together with the letter confirming the mortgage had been paid. Of course the Champagne went straight to our heads on empty stomachs, so by the time we went down for dinner we probably appeared a little the worse for wear! Anyway, that was another debt paid; hopefully we would now have the sense to avoid any more mad schemes.
At the risk of boring you yet again, I think an incident which befell the Elise is well worth relating, if only to enlighten any of you who may have experienced a similar problem, without ever knowing why. Alice and I had been out for the evening in Spalding, and had parked in her work car park. When we returned to the car the alarm would not disarm. We tried both blips, but to no avail. Luckily the system fitted to the Elise had a back up arrangement, so we were able to use that to get us out of trouble. The next day things were no different, so the car was packed off to Pat for further investigation. He could make nothing of it, and had to contact the manufacturers. They were reluctant to say too much, but eventually divulged that the frequency the system operated on had been re-sold by the government, and was now used by electricity sub-stations to communicate with their control centres. Consequently, if you were unlucky enough to park near one of these, (which we had) when it was transmitting, it effectively scrambled the alarm system on your car. The alarm had to be sent back to the manufacturer to be re-set, although I eventually upgraded to one that operated on the new frequency, to avoid further trouble. This

system was fitted to a variety of cars, and I have since talked to several other people with the same system, who had also been stranded near electricity sub-stations, although they hadn't realised they were the source of the problem at the time. So; if you had a car made in the nineties, and it left you stranded with a malfunctioning alarm, now you know the probable cause: allegedly!
Our good friends Pete and Bridget had been trying to persuade us to join them on one of their trips to Disney for quite some time, and this was to be the year we finally took up their invitation. This turned out to be an even more surreal experience than we had bargained for: if I tell you we flew out on September 10th 2001 that may give you a clue as to why.
As this was the first time I had flown on a 747, I made my customary trip up to the flight deck. The Captain was very accommodating and even had a mini globe, to illustrate why flying over Greenland was actually the most direct route, even though it appears to be out of the way, when viewed on a map. It's all to do with the earth being round apparently!
We were staying in Disney itself, so were able to go into Epcot that evening for a meal, and to see the spectacular fireworks of course. The next morning we made for Sea World, and as soon as we entered the park you could sense that something was not quite right. There were little groups of people huddled together; some intense and animated, others just looking stunned. We made for the first attraction, only to be told it had been cancelled, and then it was announced that the park would be closing at mid day. None of it seemed to make sense, so we eventually approached one of the groups, to see if they could shed any light on things for us. We were told of the horrific events at the World Trade Centre; the infamous 911 attacks, and it was immediately clear that this wouldn't be quite the holiday we had in mind. We all felt very uncomfortable, as we were outsiders in a fiercely patriotic country, plunged into communal grief, anger and mourning. You were made to feel like you shouldn't be there: how could you be even thinking about enjoying yourself after what had happened. Obviously we did

have empathy for them, but we did still have to eat, so what were we to do? I have to say that as the week went on people did seem to get a bit of perspective on the situation, and whilst things weren't exactly 'have a nice day' normal, at least the resentment seemed to subside. We must have had one of the most bizarre Disney experiences ever, as the place was virtually deserted, so we just walked into attractions which according to Pete and Bridget, you would normally have to queue ages for.

With all those potential customers I obviously didn't want to miss the opportunity to get the sales message across, and had a tee shirt made for the occasion. The front read 'If you think this place is fun, you should try driving a Lotus Elise', whilst the rear bore the legend 'shop at Limming's, near the original Boston, England.' This latter message highlighted just how insular some Americans are, and also how little they know of their own history. I had several enquiries as to the meaning of my message, and not one had any idea that their Boston was not the original; in fact some would still not accept it even after I had explained the whole Pilgrim Fathers bit! One young lady did find the whole thing fascinating however, and was really quite put out that she had not been taught any of this at school. I have a feeling she was going to be doing a lot more research into the subject.

Back at home a massive blow was dealt to the whole area with the announcement that Tinsleys was to close. For years they had produced sandwiches exclusively for Marks & Spencer, and had invested heavily to comply with the standards required by such a demanding customer. Not long afterwards they lost the contract, and hundreds of people found themselves out of a job. In an area like ours, with very little industry, this was a massive blow, and the knock on effect for local businesses was very serious.

In October we attended the usual Autumn Trade Show, to buy gardening products ready for the following year. As Tony and I wandered from stand to stand, I was sure I recognised this short, round faced man, but yet he seemed so out of context I felt I must be mistaken. The only way to be sure was to approach the guy, and as soon as he spoke I knew it was indeed Paddy Hopkirk, the legendary rally driver. Apparently he was there promoting his range of fuel cans, but naturally I was far more interested in hearing about his other job! He was incredibly modest about his achievements, allowing only that he used to do 'a bit of rallying' in his former life. He was also less sentimental about the Mini Cooper 'S', with which he is intrinsically linked, than I thought he might be, reasoning that the modern iteration was a much better prospect, with no smelly damp carpets or tendency to stutter to a halt at the first sign of rain!

Late in the year a fellow motor club member, a couple of years my junior, died unexpectedly. As I emerged from his funeral, the fact that there are no guarantees in this life really hit home, and my dilemma as to whether I could justify spending all that money on a car was sorted: an M3 was ordered without further ado!

We don't have many claims to fame, here in Lincolnshire, but one product of which we are justifiably proud is our sausages. They are obviously well regarded by the rest of the country, as you often see them advertised as you travel about. One such occasion was when we stayed at a hotel in the Matlock area, which boasted 'Lincolnshire Sausages' on their breakfast menu. I decided to order them, as much out of curiosity as anything, but what appeared on my plate bore as much resemblance to a Lincolnshire Sausage as I do to Brad Pitt. The thin, anaemic looking apologies were best described by Alice as 'dead man's fingers'. They tasted no better than they looked: if a butcher tried to pass off something similar back home he would be laughed out of town!

I didn't make a fuss, as we British tend not to do, but when we returned home I sent the hotel a pound of sausages from our local butcher, with a letter explaining why. The hotel owner took it in very good part, and confirmed that having tasted them, together with his Chef, they had immediately removed the 'impostors', as he called them, from the menu, and in future would be more careful as

to the provenance of their sausages. We haven't managed a return trip yet, but are apparently good for a bottle of something when we do, in recognition of our detective work!
Although turnover continued to decline, the fact that most of the shrinkage was on the wholesale side, meant that profits were actually better, although still nowhere near where they should be, considering the amount invested in the business. This return on investment thing was something I hadn't even considered until an enlightening lunch with our new bank manager. Once it had been established that the bank would be paying for lunch, and there would be no nasty surprise on my next statement, I accepted his invitation. The initial questions were the usual stuff about where I wanted the business to be in five years time etc., (somewhere in the South of France was not quite the answer he was looking for apparently!) but then he really threw in a curved ball, wanting to know what I intended to do with it come retirement time, seeing as how I had no natural successors. I would sell up and enjoy the fruits of my labours; simple; or so I thought! "And who are you going to sell it to?" came the unexpected response. "I don't know: whoever wants to buy it at the time I suppose." I countered. Still not satisfied, he hit me with something I had never even considered: effectively I had an un-saleable business. As he expanded his point, the logic was beyond question. In common with many small business owners, my parents and I had kept ploughing profits back in, increasing its value in small increments, but should somebody else wish to buy the whole shooting match in one go, the amount they would have to invest would not be justified by the return they would make. As my lunch companion put it; "with the return on investment you get I could offer them a better deal on a deposit account." This really hit home, and completely changed my thinking as to my likely 'exit strategy' when the time came. It was now clear the chances of selling as a 'going concern' would be virtually nil, so a way of disposing of the component parts would most likely have to be found.
Despite all the changes over the years, Holbeach still has quite a

close local community, so when I heard that one of our customer's son's who was only in his 20's, had developed a brain tumour, it was only natural to see if there was anything you could do to help. His mother said the biggest problem at this stage was boredom, as he was not able to work, and was really fed up of sitting at home. Knowing he had a keen interest in cars, I asked her if she thought he would enjoy a look around the Lotus factory, if I could arrange it. She was sure he would, and so a quick call was made to one of the contacts I have made over my years of Lotus ownership, and a trip was arranged. I thought that while we were there, it might be worth trying to arrange a look around Classic Team Lotus, who are located just across the road from the car factory and look after many of the old Lotus racing cars. I initially thought I was being 'stone walled', when the receptionist told me that only Clive Chapman (son of the great Colin Chapman) would be able to authorise such a visit, and that he was not there. To my amazement she then trotted out his direct phone number, and suggested I call him! This was like somebody ringing up to arrange a Christening, and being told to ring the Pope direct! I confess my heart was racing as I rang the number, but Clive could not have been more charming or helpful, and was only too pleased to grant my request for a visit.

Kieran found the car factory fascinating, but unfortunately the planned ride around the test track didn't materialise, as they were worried about the effect it might have on him, given his condition; the old health and safety nonsense again unfortunately. A quick call was made to across the road, to see if we could bring our visit forward, but we were told Mr Chapman was still in Norwich, and would be 30 minutes getting back. I didn't understand quite why he needed to be there, but we did as instructed, and wandered across at our allotted time.

All then became clear: Kieran wasn't going to be shown round by some underling, as I had assumed; oh no, he was to get a personal tour by none other than Clive himself. I couldn't believe how generous he was with his time, as he patiently showed Kieran

around every car, answering all his questions in great detail. At the end of his visit Clive presented Kieran with a model and poster, to complete a perfect day for him. I doubt Clive will ever know just how much he did for Kieran's moral that day, but he gave him an enormous lift, and restored my faith in human nature to boot! There was even a footnote to all this, as a short while after his visit, Kieran received an invitation from Clive to be a guest of Team Lotus at Brands Hatch, where some of the cars he had seen were competing, and as it was on a Sunday, his father was able to take him, which was the icing on the cake.
Spurred on by the kindness we had been shown by the 'Lotus Family', I decided to see what else I could arrange for Kieran. Over a period of a couple of years he went on an experience day at Silverstone, and visited Prodrive, (who built and ran the Subaru rally cars), The Donnington Collection, plus the Williams and BAR Formula One teams. The only refusals I had were from the Jordan Formula One Team, and the RAF, when I tried to get him a flight in a Hercules transport plane; perhaps that was a little ambitious! So the next time somebody vandalises your car; or wrongs you in some other way, just remember, there are still a lot of lovely people out there.

With trade still dwindling, we looked at various lines to try and increase turnover, and decided that stone ornaments and garden planters might be worth a try. This involved some investment, as we had to concrete an underutilized section at the rear of the shop, to create a display area. The range includes sundials and armillarys, which unnervingly elicit the same question on a regular basis: how do you set the time on them? I have never ceased to be amazed that somebody would ask such a thing! When you suggest they could always look at their watch and then position the sundial such that it is reading the same time, you can almost see the light go on! Perhaps I am missing the point, but I promise you what I say is true!

Another avenue we decided to explore was buying hardwood furniture by the container load. This was quite a big gamble for a small shop like ourselves, but it would mean we could sell at very competitive prices, and if the worst came to the worst, it wouldn't eat anything. As the product was made in Vietnam, the lead times were quite long, so a decision had to be made in the autumn, ready for February delivery. We agonised long and hard over the product mix, estimating that the amount of stock should last us two to three years, at our current sales levels. Eventually we decided upon a large range of product, so that we could fill the 20' container without having too many of any one item. We thought that way, if we did make some wrong choices, at least we wouldn't be stuck with too many of any one item.
On the social side, Alice and I were invited to Bob Limming's 50th birthday party. Now, I am considered quite tall, at 6'3'' in old money, but once I get amongst this section of the clan, I look like I should have six mates with me, singing Hi Ho, Hi Ho, it's off to work we go! Amongst the guests was Geoff Capes, of strong man fame, himself not noted for being of slight build, but on that particular evening he was neither the tallest nor widest present. The strange thing is, I have another Robert, on the other side of the family, and he is of similar stature. It is still my ambition to get a photograph of me with a Bob on each side, but although I have tried, I have never managed to get all three of us together. The nearest I have is a shot of Bob, myself, Alice and Penny (Bob's wife), in descending order, which in itself is quite interesting: when people first look at it they see nothing unusual; until they realise the two 'bits dropped off' in the middle are Alice and I!
Another experience was staying at a hotel in Cheshire called Frog Manor. If, like us, you enjoy quirky places, run by eccentric people, then this is; or by now probably was, the place for you! Apart from the bedroom with all manner of curios scattered about, including an old typewriter, and a secret passage into the bar, the serious stuff on the menu was interspersed with various little anecdotes, one of which I have always remembered, (well, as much as I remember

anything these days!), and will try my best to relate here. I would think, by some of the memorabilia about the place, that our host had been in the Navy at some point, and this story was from maritime records and allegedly true. I doubt its authenticity will ever really be proven, but either way it's a good story!
The incident supposedly took place off the coast of Newfoundland, and involved the Canadians and Americans. The dialogue went thus:

Canadians: You are on a collision course with us; we recommend you alter your course 15 degrees to the South.
Americans: We suggest you alter your course 15 degrees to the North.
Canadians: We strongly recommend you alter your course 15 degrees to the South to avoid a collision.
Americans: This is the Captain of the USS Lincoln, I am accompanied by three destroyers, three cruisers and numerous support vessels. I demand you alter your course 15 degrees to the North, or we will take whatever measures necessary to ensure the safe passage of this ship.
Canadians: We're a lighthouse: it's your call.

True or not, it made me chuckle!

Unfortunately August saw the closure of Hansons Bakers, a long established business in the town, and exactly the type predicted to be the first victims of Tesco arriving. It may be that they would have closed anyway, but Holbeach was adhering eerily to the pattern predicted by Joanna Blythman either way. Her other sobering prediction was that even if your business did not compete directly with them, you were still not safe. As they effectively alter the 'hub' of the town, the foot fall in the high street tends to drop dramatically, so endangering all those businesses on it.
All we could do to protect our position was make ourselves as efficient as possible, and present our wares to the customer as

enticingly as possible. To this end we started buying our Christmas stock direct from the importer, and invested in some very versatile and attractive shop fittings.
At least we managed to attract one visitor to the shop, although unfortunately he didn't part with any money! The old mental hospital, on the outskirts of town, had been turned into sheltered accommodation for people with various problems, and one of their residents became very adept at sneaking out unnoticed. Once 'free' he used to make a bee line for the shop, which on the first occasion caught us unawares. It later transpired that the lad had a real fixation with the emergency services, and would do anything to see them in action. His favourite trick was setting off fire alarms, as the fire engine put on the most exciting display. Ambulances were also on his wish list however, so on that first day, he staggered into the shop, feigning illness very convincingly, calling for an ambulance to be summoned without delay. We naturally acceded to his request, and then did what we could to calm him down and make him comfortable; although once the ambulance had been called his condition seemed to improve markedly! When the ambulance arrived the fact that the crew knew him by name seemed a bit strange, until we were enlightened by the paramedics. This was by no means his first 'emergency', and once aware of the situation, on subsequent visits we just called the home instead, and they would come and collect him. The most awkward bit was persuading him you had called the ambulance: if he suspected otherwise he could get very restless indeed!
This was not the only public service we provided. At the start of 2003 we had a steady stream of visitors to the shop trying to persuade me to join a 'get rich quick' scheme. The idea behind it was that you handed over £3,000 in cash, and then found another seven mugs; sorry, investors, to join. You then sat back, and when you worked your way to the top of the list £24,000.00 would drop in your hand, giving a profit of £21,000.
Having been about long enough to know you don't get owt for nowt, my first question was how such amazing profit was

generated: whatever sort of investment was being made? When it turned out that there was no actual investment, what scant interest I had evaporated like petrol on hot concrete.
I became so fed up with all the hype about this 'wonder scheme', that in the end I did the maths, and presented the figures to any would be canvassers/investors! I did manage to convince quite a few people not to get involved, but sadly there were also a lot of people who saw it as the answer to their money problems and got badly caught; one poor lad to the tune of £6,000, which he could ill afford.
I suppose you could say people should know better, and there were a few of course, who were in at the start who did get their money; but with no actual earnings, it was pretty obvious that for every 'winner', there had to be seven 'losers', and they were going to be the ones who came along later.
The gambling mentality is something I never will fathom. With our Kev being a keen gambler, you get to hear exchanges between him and his fellow punters, and a pattern soon emerges: they would far rather *nearly* win at say 25 to 1, than they would *actually* win at 4 to 1! I can only assume it's the lure of that big win that gives them the buzz, plus it would be a worthwhile amount if it did come up. It's just that the long odds don't seem to come up too often. For my part, I tried betting once at a horse racing meeting, and having backed every race, without a single winner, I decided maybe gambling wasn't my thing!
February saw the arrival of our first container of furniture which was stacked solid right to the doors. I have to say those Vietnamese boys don't waste a lot of space! All the boxes had to be unloaded by hand and stacked onto pallets. Then came the fun of trying to find space for it in the already full warehouse. We did eventually manage to squeeze it all in, but it was obvious that some serious re-organisation would have to take place; having a variety of products all sharing a pallet would inevitably mean that the item you needed would always be at the bottom!
Even though it was the middle of winter, I thought I would bring up

just one item, and display it just inside the shop door, so giving customers a chance to see the quality of what we had to offer, and hopefully sow some seeds, ready for the summer season. I was completely taken aback with what then happened over the next few days. Customers were so taken with what they saw that they started buying straight away, to the extent that we sold out of the Relaxer Chair I had displayed within 3 days! Responding to this we brought up more products, and as quick as we could assemble items they were flying out the door! Tony and I were like a two man assembly team, and often an item would be sold before we had even completed it; it was like some sort of feeding frenzy, with customers pouncing on items as soon as they saw them!
It soon became obvious that far from taking us two or three years to shift a container, it was not even going to last the month out! I decided to place another order, which would take 10 weeks to arrive, and we then started pre booking items, pending its arrival. Still we could not sate the demand, and a third container had to be ordered! All this was a logistical nightmare, trying to work out whose order was on which container, and how many of an item you had left to sell, but it is the sort of problem I was more than happy to wrestle with, as the increase in sales really saved our bacon.
In the midst of all this we had been to war with Iraq, and we had temporarily revived the April 1st shenanigans with next door! I had noticed that since the gates had been painted the 'beware of the dogs' sign had not re-appeared, so I thought it would be a neighbourly gesture to replace it for them. Knowing something far more fearsome lurked behind those gates than the dogs, I had the wording modified slightly to read, "Beware of the dogs, but of Lizzi be very afraid indeed". Getting the sign in place required a covert operation at midnight on the 31st, the problem being fixing the sign without alerting said dogs, (or indeed Lizzi!) Much tip toeing and hand signalling got the job done, so all we needed to do now was sit back and wait for the fall out! As usual it was all taken in good part, and to her credit Lizzi left the sign up for several years; I think she may even have seen it as a good deterrent,

especially to any would be miscreant who didn't know who or what this Lizzi was.
I also added another experience to my airborne repertoire when Alice bought me a trip in a glider for my birthday. Conditions were a bit marginal on the day, but the pilot said he was willing to take me, if I didn't mind a bumpy ride. It was a little choppy, as the light aircraft towed us up, but once we released from him it was really enjoyable, as we picked up a really good thermal, which took us up to 3,500 feet. The pilot was very good at giving instruction, and I soon got the hang of balancing the controls to keep climbing in the thermal. He even let me initiate a stall, and then guided me through recovering it. That all seemed a bit counter intuitive, as you had to point the nose of the glider towards the ground and then let it fall earthwards until you had gained sufficient air speed to re-establish level flight. I obviously didn't instil enough confidence in my companion to convince him to let me try a landing, although when he did eventually bring us in I could see why! As there was a strong cross wind, we had to come in very steep and fast, which was a real thrill for a novice like me. It transpired I had been very fortunate, as we had been up for twice the allotted time: it turned out the pilot thought the thermal we found was too good not take full advantage of, and as there was nobody else waiting to go up, he just let me keep going. I really enjoyed the experience, far more than a light aircraft, as you are on the go all the time, and have to 'read' the conditions in order to make good progress. You should really give it a go some time; if only for the peace and quiet. Sadly, this was also the year which saw my beloved Concorde fly for the final time, on October 24th. It still seems a travesty that an accident caused by another plane shedding bits as it travelled down the runway, should end the career of the greatest aircraft ever built.

Another year, another pet shop! 2004 saw yet another pet shop open in town. I had lost count by now of how many there had been, but this must have been about number seven as far as I could recollect!

Other things were also bothering me. It was becoming increasingly obvious that conventional pensions were not going to be as good as we had been led to believe. With the government robbing them at every opportunity, and returns proving to be well below predicted levels, Alice and I decided to look at alternative forms of saving for our retirement; should that day ever come!
I have long detested the long winters and non-existent summers we now expect on this island of ours; the unremitting greyness being something which really gets to me, especially when we get five or six weeks of it at a time! Putting these two elements together, we decided to look at investing in property somewhere abroad; preferably where the sun still knows how to shine! We wanted to be within reasonable flying distance, and somewhere that you would actually have proper ownership of your property. We had heard too many horror stories to risk some of the sunnier locations. Taking into consideration all the things we were looking for, the South of France seemed the best bet; the food and wine being an added bonus of course.
I started reading up on what was involved, and it soon became obvious that this would not be something to take on lightly, as the aggravation factor seemed likely to be pretty high: the French did not earn their reputation for bureaucracy for nothing apparently!
Talking of aggravation I had plenty over some lawn food we had sold to a lovely old dear. As part of the service we offer, if a customer buys lawn food from us, we lend them an applicator free of charge. This was the case in this instance, but as the lady's gardener was going to be using it, I had to explain to her that because of the way a drop spreader works, you have to allow an overlap on each breed; otherwise you end up not applying the fertiliser evenly. Whether this information was relayed to the gardener or not, I do not know, but about a week later I received a phone call from her, claiming the fertiliser was faulty, and would I go and inspect her lawn. I was imagining all sorts of horrors, but when I arrived, it was confronted with a lawn with a series of perfect yellow stripes, about 4 inches wide, a classic example of

not enough overlap being allowed. A straightforward case of operator error as far as I was concerned: unfortunately that was not the way the customer saw it, and despite me trying to explain the problem in as many ways as I could think of, she was adamant that her gardener could not have made a mistake, and that it must be the fertiliser. Logic didn't come into it: my assertion that the faulty fertiliser could not all have been applied within those yellow stripes cut no ice at all; and the fact that the rest of the lawn was a lovely rich green, so proving that the fertiliser on those parts was fine, meant nothing to her: I had sold her faulty, stripy, fertiliser and that was all there was to it.
Not wishing to alienate her further, I promised to fix the problem, and returned with a bag of fertiliser, which I then painstakingly applied by hand to all the yellow stripes. I returned a week later to find a uniformly green lawn, and a placated old dear; although she still wouldn't admit that there had been any fault on her gardener's part, and maintained I had sold her duff lawn food in the first instance! I guess the customer is always right, even when they are wrong. She was still a nice old dear though!

As more customers elected to pay by debit or credit card, so the costs associated with processing them also escalated. What a lot of people don't realise is that Debit and Credit cards are treated in different ways. On a Debit card we have to pay a set fee, irrespective of how much the customer spends, whereas with a Credit card we are charged a percentage of the transaction amount, which on something like a set of garden furniture, can amount to quite a large sum of money. This is why, if a customer tries to negotiate the price, you need to know how they intend to pay, as processing charges can swallow quite a chunk of your profit.
Being a close knit business community, such things as card processing charges get discussed, and it became clear to me we were paying too much. I suppose I had just used the bank we had been with ever since we started, assuming they would be competitive. Not being one for chopping and changing, I

approached my current provider, and explained that they would need to have a look at the rates they were charging, as I was aware they were well above what was available elsewhere. I was directed to the relevant department, who gave me pretty short shrift, informing me that I was on the best possible rate for my level of turnover, and there was nothing they could do about it. I went back to them a further two times, stressing that there were much better rates to be had elsewhere, and that I would have to move my business if they could not at least get in the same ball park with their charges.
All this was to no avail, so with some reluctance, after a 44 year relationship, I moved my allegiance to another bank. Lo and behold, as soon as it became clear that I really was leaving them, anything and everything was possible! My 'relationship manager' (I thought that was Alice, but there you go!) was full of apologies; if only I had contacted her, something could have been done. Pointing out that I had gone to great lengths to sort things out with the very people they had directed me towards, didn't seem to register. So, that was the end of a long relationship, apparently for no other reason than lack of communication within the bank.
The savings proved to be significant: our card fees had been between £150 and £200 per month, but fell to £60 to £80, and the bank charges became almost negligible, at between £6 and £8 per month.

Another avenue I explored was buying foreign currency. As our furniture was coming in from Vietnam, it had to be paid for in American Dollars. We could leave it to our supplier to purchase the currency on our behalf, at the time of delivery, but seeing how the markets fluctuated, I decided there may be an advantage to buying when the rate was favourable, and then sitting on the currency until we needed it. This can be a very frustrating venture, as you can bet your bottom dollar (so to speak!) that the day after you have bought, the rate will improve, but I have learnt to not beat myself up over it now, and if I am happy with the rate at the time I bought,

then so be it. The only thing I no longer do is leave it so late to buy: if you push it right to the last day or so, you can back yourself into a corner, and end up having to take whatever rate is available at the time you have to pay the supplier. I now have things in place at least a month in advance.
I have won some and lost some, but overall I have bought at a better rate than would have been the case at the time of delivery, so I guess it has been a worthwhile exercise. It has highlighted just how much difference currency fluctuation makes though; I have bought as low as $1.47 to the £, and as high as $1.99 to the £; so in other words, the same set of furniture could work out at £300.00 or £221.60, dependant purely on the prevailing exchange rate. You can see how the 'big boys' can get their fingers so badly burnt, or indeed, make a killing!

By now the 'French Project' was gaining pace. We had visited some sites, and started immersing ourselves in the legendary world of French bureaucracy! If ever you thought applying for a British mortgage was a rigmarole, let me assure you, it is nothing compared to the French system! They want to know everything, and not only that, they then want you to prove it, and then once you've done that they want proof of the proof!
As you may have gathered by now, I am quite keen on my cars, and one thing which I always dread is Alice's weekly trip to Morrisons. It doesn't seem to matter where she parks the car, some idiot will sooner or later damage it. Sometimes it will just be a minor skirmish with a badly controlled trolley; the result of which I can polish out, but over the period of about a year we sustained three lots of damage requiring a trip to the body shop.
After the third occasion, and feeling somewhat victimised, I decided to conduct a survey, and also garner opinion on a scheme I had devised to prevent these annoying, and expensive incidents. The questionnaire asked whether the person had ever sustained damage to their car in a supermarket car park, and secondly, would they be willing to pay a pound to park in a protected bay, with a

fence around it to prevent damage from errant trolleys, and a drop down barrier to prevent access by other people.
The principal was simple: supermarkets would construct protected bays, and as you left your vehicle a barrier would close behind you. On your return you would insert a pound coin in order to open the barrier, and every one's a winner: the customer escapes with their car undamaged, and the supermarket relieves them of yet another pound! A switched on company could even issue 'loyalty parking cards' where regular customers could get protected parking for free.
Anyway; the results of my survey were absolutely staggering. I realise the 100 people I consulted was hardly conclusive, but even so, nearly 70% of them had experienced damage, and a similar number would be willing to pay a pound to use a protected parking bay. As an aside; one lady originally couldn't see the point of it all, and was certain she wouldn't pay to park at a supermarket. About a week later she was back, wanting to know if I was still conducting my survey. She had just had her car hit in the local supermarket, and now fully realised just how infuriating it was; as needless to say, the culprit had left neither apology nor contact details!
The more I thought about it all, the more it made sense; and from a business perspective the figures don't take a lot of working out. Our local Morrisons opens 78 hours per week, so let's say each bay would turn over roughly 100 times, multiply by 30 bays, that's £3,000 per week. Even allowing for construction and running costs, that's a nice little earner. It is even the sort of scheme that could be franchised out, should the supermarket not want the bother of it.
Of course, it is no good having a plan if you don't put it into action, so I decided I needed to put my idea to a supermarket, and as my problems were at Morrisons, that's who I decided to contact. I knew it was no good talking to a local manager, or even just writing an open letter, so I decided to go straight to the top, and write to Ken Morrison himself. This would pose two problems: firstly getting the letter past his many minions, and in front of the man himself, and secondly getting the attention of an obviously

busy man.
I decided to use a tactic which had proved successful before. I used two envelopes, the outer one addressed as private and personal, and sealed with sealing wax, embossed with my trade mark 'smiley logo'. The inner envelope also had the sealing wax treatment, and it read, 'If you are not Ken Morrison you should not have opened the first envelope, and certainly shouldn't open this one'. On the second point, I did not reveal the nature of my idea; merely that I had one, and it was something that his customers wanted, and which could make him money. Knowing what an astute businessman he was, I thought that should get his attention. I don't know whether it was this technique or not, but a few days after sending the letter I answered the phone and this northern accent enquired, "Is that Patrick Limming?" I confirmed it was. "Ken Morrison here. You wrote to me."
A little stunned, I replied "I did indeed Sir Ken." "Oh, we don't bother with the Sir bit" he said, and with me now feeling more at ease, we proceeded to have a good chat about all manner of things; he even wanted to know about what I did. As it turned out he came across as a really nice, down to earth bloke, who was certainly still well in touch with his roots. He was very receptive to my idea, and even admitted that he was always wary where he parked when visiting stores unannounced, as it appears he still likes to do!
He promised to put the proposal to the board, but feared they would not go for it, as it might be seen as an admission that there was a problem in the first place; although he didn't put it quite like that obviously! Sadly I heard no more, but if you suddenly see protected parking bays popping up at your local supermarket, you will know where the idea came from!

Chapter 9 No Longer A Luddite!

Although I still hadn't done so much as turned a computer on at this stage, I thought it was about time J.W.Limming Ltd had a presence on the World Wide Web! To me surfing was something which involved getting wet and falling off a lot, but apparently a lot of people now did it in their homes, so who was I to argue.

A local chap offered to set a site up, displaying all our furniture, for £200, which seemed reasonable to me from what I had heard. This would turn out to be some mountain climb, equipped only with a computer and digital camera. I am not sure that approaching 50 is quite the right time to try sorting out your gigabytes from your Adobes©, but with help from a lot of patient people, I gradually progressed to base camp, although I fear I shall never scale the real heights of computerdom!

At first we just used the web site as a sales aid: if one half of a couple came in to look at the furniture, we could direct them to our web site, where the two of them could then peruse the whole range at their leisure, before hopefully coming back to make a purchase. This approach enabled us to find our feet, and customers certainly seemed to like the new facility, although some of our more established customers were amazed I had made such a bold move, and feared www might stand for Whaplode Wide Web!

We certainly needed all the help we could get, as Tescos continuing quest for world dominance had prompted them to apply for planning permission for a 'pop up' garden centre in their car park. Having caused severe haemorrhaging in our pet department, they now appeared to be going for the jugular that is our gardening department. Fortunately I still had the propaganda they distributed at the time they were applying for planning permission, which made all the right noises about working with the existing businesses and not against them, so I was able to remind the planning department of this. I also had tremendous support from the Federation of Small Businesses, and my local MP, John Hayes, who put in very strong representations to the council on my behalf.

Fortunately fair play and common sense prevailed for once, and the application was rejected, much to my relief, as I am not sure we could have stood another blow like that.
We are very lucky to have John Hayes as our MP. I don't think it would be entirely inaccurate to say some of his fellow incumbents of the House of Commons are not as fully committed to helping their constituents' as they might be, but you could certainly never level that criticism at John Hayes. Whenever I have asked for his assistance he has been more than helpful; and it isn't just moral support he offers; he spends his money in the town too.

Christmas was now fast approaching, and my attention turned to Alice's present. The previous year I had bought her a Tank driving experience; which bizarrely, and perhaps a little worryingly, was something she had always wanted to do. She also had a go in a Hovercraft, Buggy, Land Rover and Quad Bike, so it was quite a day for her. I decided this year's offering needed to be a little more practical, and noting all her cooking implements seemed to be in order, I considered what else she might need. Thoughts strayed to how put out she was when we were without electricity, and so I decided upon a generator: how could any girl not be thrilled with one of those? This was indeed the case, and once conversant with its operation, she was ready to challenge the National Grid at their own game! Needless to say, soon after we became 'self sufficient' a lot of the old power lines were replaced, and we now very rarely suffer power cuts; but come the day, and Alice will be prepared.

At the rate we were selling furniture locally, it seemed likely that we would eventually reach 'saturation point', so it was decided to print some advertising booklets, and distribute them to establishments which were likely to need the sort of items we had; pubs being an obvious choice. Sal spent a good deal of time typing out envelopes, and the whole lot was then entrusted to Royal Mail.
We waited to be inundated with orders, but we didn't get a single response. I know that random mail shots miss the target in a lot of

cases, but to not receive one enquiry seemed a bit strange. I decided to ring a few businesses, to see if they had received their booklet, and I kept getting a negative response. It eventually became clear that the whole lot must have gone missing, and so started the hopeless task of trying to get some form of compensation. I don't often give up on such things, but I have to admit that after months of providing reams of evidence (which they also lost!), and being pushed from one department to the next, I decided for the sake of my sanity, and what little bit of hair I had left, to throw in the towel.

As the 'Nanny State' becomes ever more prevalent, so we keep losing some of our best products. For many years we had sold a fertiliser called Nitram. This was very popular with the old boys, as it was 34.5% Nitrogen, which meant they could feed their lawns very cheaply, provided they were not too heavy handed with it, in which case they could also turn it a very nice shade of brown! All was well until various undesirables realised that it was also an excellent base ingredient for bomb making! At a stroke we were banned from selling it, much to the annoyance of the old boys, who were completely nonplussed when you explained they were no longer allowed it in case they made a bomb. You do have to wonder that we were banned from having our little bit, and yet when Alice went on her tank driving day, I couldn't help noticing there was an open barn with more Nitram than you could shake a stick at, not a hundred yards from the road. I think anyone with malicious intentions would be far more likely to plunder that source than our meagre stocks!

With the 'Nanny State' now seeming to want to interfere in nearly all aspects of our lives, I cannot believe that babies do not have to have some sort of warning sticker attached, along the lines of 'DANGER! Liable to eject unpleasant substances from multiple orifices without warning. To avoid risk of contamination, always hold at arm's length, sideways on to the handler'. That's always how it seems to me anyway; as I said, not natural parent material!

As we moved in to 2005, things were not getting any easier: I had to renew the electricity contract, as our previous two year deal had expired, and the best price I could find equated to a 45% increase. At a time when government sources kept telling us how low inflation was, it seemed that everything involved in running a business was governed by a different set of rules. At least the minimum wage, which had been increasing by three times inflation each year, was now only going up by twice inflation.

Our plight was not helped by the arrival of another national chain in the town, situated near Tesco's and selling a lot of the same products as us. Once again they were not in the main body of the town, drawing yet more foot fall to the outskirts, and away from a high street already badly affected by the 'Big T'.

Luckily we still had some lighter moments to keep moral up. I may have been challenged by the computer, but to Kev it was like something from another world. He was in a bit of a state one day, as he needed to tax his car, but had misplaced his insurance documents. I offered to do it on line for him, explaining that he wouldn't then need to produce the documents. This seemed like a good idea to him, so he stood by whilst I went through the process. You could see that it was all a mystery to him, as he studied the screen intently, and eventually he enquired how they knew he had a red car. I couldn't quite see what had prompted this assumption, but was foolish enough to ask! It transpired he had been watching the little icon which moves across the screen to show which stage of the process you have reached, and of course it was a red car, so he assumed it must represent his car, and thought it amazing how they somehow knew what colour his was! Things got even more interesting when the time came to pay, as he couldn't see how I was going to manage that trick. I explained that he would have to put his money in the slot at the front of the computer tower, and then it would shoot off to the DVLA. Cruel I know, but as I was doing him a good turn I thought I was entitled to wind him up just a little bit! I did come clean before he managed to jam the whole job up, although I suppose it would have served me right if he had.

The French project was still crawling along, and I spent my 50th

birthday looking at sites and meeting what turned out to be the most attractive bank manager I have ever seen; and no, she wasn't giving away free money!
I am always very conscious when I go to France that my lack of any sort of command of their language is really quite bad manners, so I always apologise when someone has to speak English to accommodate me. I did this with Christine, and I thought her response was charming: she assured me that if French was the international language, they would make very sure that everybody else had to speak it, so as we were fortunate enough to have that privilege, we should make the most of it. So; stunning and charming; it almost made up for all the bureaucracy....almost!
Back in England the summer was once again reminding us exactly why we were so keen to build in France, and amidst it all an old friend, who had long since emigrated to Australia, came over to visit, bringing his teenage son with him for a first visit to the home land. His son Michael, being of that age, wanted to go for a ride in the Elise at some point in their stay, as it was not the sort of car you saw too many of back home. The day duly arrived, and Michael and I set off for our jaunt. All was going well until we stopped at the traffic lights, and Michael said, "Patrick, can I ask you something?" Oh dear, I thought, this is going to be one of those awkward questions that he really doesn't want to ask his father, but feels he dare put to a stranger. I told him he could, inwardly fearing the worst, and so was mightily relieved when he said, "Is this really your summer?" It turned out that as his father is an even bigger wind up merchant than me, he thought that it was really our winter, and that his father had told him it was summer as a joke! I just looked at him dejectedly, and said, "Yes Michael, I am afraid it is". He couldn't believe that you could have a summer where it was so cold and wet: I don't think he intends moving to the U.K. any time soon!
In July somebody at the council obviously decided that there were still too many shops surviving in Holbeach and came up with the brilliant idea of introducing car parking charges for the St. Johns

Street car park, just up the road from the shop. This was the last thing we needed, and so a campaign was instigated to overturn the decision. Another trader and I took it in turns to email the council twice a day, to report on the number of cars currently using the facility. As is the case with the locals, they were not about to part with money unless absolutely necessary, and consequently the surrounding roads became jammed, as shoppers and workers alike abandoned their cars whereever it was free, whilst the car park sat virtually empty; not exactly the cash cow they had been hoping for. Fortunately, after three weeks of campaigning, common sense prevailed, and the charges were lifted!
We needed all the help we could get, as the lousy weather had seen garden furniture sales fall by a third, and that is bad news, as we are reliant on strong summer sales to put a bit of wool on our backs, ready for the quieter winter months. We also need to turn that money back into winter stock, so having a store full of furniture isn't too helpful come December.

Later in the year another trip to France finally yielded a building plot. We had a look at several locations, but none of them felt right for us, but then, probably out of desperation, Gerard, the sales agent, took us to a piece of land just outside the charming village of Villemoustaussou. The land still had vines on it, and was yet to get full planning permission, but as we stood there, looking out towards the Pyrenean Mountains, we knew that this was the place for us. There were to be 15 plots, varying in size from 1,500 to 3,000 square metres, just what we wanted.
We slept on it and then the next morning shook hands on the deal. Seeing as how we had been the first people to look at the site, we were fascinated to know how the front plot was already shown as taken on the site plan. It transpired that this had been reserved by the firm's architect, who had apparently been looking for a suitable place to build for some time, so we thought we must have chosen reasonably well. This was further reinforced when Gerard enquired as to why we had chosen our particular plot. We explained that it

was the second highest on the site, and although the one opposite was a fraction higher still, it was too large for our requirements. Next thing we knew, Gerard had bought the highest plot; it turned out he too had been looking for somewhere for quite some time!

So, at last the decision had been made. It was scary and exciting in equal measure, but I have always taken the view that if you want things in life you invariably have to make them happen, and that usually means getting off your back side and doing something about it. You just have to hope that fortune really does favour the brave. This project would mean abandoning my previous dictum of never borrowing more than half of the money needed, and would be reliant on us being able to rent out the property to help finance it. As I said, scary and exciting!

If building our house in the U.K. had been a challenge, doing so 800 miles away certainly was. By the September the plans and contracts had been drawn up, and Gerard came over to get everything signed. Just after he had left, as dusk fell, there was the sound of an engine, obviously very close by. It would get louder and then more distant, leading Alice to suspect someone was riding a quad bike or similar in the stubble field around the house. I thought it sounded as though it was above us, but obviously it was too dark and sound was too close for it to be an aircraft.

Curiosity got the better of me, and I wandered out with a torch. As I shone the beam of light down beside our hedge it illuminated a tall figure, with the complexion of a ghost! There behind him was a very small plane, obviously home built, sitting forlorn amongst the stubble. Being quick on the uptake I assumed the approaching spectre was its erstwhile pilot, who looked unharmed, although I cannot vouch for the state of his underwear!

Apparently he had been on a trip to Yarmouth, and had left rather later than intended, heading for his home airfield of Holbeach St. Johns, just over the fields from our house. With it now dark, and unable to locate the airfield, he had decided to make an emergency landing. I don't think he realised just how lucky he had been, as there are electric cables running near his landing site, but he had

managed, either by luck or judgement, to miss them.
I took him into the house, and Alice made him a strong cup of tea to calm him down a bit, before I gave him a lift to the airfield to collect his car. On the way there he was complaining that he had radioed ahead for the landing lights to be turned on at the airfield, but that there had been no sign of them. As we got closer, there was the airfield, lit up like a Christmas tree! Suitably embarrassed, I dropped him off at the entrance, no doubt already preparing his excuses for the person patiently waiting in the control tower for his arrival. We did make arrangements to meet the following morning, so I could help him load the plane onto a trailer, but he did not arrive at the allotted time, and the plane had gone by the time I returned in the evening, so I assume he had sorted it somehow! Never a dull moment at Whaplode Fen you know.

Back at the ranch, Sal had decided she wanted to take things a bit easier, and asked if she could go down to a four day week. With trade as it was this seemed like a good idea, and so she added Tuesday to her days off, so giving her a very pleasant three days off in a row. The down side to this was that with everybody else's days off, we now only had a full staff on a Friday.
Talking of ways of making economies, I like to think that I am very careful, bordering on the tight. When I go up or down the stairs at home, for example, I always keep to the left, knowing full well that everybody else will trudge up the middle, so causing excessive wear to that part of the carpet. By my avoiding this section it spreads the wear more evenly, so prolonging the life of the carpet. To me this is just logical, but I do realise that others may see it as a little obsessive!
With this in mind, I was relieved to see that there was someone on my wave length, if not even a little tighter. I was changing a till roll one day when Mel wandered in from the hairdressers next door, most likely with some job she needed doing, as was often the case; anyway, she watched me inserting the new till roll, but was then horrified to see I had only used one side of the old one! It appeared

that she always turns hers over, so as to use both sides. I think she was genuinely shocked that with my reputation, I had not cottoned on to such an obvious saving! I have never dared enquire how she goes on with her toilet rolls, but a valuable lesson was learned none the less.

Later on in the year the 'Canadian Limmings' came over for a visit. I had never met them before, but my mother and Rosie have both been fortunate enough to go over to Canada to meet them. Bud and Ollie turned out to be both good company and interesting. Having retired, Bud had taken a keen interest in the family history, and had compiled a family tree. Naturally we took them to see some of the significant family places, but Bud was particularly keen to see his grandparent's old house in Windsover Road, Spalding. It is when faced with these situations that you realise how important the knowledge of the older generation is. My mum may have been coming up to 90 years old at the time, with the short term memory of a goldfish, (I have no cause to mock, I find myself in a similar situation nowadays!) but give her the stimulation of being able to dredge up her recollection of the past, and her recall was remarkable.

Bud had an address for the property we were trying to locate, but it did not seem to tally with the property we found. We were all stumped, but mum somehow remembered that back in the dim and distant past, the properties on Windsover Road had been re numbered, and she was sure the house we were looking for was next to the butchers. We duly decamped to the butchers, and with little hope of success I ventured in to see if anybody there might remember the Limmings living next door. To my amazement the chap in the shop disappeared out the back, returning with a lady, still seemingly helping out in the shop, who must have been close to my mother's age.

Not only did she remember the Limmings, she wanted to know which particular lot we were looking for! It transpired that not only had Bud's grandparents lived there, but years later on, his cousin

Dick Limming had bought the house, not realising the connection, and then finally, his daughter, Josephine had taken it on! As if this wasn't enough, mum then revealed that she and dad had lived just across the road, in the house I mentioned earlier.
When I returned to the shop, I related this string of coincidences to Sal, and amazingly the 'Limmings house' had also been her first home when she was a newlywed, so the links continued!

As the winter months were a quiet time for the core parts of the business, especially now the horticultural sundries side was declining, we had to find something to keep the wheels turning. Like many others in a similar trade, we looked to Christmas products to bolster sales. It never ceases to amaze me how this once religious festival has now become such a major 'event', seeming to start in November, or even earlier for the 'big boys' and continuing in to January.
As we have limited space, putting up the display is quite an upheaval for us, as a lot of Summer stock has to be packed away, or compressed into just half of the usual area. Even though I say so myself, by the time we have finished, the result is quite spectacular, with waving Santas, running reindeer and chasing stars. I try not to think about the electricity bill, but the locals all seem to love it, and it does bring in quite a useful bit of trade.
The trouble with so much desirable stock is that it can also attract the wrong type of attention. So it was that when I got the call one night to report our alarm was going off, I feared the worst. I hot footed it to the shop, but on arrival there was no obvious sign that anything had been disturbed. I interrogated the alarm log, and once I had identified which sensor had been triggered, the culprit was caught red handed. It would appear that Santa had got a bit carried away in his rocking chair, and had worked his way along the shelf and into range of the sensor. Suitably repositioned, I was able to return home; relieved it had been a false alarm.
One day Kev was relating how, when he changed his car, he couldn't remember on which side the fuel filler was. He pulled up

at the fuel station, and as sods law would have it, the filler was on the other side. A little miffed, he drove around the pumps, assuming that as he would then be on the other side of them, that would have to be right, but what do you know, the blasted filler was still on the wrong side! This was all too much for Kev, so he gave up on the job until another day, when presumably he hoped the filler would play ball, and present itself on the correct side of the car!
Just one more 'Kevism', while I am thinking about it; at that year's Christmas party we went to a local restaurant and Kev had chosen the steak. Now, by his own admission, he much prefers quantity to quality, and has always maintained that one piece of steak is pretty much the same as another. All I can say in reply is that he has maybe had consistently good bits, or consistently bad, but in my experience a good bit of Fillet is a whole different animal (sorry about that!) to a rough bit of Rump. Anyway, on that particular night we were treated to a tender piece of Fillet, obviously a good piece of meat, which had been well hung. I awaited Kev's appraisal with interest, but as usual with Kev, it was not quite what I had expected! Having consumed a good portion of his steak, he came up with a classic Kevism. "These knives must be really sharp; you can cut this steak as easy as anything". The fact that you also hardly needed to chew it did not seem to register, perhaps he has really sharp teeth as well!

At the dawn of 2006 Calor Gas had hit the dizzy heights of £19.99 for a 15kg bottle, although amazingly we were still able to sell a new heater with gas for less than we had in the early seventies. Although the previous season had not been great, we still had a 40 foot container of furniture in, hoping for a better season than the last.
There was a bit of excitement when the town was approached by a television production company, with a view to making a documentary about Holbeach. They wanted to set up an experiment in a typical 'TescoTown', to see if independent shops could still

thrive in the face of overwhelming odds. In other words, was it really the arrival of Tesco which had caused the bakers etc. to close, or was it just bad management, which would have led to their demise in any case. The idea was that they would set up a baker and greengrocers, put people in them with known management skills, and then see if they sank or swam.
A couple of guys duly arrived, and for reasons I am still not entirely sure of, I was elected to show them around the town. What I hadn't realised was that they didn't just want me to show them around, they also wanted to film it and record it. Before I can conjure up some excuse about a prior appointment I've had a microphone attached and we are off; not even time for make up!
Having come from civilisation, well Brighton anyway, they just couldn't get their heads around Holbeach! The fact that we had two tattoo shops, yet no baker or greengrocer, more fast food outlets per head of population than anywhere else in the country, more hairdressers than I have hairs to cut, (that'll be about ten then) .... all these things just totally bemused them.
At the end of what turned out to be quite an interesting couple of hours they departed, promising to be in touch when they had a decision. Sadly, although it was thought a good idea, they couldn't find a television company to take the idea on and more importantly, fund it, so what could have been an interesting experiment never did come to fruition.
Another year and yet another pet shop closes, prompting a temporary uplift in trade until the next one comes along! As it was we needed all the help we could get; another wet and cold spring meant sales took another dive on the gardening front, all we could do was hope that the summer would be kinder to us. You can be as efficient as you like at running the place, but if the elements don't play ball, then you are on a hiding to nothing.
By the beginning of May petrol was threatening to break the pound a litre barrier, and a month later; you guessed it, another pet shop opened!

At least there were some bright spots, a visit from Paul, who built the shop, with his new Lamborghini Gallardo, being one of them. I think that he has always appreciated the fact that we gave him his first job as an independent builder, and as such is very generous in letting me not just have a ride in his cars, but also drive them. The Lambo was of real interest, as they had recently been bought by Audi, and I was interested to see if they had 'Audi-ised' Lamborghini. Sadly, in my opinion they had. Whilst the car was beautifully built, and nothing rattled or felt flimsy, in common with all other Audis I have driven, I found the steering to have as much feel as my fingers on a winters morning, and the whole thing just lacked any real character. I can honestly say that as a driving *experience* my Elise is better. Didn't half go though!
July brought the news that Spread, a long established wholesaler was closing. I suppose as more of us independents succumb, the wholesalers feel the knock on effect, and they too perish. I can envisage a time when we will no longer have the wholesale network to draw on, and you will either have to be big enough to deal with the manufacturers direct, or call it a day. Hopefully the few wholesalers that are left can now get a bigger piece of the shrinking cake, and continue for a few more years yet.
The high spot of the year for me personally was being sat next to that week's MD of Lotus at the club dinner. I say 'that week's' a bit tongue in cheek, as they do tend to have a bit of a revolving door style of management at Lotus! The do was at Norwich football ground; the best use I've seen for one yet! (Only joking!). Our guest speaker was Peter Warr, now sadly passed away, one time team manager of the Lotus F1 team, so a man with plenty of stories to tell. The introduction was to be done by my dinner companion who was a little unsure of how to go about it, and asked if I had any ideas. Flippantly I suggested he could mention Peter's most famous quote, which was that Nigel Mansell would never win a Grand Prix as long as he had a hole in his a**e. To my amazement he stood up and did exactly that, probably not realising that this was something Peter was not too keen of being reminded

of. Whatever, he got away with it, and Peter went on to give a fascinating talk, much of which I could not repeat here. To make the weekend just about perfect we were let loose the next day on the Lotus test track, in their cars, and all included in the price of the dinner tickets. Unfortunately they have never seen fit to repeat the event, which is understandable; as I am sure it must have made a huge loss, although it was great PR.

It has been noticeable over the years how people's buying habits have changed, and no more so than in the purchase of Fireworks. We are allowed to start selling three weeks before the fifth, but it used to be that the real enthusiasts would come in before then, to reserve some stock, before it got 'picked over'. Nowadays, nothing happens until about two days before the event, and then it is one mad rush, people not wanting to part with their money until they absolutely have to: perhaps they think Guy Fawkes might get a late pardon!
The other thing which has changed, with the decline in peoples' spending power, is the number of men who come in (because fireworks are definitely a man thing!) and exceed their allotted budget! By that I mean they will have agreed an amount that is going to be spent with the lady of the house, they would then pay for that legitimate purchase with a card, but then find some cash they had been squirreling away to pay for some illegitimate extras. Somehow we men seem better able to justify sending a couple of hundred pounds up in smoke than our more rational partners; although having said that, I do seem to be able to cope with just the ten pairs of shoes!
The close of 2006 saw the end of an era, with the demise of the Holbeach Growers Group. This was a buying syndicate, which had been formed by some of the local growers, with the idea of increasing their buying power. At its height the group boasted over 200 members, and they had considerable clout when it came to negotiating prices. In a typical month we would probably issue over a 100 invoices, which made for some late nights! We would

run an open invoice for the whole month, which I would price up on various evenings. At the month end I would finish the pricing and then add each invoice up; manually. On top of this there would usually be a similar number of 'ordinary' customer invoices; more in the strawberry season. This would usually take until 10.30 to 11.30 at night.
The next morning, my secretary would enter all the invoices in the ledger, and I would then take them round to the Group's secretary. Our target was always to get them there by the lunch time of the first of the month, and we nearly always achieved it. I have had many people try to persuade me to go on to a computerised system for invoicing, but the Group's secretary used to tell us that of all the suppliers to the Group, our invoices were always the first to arrive, and always had the least mistakes. So if it aint broke......
I think with knowing the customers so intimately, (in a purely business sense of course!) the physical action of actually reading what had been invoiced, and then writing in the price, made you really think about what you were doing: so for example; if you saw Mr Smith had been invoiced with 100 x 30 inch boxes, you would think, that's funny, he usually has 24 inch'', so you would make enquiries, and most likely, someone had indeed invoiced the wrong ones. With a computerised system, it tends to remove that thought process, or so it seems from many of the invoices I receive!

At the start of 2007 we at last had proof positive that something was happening in France, with pictures of the footings in place; the only trouble was that meant they wanted more money, and the pound was sliding ever further against the euro, now standing at just 1.48.
Luckily 2006 had not proved to be a bad year, so hopefully we would be able to keep paying the bills. Even so, I was trying to keep personal spending to a minimum, and as I am not noted for over extravagance in that department, this proved a bit of a challenge! First to go was the lottery, followed by my daily Kit-Kat and my weekly Motoring News. Together they saved over six

pounds a week, which over the course of a year would add up to a worthwhile sum.

Kev continued to amuse us with tales of his exploits, one such emerging when he mentioned a trip to see the snooker world championships. Knowing his sense of direction is not exactly in the homing pigeon league; upon leaving his hotel he took particular note of his route to the snooker venue. He turned left out of the hotel, and then proceeded across a set of traffic lights, over a couple of road ends and then crossed the road to the venue. All he would have to do after the event was turn left out of the venue, and repeat the route in reverse: what could possibly go wrong? Nothing; until that is they sent the audience out of the rear entrance of the building! Undaunted, Kev stuck to his plan, and promptly turned left. He apparently wandered for a considerable distance before an observant Policeman noticed he seemed to be a bit lost. Luckily the Bobby was able to decipher Kev logic, and realised what had happened. Suitably re-programmed Kev eventually managed to find the hotel, still not really sure quite where he had gone wrong!
Talking of people not quite understanding, we had a chap in with a bit of a mouse problem, who wanted to buy some traps. We offered him the choice of the tried and tested, but barbaric, whack 'em across the back of the neck type, or the humane ones, where they merely wander into a nice cosy container, where supper is waiting, and then amuse themselves until the nice person comes along and takes them on a trip to mouse nirvana. Apparently being a sensitive sole, he chose the humane type, and away he went. The next day the same chap walked in again, wanting another trap. Thinking he must have a few more visitors than at first thought I sold him one, and off he toddled. Next day, there he was again. By now I was thinking this is a bit strange and so asked if he had a particularly heavy infestation? "Not really'' he said, "It's just that they take so long to die." I carefully explained that the idea of the humane traps was that you actually let the mice go at a suitable site, far enough

away from your house, so that they could carry on doing their mousy business, and that leaving them to starve to death was probably somewhat less kind than the whacking them over the back of the neck option! The poor chap seemed genuinely taken aback; he just hadn't considered the fact that what he was doing was actually cruel.

Sister Rosie escaped to civilisation many years ago, but still remembers what it was like living in the time warp that is Holbeach. She was having some building work done at her house in Uxbridge, and the builders were fascinated by some sooty marks in the corner of one of the out buildings. Rosie suggested they were most probably a legacy from the copper. Being young whipper snappers, they had no idea what a copper was, so she explained it was a device situated in the wash house, where you lit a fire under a bowl of water, which would then be heated, and so provide warm water for the purpose of washing your laundry. They thought this was all a bit farfetched, and couldn't imagine such a contraption.
Cue a phone call back home, and an enquiry as to whether I knew of any coppers still in existence locally. As it happened, I only had to walk around the corner, where an old terrace still has its wash house, complete with copper. Permission duly sought, I took a photograph, and emailed it across. Apparently the builders couldn't believe such things existed, and considered themselves duly educated. I don't know what they would make of the old 'Lincolnshire Long Drops'!

A good spring saw furniture sales continue to flourish; we are so dependent upon the weather that it can literally be the difference between boom and bust, so we were just hoping that things would hold out for the all important summer season.
Meanwhile, Sal had decided that after 13 years at the mad house, she wanted to take things a bit easier, and had decided to semi-retire. Naturally this was an excuse for a party, and it was decided that we would hold it at our house, with me doing my best to

poison them all. Foolishly I gave everybody a choice of what they would like, and so on the night I finished up cooking lamb, steak and duck. Now; Sal is a bit selective when it comes to meat, and as such had never tried duck, just in case she didn't like it. Having heard me singing its praises on many occasions, she decided that this was her chance to give it a go, and so chose it for the night of the party. Now; to me there is only one way to serve duck, and that is pink. I enquired of those having it if that was agreeable, and all but Sal approved. As the blood aspect is part of what deters her from eating a lot of meats, she wanted hers a bit more done. Noting this, I committed hers to the barbecue first, giving it a good head start, before adding the other meats. Having miraculously avoided cremating anything, I served up. All was well until Sal cut into her duck. Although it had gone past the ideal pink stage, there was apparently still too much evidence that it may have once lived, and it was ordered back onto the barbecue. After five minutes or so I rescued the now somewhat charred offering, but still it didn't pass muster. I suggested that another session would see the poor morsel reduced to ash, and that maybe duck wasn't for her after all! Luckily her partner came to the rescue, and heroically tackled something which would now be more appropriate for resoling a shoe. We managed to find Sal something to eat, so she didn't go without, and a good time was had by all.
My hopes for a good summer were well and truly dashed when over six inches of rain fell in June. To put that into perspective, our part of the country usually has about 24 inches a year! This had a devastating effect on trade; people understandably spending their money on escaping to some sunshine, rather than buying garden furniture they couldn't use. I suppose the furniture had now become such a major part of our summer sales, that it governed our fortunes perhaps a little more than it should, but with the wholesale side of the business still in decline, and never likely to recover, there was not too much we could do about it, other than re-locate to the South of France, where summer doesn't seem to have gone out of fashion!

As if the weather wasn't bad enough in June, Gordon Brown was made Prime Minister. I couldn't decide whether he could do more damage as Chancellor or Prime Minister: either way it was bad news, as far as I could see. I tend to be swayed more by results than supposed policies, but as an apolitical observer, it strikes me that over the years the Labour government seems to get the country into debt, and then the Tories come along and dig us out of it; in so doing they have to take measures that make them unpopular, allowing Labour to seduce the electorate once again. The problem this time was that they had three terms in which to squander the money we haven't actually got, and as such there is a much bigger mess to clear up! A simplistic view I know, and one which could doubtless be argued against, but that is still the way it seems to me!
At the end of the day a country is like a business, just a whole lot bigger, and like a business, if you keep spending more than you are earning, sooner or later you are going to end up in trouble, or have to make yourself beholden to others in order to survive. What do they say about politics and religion?
July was bad news for both the shop (yet more rain) and smokers, as the ban on smoking in public places came into force. I really thought there would be more resistance than there was, but I have to say that not one customer came into the shop with a lit cigarette after the ban, and you could see many having a last drag outside the door before extinguishing their cigarette and coming in. Whatever the rights or wrongs, I know I enjoy a meal out a lot more now without someone's discarded smoke tainting my Creme Brulee!
On the premise that all good things come to those who wait, a month passed by after Sal left before Jack, her successor, could take up her position. Bringing a new member of staff up to speed is always a long winded affair, as the seasonal nature of the business means it is a year before they have been exposed to all the facets of the job. The only way to learn is to keep asking, and new incumbents soon learn to never assume we don't sell something, as there are many unseen treasures lurking in the depths of the stores.

By now Tesco had been in the town long enough for the powers that be to realise that it, together with Boyes, had shifted the focus of the town from the high street to the margins. Although the horse had long since bolted, at least there seemed a will to try and resurrect the town centre, and it was deemed that a pedestrian link between Tesco and the town centre, (as it used to be!) may encourage people to venture into town. The most obvious route for this link was through my Park Hall site, and so exploratory plans were drawn up for a development of new shops and community buildings to connect Park Road and its environs with High Street. As ever the stumbling block is money, so I am not holding my breath: it would be wonderful for the town if it was to happen though.

Amid all this positivity, sadly the 'new' bakery closed again, so now we were once again without a baker or greengrocer.

Nearer home, we had quite a shock when it emerged that drugs were being grown not a stone's throw away, and yet we had no idea: it did explain however why we had seen cars parked in some strange places. Being as isolated as we are this is not an uncommon sight, but usually the occupants are not there to observe the comings and goings from surrounding properties!

At the end of October, the house in France was at last finished: now the real work could start. Throughout the year we had been gradually buying bits and pieces for the house, and so on the 28th we set off for France, with the truck loaded to the gunwales! I was dreading customs, for although we had nothing to hide, loading the truck had been a long and complex task, and I didn't fancy having to take all the ropes and sheets off for inspection. Luckily they were not in the least interested in our cargo, and all went smoothly as we cruised our way down to Limoge, for our overnight stop. Our sister in law's sister has a house there, and very kindly said we could stay for the night, even though they would not be in residence. Directions had been given, with instructions that the entrance was *just* before the little well on the green, and if we went past that, then we had gone too far. Now; by the time we arrived it was gone 10pm, so we were about shattered. We eventually spotted the well, not easy in the pitch black, and there, *just* before it was an entrance, running between our accommodation for the night and the adjacent building. Even from a distance the gap seemed a little tight, but this was obviously the route in, and there was no way I could leave the truck and it's valuable cargo on the roadside, in the middle of nowhere, so I set about coaxing the truck between the two buildings, and boy, was it tight: so tight that I even had to fold the wing mirrors in. As I inched along, what I had thought to be an optical illusion unfortunately turned out to be anything but, and the gap narrowed still further. I now had a dilemma on my hands: the gap was now too narrow to open out the mirrors, and I certainly didn't fancy reversing out again blind, so I had to carry on. After much tentative manoeuvring, and the odd scraping sound, I eventually emerged out from this hell hole into a court yard, with enough manoeuvring room to line the truck up and finally reverse it into the drive. I should point out that during this performance, the French family, whose window I was loitering by, carried on as though having a truck wedged against their home was an everyday occurrence!

I consoled myself with the thought that at least the repeat performance in the morning would be executed in daylight. Inspection of our route out didn't exactly fill me with confidence, as a large stone, forming part of the foundations, would have the effect of tilting the truck over at just the point of entry. Anyway; we eventually negotiated our way out, and with much relief, continued on our way to Villemoustaussou.

There is however, a sting in the tail to this episode. When we returned home we thanked our hosts for their kind gesture, and related the drama of the passage. They looked bemused, and asked for more detail of exactly where we went. Having confirmed our route, they just kept saying, "You couldn't have done, that's impossible!" Having eventually convinced them, it was explained that we had actually driven down the footpath, the vehicular access being from the *road* before the wishing well! You would have thought the French family may have pointed this out to us, but I suppose they just thought 'crazy English!'

THE FRENCH DREAM FINALLY BECOMES REALITY

Chapter 10 Taking On Another Headache!

At the start of 2008 I suppose the seeds were sown for this labour of love, for I was asked to give a talk by a local group on the history of the shop. I didn't really think there was much to tell, and what there was, I didn't think would be of much interest, but I was eventually cajoled into it, and so I made a few notes and duly rambled for an hour or so.
To my surprise, the audience actually seemed to find it interesting, and came up with quite a few questions; I was even offered payment, so I thought I had better set to, and start reading through 40 years worth of diaries!

January 26th saw the first booking for our new 'Limlet' venture, which was a great relief, as without the rental income there was no way we could afford the house in France. The continuing dive of the pound against the euro wasn't helping our cause either. We had costed the project out at 1.5 euros to the pound, and it was now down to 1.32. Ironically, on the shop side I had just bought my dollars to pay for the container of furniture, at 1.98, which was really good, and enabled us to sell at very competitive prices.
In March I had a real treat, as Paul had bought himself another new toy, and he brought it for me to have a play with. This time the 'toy' was a Ferrari F430, and it proved to be everything the Lamborghini had failed to be. It was fast of course, but importantly, it also involved you in the whole experience, with communicative steering and a sound track that had the hairs on the back of your neck standing to attention! A lovely, lovely car; but way out of my reach, more's the pity.

In April an initiative called 'The Parish Plan' was launched. The basis of this was a document which listed all the priorities for Holbeach and the surrounding area, compiled after consulting local residents. This document was important, as it allowed Holbeach to have a bit more say in its own future, instead of being influenced

quite so much by what the powers that be in Spalding thought was best for us.
The fact there were too many fast food outlets in the town was just one of the things which was highlighted, so with the weight of this document behind us, we could now put a very strong case forward for preventing any more wheedling their way in.
Over in France there were several issues to sort out, and they really required a trip over. The only problem was that Alice could not go, so it was down to me; the non French speaker! Somehow I managed to shop and negotiate my way around with just my twenty words of French, and felt a little happier when I returned, although it was becoming increasingly obvious that all was not well with our builder.
I suspect he had been buying up more building land with the money he had been receiving from clients, rather than using it to pay for his current projects, and now the recession in Britain had stemmed an important flow of new clients, he was struggling with cash flow.

Back in the U.K. costs continued to spiral, a particular shock being a 50% increase in electricity, after my three year contract ended. I think the rest of the crew think I am a bit obsessive about switching off lights etc., but when you are faced with increases like this, it does tend to focus you somewhat!
The weather was doing nothing to help our cause, with a wet cold spring seeing takings well down on the previous year. One strange sale was a lady who came in to order three hammocks, only two of which she wanted immediately, the other one to be collected as and when, with seemingly no real idea of quite when ‘when’ might be! We gladly took her money, needless to say, and agreed to keep the third hammock until required. More of this later....much later!
The ‘other’ business was having a few teething troubles, most of which were caused by our builder, who had also taken on the role as our agent for the house, being rather more economical with the truth than was ideal. At times like these, being so far away is a real problem, and it was difficult to establish just what the real position

was: suffice to say we had unhappy clients, and that was the last thing we wanted. It all became a bit stressful, and made us start to question the wisdom of what we had done: I can find enough aggravation running the shop, without having to look abroad for it!
At least there was still Kev to offer a different perspective. I would sometimes enquire as to who he was going to put his money on for the forthcoming Grand Prix. He always has a bet, claiming he can't get interested in the race unless he has some money riding on it, so I sometimes put forward a suggestion, with the proviso that Kev never backs the favourites, as he likes big odds. At the time this ruled out the McLarens and Ferraris, so for Canada I suggested Kubica in the BMW might be a good bet; as Canada is quite a power circuit, and Kubica was a real talent, just waiting for the right opportunity to score his first win. At 14 to 1 I thought the odds were within Kev's range. I explained the logic behind my tip, and then left the decision to him. Come Monday morning, Kubica having indeed won, I expected to see Kev's pockets bulging with the proceeds from his win. Apparently not: Kubica's team mate, Nick Heidfeld was at even better odds, so Kev ignored all the logic of why he should go for Kubica and put his money on Hiedfeld, reasoning that he stood just as much chance of winning, as he was in the same type of car. It's this gamblers mentality thing again: much more exciting to nearly win at 50 to 1 than actually win at 14 to 1.

As the year progressed the economic situation became steadily worse, with the banks seemingly going into meltdown, and customers being very nervous about spending. At least the French side of things was a little better, a lovely letter from one client, saying how much they had enjoyed their stay, providing us with a much needed fillip.
It seemed impossible, but it was also rapidly approaching our 25th Wedding Anniversary; and me still just a boy! Although the budget would be limited, we couldn't just let this milestone (millstone?!) pass without some sort of party. In the end we decided to forgo the

holiday to exotic places, and put on a do. The idea of a garden party, with a jazz band, hog roast and as much ice cream as you can eat to follow, had been lodged in some cranial cavity for a long time, so we set about realising it. By coincidence, it was also Tony and Louise's Silver Wedding Anniversary: not *so* much of a coincidence I suppose; they were married on the same weekend as us! Anyway, it transpired that they were planning a hog roast at their party, the night before our do, and as a lot of the guests would attend both functions, all that hog might just be a bit too much.

We kept wondering what we could substitute the hog roast with, but none of the ideas we came up with really inspired us; then, as I was walking to the bank one day, I had a light bulb moment. We have a very good Thai restaurant in Holbeach, and I just wondered if they would fancy a bit of outside catering. On impulse, I nipped across the road and put the proposition to them. Although it was something they had never done, or even considered doing, they promised to give it some thought and let me know.

A few days later they confirmed they were up for it, and wheels were set in motion. Next the ice cream. We don't have much in Holbeach, but fortunately we do still have 'Laddies Famous Ices', who have been making ice cream for a couple of generations now. Rick was soon on board, and offered to make some special champagne flavour, as well as the usual stuff.

So, in the end all turned out well. The jazz band was just what I had envisaged, the Thai did an absolutely wonderful job, including a water melon, hand carved with Silver Wedding greetings, (apparently the poor chap was up until 2am finishing it), and the idea of as much ice cream as you could eat brought out the inner child in everybody. The rain even held off until we had finished!

I did just have to correct Alice on one point, however. She claimed I was the same man she had married 25 years before, just with less hair; but as I pointed out, I still have the same *amount* of hair; it's just not necessarily in the same *places*! I ventured that should she care to inspect any of my orifices; be they olfactory or auricle, she would find the relocated follicles alive and flourishing!

You are doubtless wondering what someone of my noted generosity would buy his spouse to celebrate 25 years of wedded bliss. Well; luck was on my side in this regard, as when we married we had a galvanised dustbin, which after a quarter of a century of sterling service had finally given up the ghost. What could be better? Silver in colour, practical and available from my 'local Limmings', the perfect gift for the girl who has everything! (Apart from a dustbin, of course!). Obviously I couldn't just hand over something so utilitarian in its raw state, so I dressed it up with a silver bow, and had it waiting in the bathroom for Alice on the morning of the big event, in all its splendour. I can't remember her exact comment, but I think it was along the lines of 'Oh; aren't I a lucky girl'. Not being completely unhinged, I had taken the precaution of concealing some silver jewellery inside the bin....

Elsewhere, the other girl in my life had been honoured by being invited to feature on the official Lotus Club stand at the 60th anniversary celebrations, held at the Lotus factory at Hethel. Given that it only featured three cars, I considered this a great honour. Needless to say, a lot of spit and polish was applied, (well, not too much spit, actually), and she looked the business. During the day I spotted Hazel Chapman, widow of Colin, wandering about taking in the atmosphere, and I would imagine feeling both proud and nostalgic. As she drew closer I approached her, and trying to second guess her thoughts, said "It's hard to believe all this is because of one man, isn't it." Instantly she fixed me with a penetrating stare, and rebuked me with the reply, "And one woman!" She may be past the first flush of youth, but is still as sharp as a knife. I realised it had been an inappropriate thing to say: although Colin was the star of the show, it was obvious that Hazel had been very much a part of the success. (If you wanted to be corny, I suppose you could say she was 'the wind beneath his aerofoils', although that would give lift, not down force of course!) Not wishing to miss the opportunity, I asked if she would do me the honour of posing for a photo with my girl. She agreed, but only on condition I made a donation to the charity the Chapman family

COLIN CHAPMAN'S WIDDOW, HAZEL, WITH MY GIRL AT THE LOTUS 60th ANNIVERSARY CELEBRATIONS. A VERY PROUD MOMENT FOR HER!
(THE CAR, NOT HAZEL!)

supports; as I said; sharp as a knife. All this activity aroused the interest of the Italian Lotus Club, whose display was next to us (lovely people, but as mad as a bucket full of frogs), and they enquired as to who this lady was. When I revealed her identity, they reacted with typical Italian brio and wanted anything and everything signing! So, we ended up with the surreal scenario of me negotiating the donation levels while Hazel signed everything from car chassis to jackets!

Later in the year we were invited 'next door' for dinner, and realised we seemed to have a gift of some sort for everyone bar Lizzi. We didn't feel we could exclude our hostess, and yet what to give her? Then another of those worrying ideas invaded my head. When we had been showing Lizzi some photos on another

occasion, there was one of me emerging from a hot tub, which elicited the sort of comment someone with my physique might expect.
What could be more fitting therefore, than a 'Hunks Calendar', featuring that very 'photo? I duly ran a copy off, and presented it on the night. From her reaction when she opened it, I guessed it was a success, although Holt didn't seem so keen! The trouble is, this has now become something of a tradition, and we have to think of something for Lizzi's calendar every year now.

Back at the shop, one of our long standing suppliers had a new hand on the helm, following the sad death of their much respected predecessor, and they decided they wanted nothing to do with the small fry like ourselves, and unceremoniously dumped us. Fortunately another wholesaler was more than pleased of our business, so we were able to agree terms with them, but that was yet another source of supply gone.
As the year wore on, Holbeach lost its travel agent, one of its estate agents, and yet another pub; and then to cap it all, Woolworths went bust, which was a real blow for a town like ours, as it was one of the shops that people would come into town specifically to visit, and then hopefully patronise some of the independent shops whilst there.
Things weren't much better elsewhere, with Iceland going into meltdown (so to speak!), and our builder in France finally throwing in the towel. Just to put the tin hat on it, the pound had fallen so far against the euro that they had all but reached parity, which for our lettings venture was a disaster.
All this financial turmoil had a big effect on our furniture prices, as it had to be paid for in Dollars, and where as the previous year we had bought them at 1.98, this year the best I could do was 1.48, which even without any 'normal' price inflation, meant we had to put it up by over 30%. It is very difficult to explain an increase like that to your customers, and inevitably it would impact on sales. I kept thinking 'surely the pound can't fall any further', but it turned

out it certainly could! The only consolation was that it fell to 1.37 five days later, just as Obahma was made president of the USA, so it could have cost me another 700 quid!
At least the cold winter weather was helping fuel sales: I think a lot of locals were really feeling the pinch by now, and where as previously they may have had enough disposable income to buy a few treats along with the essentials, now there was barely enough money for those essentials, and so purchases had to be rationalized and prioritised, which meant that when it wasn't *really* cold, they would make do without coal, but now it had turned *really* cold, fuel moved up the priority list. This may seem like fantasy to some of you reading this, but I can assure you, to some of our customers, there were some very difficult choices to be made. A lack of funds also meant they could not afford the outlay to buy a ton of coal, so they would come to us for a bag or two, as and when their finances allowed.
I remember one particular evening there was a youngish couple sat outside the shop in their car, and I couldn't help but over hear their conversation; which revolved around whether they should buy a bag of coal, or go to the nearby supermarket for some food items. After careful consideration, the lad said 'I think we really have got to have some heat tonight', and the bag of coal won the vote.
I really did feel for them, and seriously considered giving them the coal, but that can then create its own problems, so in the end I decided it was best to let them sort things out for themselves.
One unforeseen spin off of the rapid increase in the price of fuel was that a surprising number of people stopped using their central heating, or if they did, they would keep the thermostat very low, and then boost the heat in whichever room they happened to be using. This scenario lent itself perfectly to the portable gas heaters we sell, and it was noticeable how sales of these improved.

Woolworth's demise meant that there was now a sizeable shop empty on the high street, and what should be done with it came up for debate at one of the Business Forum meetings. It was no secret

that the council had received a sizeable chunk of money from Tesco's as a 'good will' gesture (careful Patrick!) when planning permission had been granted for their store in Holbeach, this money supposedly to be spent for the good of the town.
I suggested that if this was used to purchase the premises, then half a dozen or so 'shops within a shop' could be created, and rented out to micro businesses. There could even be a 'community unit', where say, for example, one day somebody could sell their honey, the next maybe someone their woodcrafts, and so on and so forth.
I even proposed replacing the end wall with large doors, so that a cafe could spill out on to the adjacent large paved area on Market Hill. (Eight feet above sea level you know, that's nearly a mountain here in the Fens!)
The idea seemed to be well received by the members present, but it transpired that all the Tesco money had already gone, and there was none to be had from anywhere else: so we eventually ended up with one of the price cutting multiples, who sell pretty well what was already available in the town, only at prices we independents can't hope to compete with; well, on most of the items anyway: we still give them a run for their money on some things, the trouble is people just assume the multiple will be cheaper, and don't even give you a chance in many cases.

The start of February 09 was very traumatic. Although mum was now nearly 93, she still lived on her own, which suited her independent nature. On the fateful morning I received a phone call from one of my mother's friends who had been unable to raise her for her lift to Church. As this is something mum would not normally forget, I thought I had better investigate. The timing couldn't have been worse, as Tony and Jack were away at a trade show, so there was only Kev and I to man the shop. On arrival at mum's I let myself in, and called out. Eventually a feeble voice came from the bathroom. I asked if she was alright, and she insisted she was still getting ready, and would be out in a minute. Quite some time passed, but still she did not emerge; also worrying was

the fact that her voice appeared to be coming from low down, and close to the door. Despite her insistence that all was well, I decided to go in, and was met by the sight of mum collapsed behind the bathroom door; obviously very weak, and disoriented.
I called an ambulance, and the crew quickly established that she was badly dehydrated, amongst other things, and definitely needed hospitalising. This did not go down well with mama, and if I hadn't been in enough trouble for calling the ambulance in the first place, I certainly was now!
While all this had been going on, poor old Kev had been manning the fort single handedly of course, and had done very well to cope.
This incident effectively ended mum's independence, as she has never recovered enough of her faculties to live independently, which is a shame.
The tie up between Sommerfields and CO-OP meant that they had to transfer some of their shops to other groups, in order to avoid a supposed monopoly position, which unfortunately meant we lost the Sommerfields just up the road from the shop. I had always held the view that they did us more good than harm, as they didn't compete with us on many items, but did bring a lot of customers down to our end of town.
Their replacement, Budgens, whilst having a nice range of quality products, unfortunately started off on the wrong foot by being perceived as too expensive. They later took steps to dispel this view, but the trouble is, especially with Holbeach people, once they have decided you are not right for them, you have a job on your hands luring them back.
The upshot of all this was a dramatic drop in footfall at our end of town, and doubtless a very happy Tesco manager! Hindsight is a wonderful thing; but knowing they were taking over from a brand with a reputation for keen pricing, maybe Budgens should have started out with a few loss leaders, and some 'value' products, to retain those customers who had previously used the store, rather than having to attract a new group, more appropriate to their more 'up market' offering.

I am not exactly unaccustomed to putting myself in embarrassing situations, but I excelled myself one day with a young lady I had known since she was a young girl. Making conversation, as you do, I enquired as to what she did for a living now days. She seemed reluctant to tell me, but being the dim wit I am, I kept labouring the point, until she eventually declared that she was an escort! Now; even I could work out that she wasn't talking about the sort that Henry makes, so there followed something of an embarrassing interlude; for both of us. Anyway; now the ice had been well and truly shattered, I felt I could enquire as to how things were going: it's a bit difficult to know how to be in this sort of situation, as you want to show *interest*, without sounding as though you are *interested*! I should also mention at this point that she also breeds dogs. A few weeks later I enquired as to how things were, and received a very succinct reply: "Well; Bertie has been getting more s***s than me, *and* he's been getting paid more for them!" There really is no answer to that! The name of the dog has been changed, to protect the innocent.
At the end of July I became the only member of the family still in full time employment, as Rosie decided to call it a day and retire to a life of dusting and polishing, or there again, probably not.
The magnificent summer continued, with 2.5 inches of rainfall in a day, which was a bit extreme. It is the first time, as far as I can remember, that houses have been pumped out in Holbeach. All this helped us to also record the worst day's takings I can remember!

The house in France was still taking its financial toll, and leaving Alice and I sailing a bit closer to the wind than our naturally cautious natures were happy with. I decided to bolster funds by drawing the tax free lump sum from my meagre pension pot. This at least gave us the peace of mind that we had something behind us again, and if I should do the same silly trick as dad, and snuff it at 64, at least I have had some of my cash!
As technology has gained more of a hold over our lives, I think Alice and I are amongst the very few who still seem able to exist

without a mobile phone constantly by their side. We still have a 'pay as you go' affair, which we bought for emergencies, and use for such, hence we fritter about £10 every couple of years on calls, and seem to cope quite satisfactorily doing so.
This subject came up at a dinner party one evening, and one of our guests, who is rarely seen without her 'third ear', concurred that she also used her phone for emergencies only. This assertion was greeted with an uneasy silence, until her husband, noted for his dry humour, piped up with. "Yes; the only trouble is, she has a shedload of emergencies!" Quite so.
In defence of our geriatric old Nokia, it may be the subject of ridicule, but at least it works as a phone. There have been several occasions when these so called smart phones have been unable to get a signal, and our old relic has had to come to the rescue. It may not be able to tell me the temperature in Istanbul, but it is good at making phone calls, which funnily enough, is what we bought it to do! In these situations it is tempting to say of its modern rivals 'not so smart now, are you', but I try to resist!
According to a friend who works in the industry, there is actually some basis to my assertion, as the modern phones have so many other bits and pieces in them, that there is limited room for the actual phone bit, which is why the old ones tend to work better.
Before we leave the dinner table, I must relate a story concerning another friend with a dry sense of humour. Tink, bless her, does like her car boot sales, and usually comes back with a collection of treasures. She was regaling us with stories of her latest finds, and reassuring Richard that they were real bargains. To reinforce her point, she mentioned a few previous purchases, which had now increased in value. As usual in these situations Richard let her have her head, and then, just as Tink thinks her case proven, Richard, calmly rounds the story off with the foot note: "What she doesn't tell you about is the other £3,000 worth of rubbish we've got stuck up in the loft!" Doesn't say a lot Richard, but what he does is usually priceless.

In December Holbeach's slide down market continued with the opening of a pound shop. I suppose such shops do have a place on the high street, but you don't see too many in Knightsbridge, do you?

Chapter 11 The First Half Century

2010 was the 50th year of trading for the firm, which in these troubled times had to be something worth celebrating. At the start of February, I decided to start a countdown to the anniversary day, all very low key, I just wrote '23 days to go' on the sign board we have standing out on the frontage, and thought no more of it. I never would have believed the amount of interest it generated! Before I knew it there was a steady stream of people through the door, trying to second guess what the message meant. A rather worrying number thought it was the number of days until we closed down, whilst others thought it to be anything from the start of a sale, (obviously they didn't know me too well) to my birthday.
I refused to confirm or deny any of these predictions, which just made people even more inquisitive of course! Eventually the local paper latched on to the story, and ran an article about this mystery count down. Seeing the potential this situation presented, I decided to run some 'teaser' adverts in the paper, which stoked things up even more! Gradually one or two people began to do their research, and came in triumphantly to announce they had 'cracked it'. Although the publicity created was not initially planned, I still think it is the best return I have ever had on a piece of chalk!

Just before the anniversary day I was asked to give another talk about the shop. Apparently some of the people, who had been at the first effort, were also members of another group, and they too now wanted to hear the story; now that's what a call being a glutton for punishment! Anyway, I decided that if I was going to do it, I ought to make a proper effort, and enlisted the help of a couple of technically minded friends to make up a slide show of some of the old photos I had. Nick was even kind enough to accompany me on the night, to look after the 'magic lantern' side of things. Yet again there was no sign of snoring, and payment was also offered. It even occurred to me that I might be better giving up the actual shop keeping, and just talk about it instead!

When February 23rd finally arrived, we gave our customers a treat with some very good offers, and even gave away some rather posh hessian shopping bags. Although I say so myself, these were a cut above many you see, being sturdily constructed with thick, soft handles. I still see a lot of them on my travels and it's nice to think you have given people something they actually wanted: I do like practical gifts.
One sad bag related tale came from a customer whose house had been broken into. He told us that what had really upset his wife was that they had even stolen her Limming's bag to take some of their haul away in. He enquired as to whether I might have one left he could purchase, to at least cheer her up a bit. At first I thought I would have to let him down, but then I remembered I had secreted one in the truck, just in case we delivered to a customer who had 'missed out' when we were giving them away. Even I didn't have the heart to charge him in this particular situation.

I am well aware that as I get older, I become more 'grumpy old man' about technology, but sometimes it really does astound me how ill thought out some of the systems are. One particular gripe of mine is taxing a vehicle on line. The first time I tried to do so with the truck, it wouldn't accept it was insured, for although it was insured at the time I was trying to make the purchase, the insurance would have run out by the time the tax disc came into force. Fair enough: I could see the logic in that. The following year, determined not to be beaten by 'the system', I re- insured the truck well in advance of the due date, so that the data base would be able to see a seamless continuation of the insurance. Not so! Still it insisted the truck would not be insured at the time the tax disc came into force. Thinking that maybe my broker had been a little tardy in renewing the policy, I made enquires, only to be told that the data base is only updated on the actual day the insurance comes into force, and so as far as the DVLA system is concerned, even though the premium has been paid for two weeks, you are still deemed to be uninsured. How stupid is that. Surely something can be done:

think how many people this must effect, as millions of cars are sold, and therefore originally taxed and insured, at the start of the same month. There are ways around it, I realise: you can wait until the new insurance starts, and then tax the vehicle a little late, or tax for six months, or even alter the insurance; but why should you have to?

My much loved BMW M3was now coming up to nine years old, and although it had been reliable, I realised that if it did ever go wrong, it would not do so cheaply. As usual, Alice was the voice of reason, and convinced me that as she covered the vast majority of the mileage trundling back and forth to work, the M3 was a bit of a waste anyway, and we ought to look at something which would fit our pocket and needs better.
As usual, a short list was drawn up, and eventually the Volkswagen Scirocco got the nod. It has turned out to be a good compromise, as Alice loves driving it, and I love the size of the bills. I still miss the sound of that M3 engine at 8,000 rpm though!

After all the teething troubles, the French adventure was now proving less stressful, although there were still the problems you would expect with any such venture. Being very hands on, if not border line control freak, I do find it very hard to delegate all the jobs: no matter how good the people are who look after the house, you still don't have that ultimate command over events there.
One recurring problem we did have was with the drains. They would seem to be fine for a while, and then suddenly there would be all sorts of problems. We tried everything, including the French equivalent of Dyno-Rod, who did retrieve all manner of building debris, including part empty concrete bags, but still no lasting remedy was found.
Luckily, when we went over at Easter, the drains actually worked their magic for us, with all sorts of gurglings and shower shenanigans. We decided to try a trick which had worked for us at a property we had rented in Portugal, many years earlier. Every sink,

and the bath was filled with water, and they plus the toilets were each manned by one of our guests. (Funny, people never seem to want to come over a second time!) On the command they all released their salvos, as I stood by the open drain, rod in hand. You could hear the torrent that had been released approaching, and as it cascaded by, suddenly this red shape appeared amongst the maelstrom. Instinctively I stabbed at it with my drain rod, like a hunter spearing a fish, and managed to restrain it until the waters had subsided. Once retrieved, the item could be identified as one of the bungs they insert into open pipes, to stop debris entering them during the building process. It didn't take long to realise that this would be exactly the right type of obstruction to cause the intermittent problems we had experienced. Most of the time it would position itself such that water and small items could pass by, but then obviously something a little more substantial would present itself, (I will leave you to form your own images at this juncture!) and then the bung would flip through 90 degrees, and block the drain. Following removal we have experienced no further problems, so hopefully we have at last found the culprit of our drainage disaster.

After May's election we eventually ended up with a coalition government, which whilst it wasn't perhaps the ideal situation, at least meant we were at last rid of Gordon Brown! I never could decide whether he was trying to bankrupt the country on purpose, or was just spectacularly incompetent, but either way, he and his cohorts had left a hell of a mess to clear up. It is sobering to think that when Margaret Thatcher left office our debt was 26% of GDP, and by the time Brown went it was double that, and set to keep rising, until drastic action was taken to bring things back under control. I find it incredible that politicians talk about a national debt of nearly a trillion pounds as though it is a few quid: as I say, a country is in effect like a big business, and even I know that if you consistently spend more than you earn, and keep borrowing to fill the void, sooner or later there has to be a day of reckoning, and now that day had arrived; all be it about ten years too late!

In our own little world, we were treated to another snippet from 'Kev world'. Tea breaks at the shop tend to be random affairs, taken when there is a quiet spell. As I don't partake of the hot stuff, I usually try and serve, so that the others can enjoy an undisturbed cuppa. During this time any manner of subjects comes up for discussion, and on this particular day the conversation revolved around electric toothbrushes. Tony had been given an all singing and dancing model, and we were all agreed that they were a pretty useful gadget: all but Kev that is. When quizzed as to whether he had actually tried one, he confirmed that he had, but just couldn't get on with it. By now I really should know better, but foolishly I enquired as to what he found so off putting about them. The answer was classic Kev: "Well, the toothpaste goes everywhere, doesn't it?" For just a second I was a bit perplexed, then, remembering Kev has 'logic dyslexia', I enquired as to whether he put the toothbrush in his mouth *before* he turned it on. Well, his face said it all: I guess not! He really is a one off our Kev, but at least he brightens up the day.
Another wet spring had done nothing for trade, but that is the risk you take with selling weather dependant products. The problem is that a consistent run of bad weather knocks consumer confidence, and they quite rightly decide it is a waste of time investing their hard earned cash in something they are unlikely to use above a couple of times in the summer. The effect on takings is drastic: for example, on the end of May bank holiday Saturday, we took just one third of what we had the previous year, and that was almost entirely due to the weather.

Living in the country has many plus sides, one of which is the number of birds and other creatures you are surrounded by. This is fine while they stick to their bit, but every now and then they decide they like you that much they want to move in. Alice once returned home to be greeted by two baby small owls, which had fallen down the chimney in the sitting room. They were completely unfazed by their new surroundings, and just looked at her in that quizzical way they have. They were not overly keen to leave, but Alice did eventually manage to return them to their proper environment. On another occasion, one summer's night, I opened the bedroom door, only to be buzzed by a couple of bats, who were putting on a splendid display of acrobatic flying. Persuading them to leave proved somewhat of a challenge, but after much trial and a lot of error, they did eventually exit through the same window they had used to enter the bedroom.

In late summer Alice and I took a trip to the Hampshire/Sussex area, and decided to re-visit Hook by Warsash, where I had spent many happy teenage holidays, as a guest of the Cauleys. As is usual with these nostalgia things, it was a bitter sweet experience: the bungalow, which held such happy memories, although still occupied, was now dilapidated and the garden unkempt. As for the small holiday village, where I had honed my trampolining skills, this was now a sprawling collection of mobile homes and chalets, all far less intimate than I remember. What did interest me however, was the apparent encroachment of the sea. Although it had been the best part of 40 years since I was last there, I am sure that the tide did not used to come up as far as it was now. It could be to do with the time of year, or other influences of course, but on the face of it, there seemed to have been a definite change in that respect.

It is funny how your life drifts seamlessly from one stage to another, without you really noticing it; other than by the change in conversational subjects at social gatherings! Up to the quarter century mark it was all about where to go and what to do, then it became marriage and mortgages, then kids and schools, quickly followed by grandkids and the attendant disruption, now the conversation often seems to focus on retirement!
Already Tony's wife Sue had reached that stage, and Tony himself had also started his seventh decade. By now I should have been just five years away from the sun and sandals stage of life, but looking

at the way trade was going, this seemed increasingly unlikely to happen. I am at that age now where if I bend down to tie my shoe lace, I try and find another job to do while I'm down there, to make it worth the effort.

I don't know quite what the reasoning was behind our building society's decision to offer business accounts in the first place, but given that benevolence isn't a trait usually associated with any financial institution, I always assumed that part of the reason was that they wanted the cash we deposited, to save them having to 'buy it in' from other sources. I may be completely wrong of course, but it did seem strange that as the use of cards has become more prevalent, and therefore the demand for cash less, that they should decide that we could no longer bank more than £5,000 in cash at a time, and not only that, we may only make two deposits per month.
There was the excuse that this was meant to be a savings account, but they had been pleased enough of our cash for all those preceding years!
Something else which had become obvious was that the internet was growing at a phenomenal rate, and that this would pose the biggest threat yet to the high street. Up to now, as long as the 'big boys' were a fair distance away, people would use the local shops, rather than spend any savings they may have made on travelling. Now these 'big boys' were literally in their own homes, and that alters the game plan entirely. The other problem this creates is that you now often don't even get the chance to put your offer forward, with the customer either just assuming the internet option will be the cheapest, or not looking at the whole picture. As an example, you may get someone who looks at a barbecue, the same as we sell, and it seems to be say, £60 cheaper; so they buy it. At the end of the transaction they have a £30 carriage charge, but that is OK., as they are still £30 up. Their purchase duly arrives, but has no regulator, so at this point they need the help and advice of their local shop keeper. Invariably they have no idea as to whether their

new acquisition runs on butane or propane gas, or which size of bottle they need. Ah; the bottle. Now; our barbecues are all priced to include the bottle and regulator, so there is another 40 odd quid they need to find. By the time you have got them all sorted out, they have usually realised that it would have been cheaper to buy from us, (other barbecue retailers are available, as the BBC would say!) but it is too late by then. I still can't help myself pointing out that had we supplied the barbecue, we would have assembled it for them, supplied the correct regulator and gas, and delivered it to their door, if required. All very frustrating, but that I am afraid is the direction in which we are inexorably heading. People ask me what we intend to do about the situation, and I liken it to the chap who used to go around lighting the gas lamps. He doubtless thought he had a job for life, and then some blighter went and invented electricity; well, retailing is in much the same situation with the internet really, and as it is unlikely to be disinvented, I suppose we will just have to deal with it as best we can.
You may say if you can't beat 'em then join 'em, which we have tried to do. We invested quite a lot in a new web site and even paid someone a lot of money to do all the search engine optimisation etc, but it became apparent after a while that although you may drag yourself up to page 31, or whatever, you are never going to get onto those first few pages on merit, and even if you did, there is no way you can compete with the big boys on something like garden furniture, where their superior buying power, on both the goods, and the carriage, enables them to undercut you.
Talking of rates, the government had introduced a scheme, designed to help small business such as ours, by allowing exemption from rates on properties below a certain rateable value. At first I thought that this would be of no use to us, as it only applied if you owned or occupied one property. On giving the matter more thought however, I realised that as the company owned the shop, and I owned Park Hall, effectively I did only own one property, and as Park Hall was used to store goods for other than just J. W. Limming Ltd, they only as such rented space, and

were not therefore the occupier.
Once this was all sorted out, quite a significant saving was made, which with things as they now were, was very welcome. I have always believed that when things are going well, it is quite right that 'the boss' should be the biggest beneficiary, but it therefore follows that when times are tough, they should also take the biggest knock. With this in mind, when the time came for the pay increases, there was no more in the kitty to finance them, so the only answer was for me to take a pay cut equivalent to the rest of the crew's combined increases. As my wage had resembled the Arctic Circle these last few years anyway, this meant the belt going in another notch. I had for some time not been paid the highest hourly rate on the firm, but now I was no longer the highest earner, period.
It was difficult to see where we could make many more cut backs in our living expenses, but with heating being a major outgoing, we decided to tackle that. The thermostat had already been gradually wound back from 21 degrees to 17, but we now decided to add yet more loft insulation, in the hope that enough heat would then be retained overnight to be able to cope without heating in the mornings. This we now do, although I have to admit it makes you nip about on some of the chillier ones!
Another down side to this was un-spreadable butter. We can't be doing with this substitute stuff, so some way needed to be found of making the proper stuff more malleable. Eventually I came up with a solution. If we put the butter in the airing cupboard when we go to bed, when the heating has gone off, then by morning it is the perfect consistency for spreading: problem solved.

Unfortunately the local economy suffered another heavy blow when Greens Structural ceased trading. We do not have that many big employers in the Holbeach area, but this long established family firm had been one such, and its closing affected a lot of local families. The recession was not just weeding out the weak and inefficient, it was robbing us of some good companies, many of them failing through no fault of their own, merely being victims of failures further up stream.

It is amazing how sometimes just a casual comment can open up a whole new avenue. One day a lad wandered into the shop to buy some fireworks, having been sent by Holbeach Tyres, who were sorting out a pneumatic problem of some sort for him. I noticed his jacket bore the DTV legend, something which I thought strange for someone of his age, as they were a racing team from the seventies. Curiosity got the better of me, and I said, "DTV; that's Gerry Marshalls era, what are you doing with a jacket from back then?" I should maybe explain at this juncture that Gerry Marshall was a legendary figure in club racing, winning over 600 races before his death in 2005. He was also part of a triumvirate which was infamous for their exploits both on and off track. Anyway, I could tell from the lad's stunned expression that I had struck a chord and after a moments silence he also stunned me with his retort. "Gerry Marshall; he was my dad!" Needless to say, not too much work was done for the next half hour or so! Gregor, as Marshall Junior is called, turned out to be a really nice lad, and it was a real treat and privilege for me to be able to exchange stories about his father with him. Just to bring the story full circle, Gerry's most famous car, Baby Bertha, is now owned by a local farmer, who also calls in the shop from time to time.

Taff had long wanted a dog, and he eventually wore his better half down, and Grommit, a leggy Labrador, duly arrived on the scene. Taff brought Grommit round for a visit, but no sooner had we cracked open the front door to greet them, than Grommit was in, like a rat up a drain pipe. He tore through to the kitchen, back through to the sitting room, then up the stairs, where he summarily checked out all the rooms. Still not content, he made it quite clear he now needed access to the dining room. During this performance poor old Taff alternated between trying to bring Grommit under control, and apologising to Alice & me for his actions.

What I haven't told you up to this point is that Grommit had just retired....as a drug sniffer dog! The good news is that he didn't seem to find anything to arouse his suspicions.
Back in the metropolis, the baker who had been standing on Holbeach market, decided to take the plunge, and open a shop in the town. It was really refreshing to see a new business opening, instead of the usual closures, and especially so as it was something the town actually needed.

Our Kev was still finding new ways to challenge conventional thinking, and on this occasion it involved gas cylinders. He had taken two propane cylinders to a customer, and was complaining about the difficulty he had with removing the second one; so much so that he had sought help from the customer, who came to the rescue with a seriously big spanner. The customer undid the nut on the cylinder with little or no effort, which left Kev nonplussed, as he had been giving it his all, and getting nowhere. He explained how he had been pushing the spanner away from him with all his might, just as he had with the first cylinder, but it just would not budge. Now, usually with Kev, there comes a point in his story where the mists start to clear, and on this occasion it was now. You see, propane cylinders are left hand thread, and when there are two of them, they are installed with their fittings facing each other. It therefore follows that if you have to push the spanner away from you for one, you will have to pull towards yourself for the other.
I put this to Kev, but he was adamant that he always pushes the spanner away from him when removing cylinders. Now, once he gets a bee in his bonnet, you've got a heck of a job to shift it. Often you just let it go, as trying to convince him can be a draining experience, but on this occasion, as we were dealing with irrefutable fact, I decided to prove the point. I fetched a cylinder, screwed a regulator into it, and then got him to remove it. He did indeed push the spanner away from him, as he claimed he always did. I then re-attached the regulator, turned the cylinder through 180 degrees, and asked Kev to have another go. What do you

know; he now had to pull the spanner towards him. Point proved; or so I thought! Even this practical demonstration didn't convince him, and he was still adamant that when he was out on site he always pushed the spanner in the same direction. Oh well, you can't win them all!

As winter proper got into its stride, the temperatures plummeted, dropping to minus 10 degrees centigrade, and below. It's an ill wind, as they say, and for us this was a real bonus, with solid fuel and gas sales rocketing, the only problem was getting sufficient supplies of gas. It was a real hand to mouth operation, with us having to make lists of customer's names, so that we could call them as soon as fresh supplies arrived. This went right down to the wire on Christmas Eve, when we had a shop full of customers waiting for a delivery, which eventually materialised at 5.30pm. Boy was I pleased to see that, I think I would have had a riot on my hands if it hadn't arrived.

For quite some time I had been monitoring customer flow between 5.30 and closing time at 6pm. This led me to the conclusion that the cost of being open was far greater than the revenue it generated. Realising that this is only part of the picture; we are there to provide a service after all, I quizzed the few 'late birds' as to whether closing at 5.30 would inconvenience them. Nobody seemed to think it would, so I made the momentous decision to close at 5.30 in the New Year. Had dad actually been in a grave, I am sure he would have been turning!

To finish off the year, we were invited to a New Year party, with a 70's theme. I was asked what I was going to do about acquiring a costume, but for me it was simple: I would just have to select something from the right hand side of the wardrobe! I do have a bit of a reputation for extracting maximum value from my clothing purchases, as Alice reminds me on occasion; like the time a while ago when I was complaining about a jumper, which was starting to come apart at a seam. My complaint was dismissed with the comment, "well I did buy you that for your thirtieth birthday you know." Just my point: the thing was nearly new!

Another new year, another new VAT rate: In their infinite wisdom, the government had decided to tinker with the VAT rate yet again, now setting it at 20%. I don't know whether they realise, or indeed care, how much upheaval these changes cause the retail trade, but for a small business such as ours, it is better to take a 2.5% hit, and leave the prices of existing stock as they are, than change thousands of price tickets. Now they have at last settled on a round figure, let's hope they stop tinkering with the rate every couple of years!

At the beginning of February I at last made a start on the ramblings you have so selflessly given your valuable time up to read! With so many other demands on my time this is very much a project which has to be fitted in around everything else, but hopefully it will reach a conclusion before I do.

Even though fuel prices had gone through the roof, with paraffin now £4.50 per gallon and a 15kg bottle of gas £32.99, the takings did not reflect this. People just had a fixed amount of money, and that was it: if the prices went up, they just made what they did buy last longer. Of course the other alternative was to not pay at all, and to this end we really had to toughen up a bit, and not be quite as trusting as has been the case over the years.

It is amazing how artful some people can be, and one young lady in particular caught us, (and as I later found out, many others) good and proper. Using a combination of cunning and downright lies, she worked a system for quite some time, before I rumbled her. As usual with these things, it was by trying to help her that we set ourselves up. She used to come in to collect gas cylinders in her car, nothing unusual in that, other than these were the big 47kg jobbies, which with the cylinder and contents combined, weigh closer to 90kg.We would of course load them at our end, but concerned about what happened when she got home, I enquired if she had someone to unload for her. It turned out she didn't, and we were then regaled with the whole saga of the abusive partner who was now in prison etc.

I convinced her there was no way she should be trying to handle these sorts of weights, and that in future we would deliver and fit the cylinders for her. This we did, and each time she would tell Kev she would call the shop and pay on her credit card. Being the trusting sort, Kev assumed she would be true to her word, and that this was what she had done. For my part, I assumed she had paid him on delivery. So, through a combination of lax systems and lack of proper communication, plus a bit of naivety, she managed to work this system for quite some time.
It was not until I had to make a delivery one evening that her scam unravelled: the shop was closed, so with some reluctance from her, I took her card details, so that I could process the payment the following day. Needless to say, the card was declined, and only then, when I brought the matter up with Kev, did it transpire that he had not been taking payment from her. I tried to recoup the money, but it turned out that behind that sweet, vulnerable exterior, was a scheming young madam, who was as hard as nails, and could lie to your face without so much as a flicker of conscience. All I could do was to warn other local traders, in the hope that those who had not already been caught would avoid being so in the future.

During September the previous year, I noticed some markings on the road, throughout the town, and wondered what they were for. Come April I found out! To my horror, I arrived at the shop one day to see shiny new yellow lines, right along our frontage. I was far from amused, as kerb side parking is essential for our business, with so many heavy items to load into customer's cars, so an email was soon winging its way to our local councillor, expressing my disgust that we had not so much as been consulted about this catastrophic change to our circumstances. Nick, the councillor in question, is usually pretty good on such matters, but seemed equally nonplussed as to why these lines had suddenly materialised. It was not long before he was back in touch: it appeared there had been what I believe is known in local planning circles as a cock up, and the lines in front of our shop, and indeed throughout the rest of the town, should not have been there at all! We then had the job of trying to explain to our customers that they could carry on as normal, without fear of a parking ticket, until such time as the council got around to painting the lines over with black paint! I don't doubt the person responsible for said cock up offered to meet the cost out of their salary.

Tony sometimes used to reckon there wasn't a recession at all; it was merely that I had wound that many customers up, that I was running out of victims. Although a little harsh, I suppose he did have a point, but as I have said, these things just seem to slip out before I can edit them. On one such occasion a chap made a perfectly reasonable enquiry; to whit, "Will your post hole borer be free tomorrow?" Before I could utter a word, my alter ego jumped in with the reply, "No. It will be £5.00, the same as any other day." To be fair the chap took it all in good part, which is just as well really.

Easter lulled us into a false sense of security. A combination of exceptional weather, and pent up demand, saw us have our best day ever in the shop. It was a fantastic feeling to be absolutely flat out again, something we hadn't experienced for a very long time. The whole thing must have been a bit much for me, as I was even moved to give the staff a few quid to celebrate the occasion with. As it turned out, this proved to be a false dawn, but at least Jack now knew what a properly busy day felt like; the first we had seen since she started working with us.
Selling stuff was difficult enough, but trying to source it can be a headache as well. As I said previously, one of our long standing wholesalers was no longer too interested in dealing with us, but there was a particular product of theirs that I was keen to keep selling, so I tried to buy some stock on a pro forma basis (where the goods are paid for in full, before being dispatched), but they didn't even want to know about that. Not being one to take no for an answer, I thought I would try skinning the cat a different way, and

contacted an old business associate, who managed a garden centre. He agreed to lump my order together with his, and I could then collect our portion of it from him. All seemed well, until he placed the order, and found they thought him too insignificant to deal with as well!
I really cannot understand any organisation turning away good business purely because you are not going to spend £50,000 a year with them. If someone wants a 60 pence flower pot, I am more than happy to take their money; in my book, (which this just happens to be) it all counts!

For my birthday, Alice had arranged a surprise visit to see my cousin Trish in Bath. (Not in the bath, you understand, that would be a bit weird). She is very good like that, as our family are maybe not the best at keeping in touch: we get on well when are paths do cross, it's just that we are not good at walking along those paths in the first place.
We had a thoroughly enjoyable time, and even took the opportunity to do a bit of shopping. Top of the list was what were to become known as our Bryanair jackets. (They may actually be called something that rhymes with that name, but you get the idea). As we now had quite a few clothes out in France, we could get away with just taking hand baggage, as taking anything more is a definite financial no no on the budget airlines. We therefore scoured the shops for a couple of lightweight jackets, with as many pockets as it is possible to attach to one garment. You really do have to play by their rules, and if the baggage limit is 10kg, then anything above that has to be somehow accommodated on your person. I do find it strange that a 12 stone person with an 11kg bag faces draconian penalties, whilst a 20 stone passenger with a 9kg bag is apparently absolutely fine. I know all about safety with the overhead lockers and all that, but it does seem just a bit petty. The other contentious issue is the accuracy of airport scales. I have checked my bag on our Trading Standards certified scales at work on several occasions, to confirm it complies, only to find that when checked at the

airport, it has miraculously gained a kilo or so. I now limit myself to a true 9kg, just to be on the safe side, sometimes the scales agree, but it is not always the case (no pun intended!). I have even had it where I have left a few items out in France, and yet my baggage allegedly weighs more on the return journey: all very strange.
There is of course a simple solution to all of this. If local Trading Standards teams were to set up certified checking stations in airports, then for a fee, they could confirm the weight of your bag, on a properly certified scale, which was calibrated daily, and then put a couple of straps around the bag, bearing an official seal, and this would have to be accepted by the airlines. This way it would stop all the arguments, and feelings of mistrust. It would also be a nice little earner for Trading Standards, given their hard pressed budgets. Although airport scales are subject to checks by trading standards, it would appear, from what I have read, that it is far from guaranteed that they will be accurate.

July saw a really proud occasion for 'my girl' and me, when she was selected from over 40 applicants to appear in an article about Lotus in *Classic & Sports Car* magazine. The photo shoot took place at a dull and drizzly Snetterton race circuit, where we spent the whole day being interviewed and photographed. Fortunately, the wonders of Photoshop made the day appear considerably more clement than it actually was. Apart from a near riot when the promised lunch failed to materialise, the day was a lot of fun, spent with a group of likeminded people - or 'saddos' - depending on your point of view!

As summer wore on the financial turmoil continued, with the American debt crisis managing to wipe 113 points off U.K. shares in one day. From our standpoint, furniture sales had been so slow that we struggled to scrape enough of an order together even to fill a small container. As an increase in sales seemed unlikely any time soon, I needed to look for yet more economies. For many years I

had been on a really good tariff for the electricity at Park Hall, whereby I paid an inflated rate per kilowatt hour, but paid no standing charge. As we only turn a light on about six times a year at the store, this was a really good deal for us: so much so, that we had been years working off a small credit after an over estimated bill. Unfortunately, the electricity company decided to review its tariffs, and this one, not unsurprisingly, got the chop. As usual, I tried to reach some form of mutually acceptable compromise with them, but predictably, they were not interested. My contention that by paying their standing charge it would cost about £10 every time we turned a light on was of no interest to them, and so I had no alternative but to ask them to disconnect the supply. This they did, but of course they were still able to have the last laugh, by stinging me with a £189 disconnection fee, not bad for 10 minutes work. Even so, I will be in pocket in less than three years.
It would of course be a lot easier if I was a government: when they get a bit tight on money, they just print a load more, and call it 'quantitive easing', or 'financial delusion', as it's known in the real world! Another 75 million was thrown at 'the problem' this time.

Meanwhile, a new product caused Kev a bit of conflict. We had been asked to stock a new type of poultry food, called garden chicken blend. It was available from our usual supplier, and so we decided to take it on. It seemed to go down quite well, and as it could be fed in place of standard wheat, or mixed corn, we pointed it out to buyers of those products as an alternative. I noticed that Kev wasn't promoting the new product, and quizzed him as to why. As usual, Kev logic was being applied, and he reasoned that if we kept turning people away from the wheat and mixed corn, we would not need sufficient bags of them to reach the minimum delivery quantity. He had somehow forgotten to factor in the bags being sold in their place!
In October, our long standing neighbour, and fellow tight wad, Mel, announced she was moving her hairdressing business to new premises, in another part of town. We discussed the various

ramifications of the move, and amongst the many plus points of staying in the town, was the fact that she could take her phone number with her. Kev thought this was a really handy thing to be able to do, but concluded it would be an option unavailable to them, as their phone was fixed to the wall!

For the Holbeach Christmas Fayre, we had for several years had Santa in attendance. The cost of visiting him in one of the posher establishments is too great for some families, so we had a very simple set up, with our long suffering Santa squeezed into a hastily vacated corner of the shop: one day dog food, the next Santa. We don't charge to visit our realisation of the bearded one, and the children always seem happy with the small gift they are allowed to choose.

As you do with these things, we got to discussing how we could improve the show, and rather recklessly, I suggested attaching a gazebo to the side entrance of the shop, so creating a three metre square Santa's Grotto. Like many such ideas, once we started on the project, it grew in ambition, until we ended up with a cosy little haven, complete with lining to keep light out and heat in, carpet, (kindly donated by a local firm, even though I went with the intention of buying it) Christmas lights, cheerfully glowing heater and even a lit reindeer.

This far more up market effort was much appreciated by both parents and children alike, and a letter from one of the parents, expressing her heartfelt thanks for the effort which had obviously gone into the project, made it all worthwhile. It is so rare nowadays that people take the trouble to express their gratitude in such a way. The only trouble is there was now no going back, so every year we write off two man days to do something that actually costs us money: I must be going soft in my dotage!

As with any group of people that get on well together, there is a fair bit of banter during the course of a day. I suppose Tony and I are a sort of good cop, bad cop set up; in so far as he will pay our Jack a compliment, and I will then put a counter point: purely in the interest of balance you understand. This also applies to the group of customers, who also tend to festoon her with compliments. Naturally I direct them to the local opticians, but still they persist. One such is our local undertaker, who always comments as to how radiant Jack is looking. On one occasion, his compliments had been particularly effusive, and I thought they really needed tempering a little; so once Jack had been allowed a suitable period of indulgence, I did just have to remind her that as Derek spend most of his time with corpses, maybe his point of reference was a little skewed! Such comments usually elicit the response: "Oh; you are a nasty man", and I then have to await the retribution, which will surely come at some point!

Although we think of ourselves as a garden and pet shop, we do get asked for all manner of things, totally unrelated to our trade. Often the customer will continue to describe their problem, even though you have established you do not stock the type of product they require. One such was a chap who was looking for plumbing bits. Although I told him we did not stock them, he still went on to tell me he had a leak in his airing cupboard. My response: "Well I suppose it could be worse: it could have been a marrow". Well; we are a gardening shop....

Thinking of things vegetable, we have this one particular smallholder who really is a one off! He came in one day, asking if I had the new season's seed catalogue. I did, but the company had only sent me one copy, so I couldn't let him have it to keep. Undaunted, he asked if he could borrow it for the evening. This he did, returning triumphantly the next day, having had all 144 pages photocopied, regardless of the fact that much of the catalogue contains flower seeds, which as he doesn't grow them, were completely irrelevant to him. Anyway, a few days pass, and in he comes again, ready to place his order. He had not brought his copy of the catalogue with him, so we used the original copy. Compiling his order is always a steady old job, but on this occasion it was proving particularly so, as he couldn't locate the particular cabbage

he was looking for. Most people would have made a list of course, but that would be a step too far for our hero. So, after an exasperating fifteen minutes or so, he concludes that this particular cabbage cannot be in my catalogue, and decides he will have to go and fetch his copy!
I tried to explain that as his catalogue was a photo copy of the one he was looking at, it was highly unlikely it would be in there. Logic however was futile, and off he went to fetch his copy. A while later he returned, triumphantly brandishing his catalogue, complete with the elusive cabbage. His face was as red as his language was blue when I pointed out the same item in the catalogue he had been studying before: all part of life's rich tapestry I suppose.

Elsewhere, back on planet earth, U.K. debt had now reached a Trillion pounds: I mean, that's £1,000,000,000,000, which is a lot of dosh in anybody's language. If we were to pay off a pound of that debt every second, of every day, how long do you think it would take us to clear it? I will let you have a think about it, and come back to you later on with the answer!
When faced with such enormous figures, I try to bring them down to a manageable level. According to government figures, there are about 29 million of us working, who will presumably have to pay off this debt, one way or the other, (I realise there are other groups who also contribute to the coffers, but many also draw on them, so let's call these neutral) so that's £34,482 each. Now, if I personally had that much debt around my neck, and more importantly, it was growing, day by week by year, if somebody asked for financial help, I think I would have to say that until I got my own house in order, I would be unable to contribute. What I can't therefore understand, is why we as a country, burdened with unimaginable debt, still give money to countries, many of which have far more buoyant economies than our own. Answers on a postcard please!
I know far brighter people than I rationalise our situation by assuring us the interest is a small proportion of our GDP, and therefore quite manageable, but to my mind the cheapest money is

still your own, and I reckon the country's current 'life style' is unsustainable.
In February the last of mum's siblings died. This really hit her hard, as Jean was ten years her junior, so she thought it very unfair that she should still be here at 96 years old, when Jean had gone. People think I am uncaring when they say it is marvellous my mother has reached such an age and I disagree with them, but she will often tell my sisters and I that she is more than ready to go, and that these past few years have been a case of just sitting around, waiting for the inevitable. As far as she is concerned her quality of life no longer warrants being here. That is not to say the staff at Holbeach Hospital do not do their best to make her life as fulfilled as possible: they are a marvellous bunch, it is just that she has had enough.
I do find it fascinating how we can apply logic to our animals, but cannot transfer this to our loved ones. When we had to make the decision to have Walt put to sleep it broke our hearts, so much so that to this day we still cannot even consider having another dog, we just never want to have to make that decision again; and yet we did it because we knew it was the best thing for Walt: you only had to look in his eyes to know he had had enough, and it was the only humane thing to do. Substitute a human being, however, and we are prepared to keep them hanging on, sometimes for years, unable to show any signs of intelligible life. I realise there are all sorts of moral and legal issues, but even so, it just doesn't make sense to me: as people say 'you wouldn't treat a dog like it'.
Holbeach made the news on February 11th 2012 by being the coldest place in the UK at minus 16 degrees centigrade. This spell of cold weather was very much a double edged sword for us, for whilst it helped enormously with fuel sales at the shop, out in France, similarly freak conditions had caused havoc with many properties out there, ours included, with the boiler and pool heater both falling victim to the big freeze. You just don't expect temperature of minus ten for over a week in the South of France. This was obviously an expense we could well do without, but,

doing the glass half full bit, we had escaped far more lightly than some of our neighbours.
You could tell just how cold the weather was by Kev actually resorting to wearing his store coat - some of the time! This is something I haven't touched on before, but he has an absolutely incredible resistance to the cold. In all the years he has worked with me I have never seen him wear a jumper. Even in the midst of winter he walks around in nothing more than a short sleeved shirt. (Well, trousers as well, obviously). Being at the opposite end of the thermal scale, it chills me to the bone just looking at him. Kev puts this phenomenon down to having worked in a chiller room for many years in his younger days, but it still astonishes me; and many of the customers, it has to be said. You really have to admire his resilience though; he never seems to get a cold, yet alone have a day off ill.
In April my long serving (suffering?) book keeper, Eileen announced her intention to retire. Initial thoughts were to look for a replacement, but with 20 shops a day now closing, I decided it would be better to try and save a few pounds on the wages bill, and take the job on myself. I would now be wearing that many caps, it was a good job I have such a big head!
The timescale was a bit tight, so there followed a crash course, like a plane falling from the sky, on book keeping. So, after about five hours tuition, I was on my own; well almost on my own: fortunately I had Alice as my mentor when I got a bit bogged down.
Given that the book keeping system, manual of course, had changed little since dad had first devised it, even with my lack of experience, I could see that it had become a very cumbersome and inefficient system, having had everything from VAT to e-commerce tacked onto it over the years. I had Alice look over the whole thing with me, and we agreed that a complete overhaul was needed. I wanted to keep all the good elements about a manual system, i.e. not losing the vital thought process, whilst simplifying the whole thing.

Alice set up a spread sheet system, which would still allow me to price the customer accounts up manually, but enable all the figures to be presented in a more accountant friendly format, and therefore hopefully make further savings in that direction as well. I don't look forward to my annual meeting with him as much as I used to in any case. Nothing personal, you understand, he is a thoroughly nice chap, it is just that he is not the bearer of good news he once was. I already know I would be better off selling up, investing the proceeds, and working at the local Pizza factory, but it still isn't what you want to hear from your accountant. I reckon I am pretty well unemployable anyway!

Having no line of succession, Alice and I are aware we need to make clear what we would like to happen to our few worldly possessions when we shuffle off this mortal coil. As it had been some time since we had made a will, we decided to update it; after all, there was all my Lotus memorabilia to think about!
The reason I mention this is to do with why we made a will in the first place. A story was related about a local couple who tragically both perished from injuries sustained in a car crash. The nub of the story however was that the husband pre-deceased his wife by a few hours, and as he died intestate, the whole estate passed to her side of the family. This really made me think, as should the same happen to Alice and me, her father would take over the majority stake in the business, putting my mother in a very awkward situation, particularly as his track record in running a business wasn't exactly exemplary. I know the chances of such an occurrence are slim, but for what it costs to make a will, the peace of mind was well worth it.
Of far greater concern was the fact that my beloved Lotus were in trouble again! A couple of years under the stewardship of the charismatic but misguided Dany Bahar had once more brought them to the brink. His confrontational management style and fantasy aspirations for the brand saw many of the people who make Lotus what it is leave, to be replaced with people who although

talented in their own right, did not understand the ethos of the company. I have no doubt they will survive, but all these distractions delay still further the new product they desperately need: there are only so many rehashes of the Elise and Evora they can do.
In my fantasy world, I would love to form a partnership with a really clever guy, with proper knowledge of the car industry, so that we could sort Lotus out once and for all. We would run it like a proper business; him dealing with the management side and me with the 'grass roots' common sense stuff, something which has been lacking for many years now. It is such a shame that a company staffed by such passionate and talented guys endlessly wanders from crisis to disaster like a rudderless ship: tragic.
The late spring weather was once again abysmal, so much so that one farming group resorted to planting potatoes by hand for the first time in 40 years. Fortunately it did cheer up for Holbeach's big event: we were on the route for the Olympic Torch. The council decided they wanted to spruce up the town with bunting, and one poor girl was given the job of sorting it all out...about six days before the event! She had been put in touch with me, owing to my involvement in the town's Christmas lights. It soon became obvious this was a well planned idea: she had no idea what the bunting was going to be attached to, how she was going to get it up there, and as for applying for a road closure order, to ensure the workers stringing the bunting across the road could work in safety; well...
Fortunately there is still a community spirit in the town, so Paddy sorted out some men and machinery, and the job got done, but what a performance.
For our part, we provided the gazebo and seating for the VIP's, including our very own Olympians, Geoff Capes, Stewart Storey and Sally Reddin! Needless to say the furniture carried prominent Limming branding, much to the amusement of Geoff, for whom I had provided a particularly robust oak bench, complete with budgie logos.

LIMMINGS PROVIDED VIP SEATING & SHELTER FOR THE OLYMPIC TORCHE'S PASSAGE THROUGH HOLBEACH

The day itself was a huge success, with more people in the town than at any other time I can remember: the pavements were thronged from one end of the town to the other. As I said when interviewed by the local radio station, if we could get a tenth of those people to shop in the town on a regular basis, I would be well happy.

At the end of August I came to the conclusion that e-commerce was not going to work for us, as we were throwing far more money at it than was being earned. I felt we had given it a fair chance to perform, but with money now so tight, I wasn't prepared to keep funding all the optimisation and other costs, so with some sadness, I pulled the plug. I have to say that since withdrawing the support elements from the site, we still sell about the same amount of

product through it as we did before. Generally speaking, if a customer comes to us, it is generally for a niche product they can't get from the 'big boys'.
We have always considered offering free local delivery as being part of the service you offer customers, but how much longer we will be able to do this I am not sure. In September, it cost over £100 to fill our truck with fuel, which makes delivering a £3.99 bag of compost to Holbeach Hurn a loss making exercise; something one elderly customer was unable to grasp: she saw no reason why we shouldn't instantly deliver said bag of compost. I tried to explain about the cost of fuel, but she retorted that she didn't run a car, so this didn't affect her!

The town has a Business Forum group, with the aim of promoting Holbeach and its businesses. One perennial topic, (apart from parking!) is how the town is declining, and what can be done about it. Seeing all those people in town for the Olympic Torch event, had made everyone realise that there were still people out there, they just needed a real incentive to come into the town. This discussion, together with a comment made by one of the members, who has an office opposite the entrance to Tesco's, really got me thinking about how we might persuade some of them to return. The person in question assured us there was no shortage of visitors to Holbeach; it was just that the vast majority of them ventured no further than Tesco.
These two factors set me thinking; how could we get all those potential customers to venture from the periphery, into the town itself? Realising that me jogging through the town brandishing one of our garden torches may not draw too much of a throng, I hit upon the idea of a Holbeach Promotion Day, where all the traders in the town could join together and offer some really special deals. I reasoned that whilst it may not be worth someone making the effort to come into town for one shop's promotion, if they could visit a number of shops, all offering really good deals, it may just persuade them to come. Of course, we would also have to persuade

Tesco to let us target their customers, something I was not convinced they would be too keen on.
I put the idea forward at the next meeting of the Forum, and it seemed to be well received, so somewhat impetuously, I volunteered to organise the day.
Expecting Tesco to be the biggest stumbling block, I made them my first port of call, and to my surprise, the duty manager agreed to let us distribute flyers advertising our event in their entrance foyer.
Once I had all the details sorted; special advertising rates with the local paper, cost of printing the flyers etc, I took a booking form to each of the businesses in town, so they could register their interest, book advertising space and so on.
As the date for the event drew nearer, I had received a very disappointing response, and aware of the lead times for printing and distributing the fliers, informed the lady coordinating the advertising that it was unlikely there would be enough businesses to make the event worthwhile. Undaunted, she volunteered to visit people, to see if they could be persuaded to join in. As she went round she was continually met with the response, 'Oh yes. We are going to take part, we just haven't got round to returning the form'.
With the event now viable, a mad rush ensued to get everything organised in time. The other problem was finding enough man power to get the fliers distributed at Tesco. For my part I found it fascinating, and just couldn't believe how many people passed through their doors in the four hours I was there: as was said; there is no shortage of people in Holbeach!
Tony came up with the good idea of each business putting a sample of their offering in another shop; so Swepstones butchers might have samples of our wild bird seed, whilst I would offer samples of the Flower Basket's Belgian chocolates: a sort of cross pollinating I suppose.
Come the day, and the town certainly was busier, and for our part we put on some super offers: we wouldn't make any money on them, but as I had tried to impress on other shop owners from the start, the idea of the day was not to make money, but to incentivise

shoppers, in the hope that they would return in the future.
The fact that we took over two and a half times what we normally would on a Thursday, marked the day out as a great success for us, but I have to admit that many other business owners were far less enthused; so maybe it wasn't such a good idea: but at least we had tried to do *something*. I also think not everybody put quite as much effort into the day as they could have, but that was down to personal choice.

With the sad demise of Halstead & Fowler, the shed at the rear of our Park Road store came up for auction. The receivers had been trying to sell it on the open market for some time, but with no independent services to it, and the only way to connect them requiring access across my land, there had been no takers.
It was bought at the auction by a surveyor from London, who considered it an absolute steal at the price he paid. Unfortunately London is a whole different ball game to Holbeach, and when I made him aware that there had been no interest at half the price he perceived it to be worth, he seemed a little deflated. Suffice to say that over a year later the shed still stands empty.

A real highlight of the year was an event in Bourne, celebrating 50 years since BRM won the Formula One World Championship. This marvellous pageant encompasses everything from Raymond May's ERA's to the last of the BRM's being driven through the Bourne streets. After the last one, held in 1999, I didn't think there would be a hope in hell of a repeat, as the police were less than pleased about the conduct of some of the drivers. Given that speed is in their blood, some of the racing drivers exercised their charges with maybe a bit more enthusiasm than the legislated 30mph maximum limit allowed, much to the delight of the enthusiastic crowd, it should be noted.
Refreshingly, the 'Nanny State' mentality did not prevail, and the event proved bigger and better than the last one even, with thousands of people flocking into the town. Highlights included ex

BRM driver Sir Jackie Stewart demonstrating not only a BRM, but also his Tyrell, and Damon Hill giving his father's championship winning car a spin. And as for the sound of that V16 BRM....

The regeneration of land, which incorporates our Park Hall site, is something which has been on the agenda for some time, but lack of funding has always confined it to the back burner. Councillor Nick Worth shares the view that the project would be of great benefit to the town and has always championed its cause. As part of his efforts, he explored the possibility of gaining lottery funding for the restoration of Park Hall itself. A meeting was arranged at their Nottingham offices to discuss the possibility of the building being eligible. Things seemed to be going well, with their representative finding the building and its history interesting. Then came the reality check: as this would be quite a large project, they first wanted proof that we could deliver, and suggested a smaller undertaking, which could then be assessed, and if deemed successful, lead to approval for the one we wanted to do in the first place! Likely time scale: about seven years!

I often find it difficult to buy suitable cards for birthdays etc, and sometimes resort to making my own, usually complete with an inappropriate verse. One such example was when a friend went in for a knee replacement. Surprisingly I couldn't find a get well card which depicted a replacement knee joint, so I made one, complete with the caption: 'A friend re-kneed, is a friend indeed!' This seemed to cause great amusement amongst the nurses, and was even taken off to show other patients who were there for the same operation. Perhaps that could be another business opportunity; condition specific get well cards.... They tell me that your leg is broke, and through the skin, your bones do poke. But look on the bright side, it could be worse, at least you're not riding in a hearse....that sort of thing: OK; maybe not then!

At the end of November my path to retirement took another blow, when Tony announced his intention to retire at the end of June the following year, two years sooner than I had anticipated. Back in the dim and distant past, I had decided to hedge my bets against an early demise by retiring at 60, in the hope that it would increase the likelihood of me enjoying a few years retirement. In view of the fact that I would have already worked far more hours than had I done a normal job, I felt this was justifiable. My assumption had always been that Tony would retire at 65, so coinciding conveniently with my 60th.
The situation was now very different of course: retiring at 60 just isn't going to happen for me, so with Tony calling time two years earlier than expected, we would have to soldier on with a new second in command. This was hard to envisage, as Tony and I had been a team for as long as I could remember, and with that length of partnership comes an almost intuitive way of working together: it was going to be a hard act to follow, and it was not a challenge I exactly relished.
From Tony's point of view, I didn't blame him at all: life is too short to spend more of it than is necessary working, and if your situation allows you the freedom to escape from the ties work imposes, then why not go and live a little.
At least we still have Kev to apply his own brand of logic to the world around us. One day I commented that a large man passing by on a bike could do with some exercise, in order to lose some weight. Kev observed that at least he was making an effort by cycling. The fact that the chap was riding a *motorised* bike was what had prompted my comment in the first place! Kev did see my point and conceded that without the peddling bit, maybe the chap wasn't getting as fit as he might.
On a different tack, I felt really sorry for an elderly lady who came in one day. She had a problem with cat poo on her gravel drive, which in itself is not unusual. Where her situation differed was that it wasn't a cat that was depositing it. It transpired that she had some new neighbours, who she found quite intimidating, and as such

dare not approach; but apparently they were collecting gravel from her drive, using it in their cat litter tray, and then depositing it back on the drive, complete with additions, as they replenished the tray with unsoiled gravel. The poor lady was desperate to find something which would make the gravel unattractive to the cat, in the hope that it would stop this inexcusable practice. I am usually pretty mercenary, but it seemed so wrong that she should have to spend what little she had on such a thing.

It often amuses me how people rationalise things they do, but with which they are maybe not completely comfortable. One such is eating meat. I think probably the best conscience easer I have heard on this one was from someone who insisted he only ate meat from animals which were vegetarian; and no, it wasn't Kev who said it!

Thinking of twisted logic, another customer pushed the boundaries of reason when I tried to save him some money on a purchase. The customer in question was a smallholder, who wanted to buy some rat poison. Owing to a pricing anomaly, if he purchased a 500gram tub, it would cost him £9.50, but were he to buy five 100gram sachets of the same product; it would only cost him £6.50, for the same weight, so saving him £3.00. He decided upon six of the 100gram sachets, but then hesitated, and put one back. Expecting there to be a logical reason why, I posed the question. Apparently it had dawned on him that if he had bought six sachets, he wouldn't have saved the full £3.00: of course; silly me.

It was around this time that there had been a hoo-hah in the insurance world about women getting cheaper car insurance than men. Now as far as I know, there has always been a good reason for this: whereas the fairer sex are statistically more likely to scrape the Morris in Morrisons, we chaps tend to total the Toyota in Tewksbury, which is why we pay about 16% more apparently: fair enough. However, now we have sex equality, (must remind our Jack of that, next time a bale of peat needs loading!) it appears us blokes must be charged the same rate as our more careful counterparts.

All this was fresh in my mind when my insurance broker came in for a bag of salt. When it came time to pay, trying to look as serious as possible, I announced, "Sorry; I won't be able to knock your usual 16% off, I'm not allowed to discriminate anymore!" Poor old boy, I think he was already fed up with the whole nonsense.

It's a bit like the email I received, urging me to contact the sender 'if I wanted more infuriation'!

Amongst all this frivolity, Jessops, HMV and Blockbuster had joined Comet on the ever growing list of retailers who could no longer survive the harsh trading conditions. In the world of independents, as we small fry are known, there were now about 30 a day closing.

At least there was still some buoyancy in the area: with interest rates so low and a lot of wealthy people wanting something safe in which to invest their money, land prices had rocketed, with £20,000 per acre now being talked about for the best land; that's treble what it was not that long ago! At this rate it will soon be worth us demolishing our house, and turning the plot back into arable land.

Talking of money, did you work out how long the Nation's debt would take to clear? It shocked me when I worked it out, and although I'm no Einstein, I reckon the answer is 31 *thousand* years, give or take a day or two; and that's without the interest!

With the internet, telephones and credit card machines to contend with, our poor old phone line struggled to cope, and compromises had to be made. This could be really frustrating, as you couldn't use the phone at the same time as the credit card machine. This all came to a head one day when I had to keep a customer waiting whilst another member of staff dealt with a long winded phone enquiry. Enough was enough, so I contacted our card processor, to see if anything could be done. As it turned out there was: it could be connected to the internet. So with just a simple bit of rewiring, and a quick re-programme of the card terminal, we were up and

running; now we could use everything at the same time.
What amazed me about all this was that not long before, somebody had come from the processing company to install a new terminal; wouldn't you have thought he might just have mentioned the fact that it would perform far better if connected via the internet?
Later in January Alice's youngest sister celebrated her 50th birthday. As the nominated brother in law for winding her up, it fell to me to make sure her neighbours knew she had reached such a significant milestone. Remembering how well the anti wrinkle cream had gone down on her 40th, I thought I had better keep it low key; so I limited my activities to stencilling the glad tidings on the road at various points along the route to her house, complimented by a very subtle string of letters reinforcing the message. There was also Sarah of course....Being of Dutch decent, it seemed appropriate to add a bit of their culture to proceedings. In Holland, when you reach the big five O, men supposedly see Abraham, and the ladies see Sarah; so an effigy is made, supposedly depicting the victim...I mean lucky recipient... to acknowledge as much. I think the neighbours thought it all a bit strange, but found it amusing all the same, as did Berny of course!
Meanwhile, the cost of raising a child had now been calculated at £222,000, so that was even more money Alice and I should have somewhere! It just baffles me how we are supposed to be saving all this cash and yet there is still no Ferrari in the garage: I guess we just don't earn the money in the first place.
February saw the opening of Holbeach's third Polish shop. I am surprised there is sufficient trade for them all, as they sell similar things, but no doubt they know what they are doing: perhaps they could give me some tips!
A trip to stay with friends in Cornwall was a real eye opener, both for the price of property in this sought after area, and what some of the gifty type shops were offering for sale. One particular store had six dolly clothes pegs, tied up with a bit of ribbon for £3.50: it was only a couple of years ago we stopped selling them at 99p for a pack of 24! It must be the bit of ribbon that makes the difference.

I don't know how I drop in for these things, but one of our trade organisations asked if I would be prepared to talk to a journalist from the *Guardian* about how changes announced in the budget would affect us. I duly gave my opinion over the phone, and next I knew a photographer had been dispatched to take photos of me in my place of work.
When the local paper has done this sort of thing, the photographer is usually in and out within a few minutes, keen to get to his next assignment. Not this chap! We had lighting rigs and the lot: I think he photographed me everywhere in the shop apart from the loo! He seemed genuinely interested in the place, and was particularly taken with our old set of scales for some reason: we had lots of shots of me with them.
A while later my opinion was sought again, this time about the chances of a triple dip recession: I told them we were still trying to drag ourselves out of the bottom of the first dip, never mind a third one!
With working most Saturdays, it is very rare that Alice and I spend a weekend doing the sort of things normal couples do; like shopping together on a Saturday for instance. This is something I am not that keen on in any case, largely because it invariably involves parting with money. We did however venture to Lincoln on one such trip, and whilst waiting for Alice to return from a comfort break, I noticed a shop proclaiming they bought tablets. I thought this a bit strange, but I had an Asprin and a couple of Paracetamol on me, so thought it worth getting a price for them....not that sort of tablet apparently!
Holbeach was very honoured in June to be chosen as the launch venue for an arts initiative called Transported. The idea was to take the arts out into areas usually not over endowed with culture: that would be Holbeach then!
Carters Park was the venue for most of the activities, including a very impressive Luminarium. As most of the events took place on the Sunday, when the vast majority of the shops are closed, the organisers agreed to do something in the town itself on Saturday.

One of the attractions turned out to be human statues. It was amazing the effect these motionless, staring, beings had on some people. A couple of them sat on a bench outside the shop for a while, and a few customers where so disturbed by their other worldly aura that they wouldn't go anywhere near them and couldn't even look at them; strange.

Remember that lady who bought the three hammocks in 2008? Well; her husband turned up for the third one, just five years after the lady had ordered it! The best bit was the way he just wandered in and announced he had come to collect Mrs. Whatsits hammock; like it had been ordered a couple of days ago! Apparently the patio on which it was to go had taken a little longer to construct than planned....

Our annual trip over to France gave us a much needed break from routine before facing up to the biggest change in the makeup of the business since dad had died. In June yet another Kevin joined us, so that he could have three weeks working alongside Tony, in order to at least get some insight as to what the job entailed. The trouble is, with being such a seasonal business; it takes a year to see the whole spectrum of what we do: the shop is a completely different layout in December to that in June.

I think Kevin's first impression must have been that it was just one big social whirl, as we had a leaving party at ours for Tony at the weekend, and then Kev's 50th birthday party a few days later. As Jack's partner is also a Kevin, it was a bit like the old Monty Python sketch, with all the Bruce's; very confusing.

As usual Kev kept us entertained at his do. Whenever Tony's sister is present, she brings out the best in Kev, and this evening was no exception. This time he sought her advice about his new mobile phone. He had been to Hunstanton, and decided to take some pictures with his phone, but when he reviewed them later, it was as though he had someone else's phone, as none of the pictures were of what he had taken: no pier, no seascape, just a load of buildings and such. Even more perplexing was the fact that he was somehow

in some of the pictures.
A quick look at his snaps confirmed the already obvious: he was of course holding the phone the wrong way round. There seems to be this obsession with some of the more attention seeking celebrities for what I believe they call 'selfies', so I suppose Kev was right on trend really, just not intentionally. Kev seems to have quite a bit of trouble with things technological: he once bought a video recorder cheap from a car boot sale. Predictably, it didn't work when he tried it out, but no matter, the price he had paid would allow for a bit of maintenance, so he took it to the repairers. Unfortunately they were not able to resurrect it; something to do with the workings having been substituted with a house brick apparently....
Tony finally took the plunge into retirement on the 28th June; it was going to leave a very big hole after so many years: his knowledge of the workings of the business was such that it could operate seamlessly, whether it was he or I at the helm, and knowing the various seasons as well as I, we rarely needed to discuss what had to be done, as each of us would organise our own bit of the business, knowing exactly who did what and when! It takes so much of the pressure off when someone is self motivating, and just gets things done.
I think when you lose your father at an early age, as both Tony & I did, it alters your perspective a little, and as he realised, later in life is perhaps now! If you are not careful you keep plodding on in the same old way, and suddenly it is too late to do all those things you were going to do....later.
Tony is still fit and active, and will hopefully be able to enjoy some good years of doing what he wants with his time, and whatever happens in the future, at least he has had a couple of years head start. Hopefully there will be aspects of the shop he will miss, we did have a lot of laughs together, but I am sure there are some he won't; like having to put all the display stock outside the shop and then dragging it all back in again at closing time. Then there are some of the more 'challenging' customers, like the chap who had Tony show him virtually every bit of garden furniture in the place,

before deciding on a sun lounger. Then; just when Tony thought the deal was done, the customer decided that the colour of the fabric would not compliment his wife's skin tone, and the deal was off!

Chapter 12. Shop Life Goes On

With Tony gone, the dynamics of the business would never be the same again, and no matter who followed, they would not have grown with the business, and have quite that same connection with it, but this is now and that was then, so we would just have to re-adjust our perspective, and get on with the job.

Holbeach's gradual decline continued with the closure of the Natwest bank in June, together with the announcement that Barclays would follow suit in October. This would now leave just Lloyds and HSBC. A lot of our customers were angered by this, but seemed unprepared to do anything about it. Luckily my bank was one of those still staying...for now, but had I been a customer of one of the others, I would have changed to a bank that was still supporting the town, and then have written to the area manager, to explain why I had done so. At least in that way the powers that be realise that they do lose customers if they close branches, plus if those that remain gain customers, they are more likely to be viable.
It is all very well telling customers they can do their banking on line, but I have yet to find a way of extracting the change I regularly need for the tills from my computer.
Another piece of news also had potential ramifications for the town, as Andy Hawkins, owner of one of the towns longest established businesses was looking to sell up and retire. Andy, like me, is second generation, and oversees a proper ironmongers shop, stocking all the obscure bits and pieces. He has eventually managed to sell the business as a going concern, but it remains to be seen if the new owners are able to stay on the tightrope. Andy was finding it tough with all the benefits of being established, so it is going to be tough for the new owners. Meanwhile we had our own problems, as the meddlers had now decided that they were no longer going to allow the import of Keruing, the wood our furniture is made from, into the country; irrespective of whether it is from managed sources or not.

This effectively spells an end to what has been a very good line for us. Ironically we can still get Teak and Oak, but price rules them out for most of our customers. A corollary of this was that we would also not be able to get the spare covers, the one thing that we had carved out a niche for on the web.
We are always on the lookout for new lines, so when a customer asked if we could get chickens feet, apparently irresistible to her dog, we were pleased to oblige. These soon became a popular line, although some customers thought them a step too far. Buoyed by their success however, we decided to move onwards (and upwards) to chickens necks. I was trying to convince a customer, who had already balked at the feet stage, of their merits, but they were not impressed. This was at the time when the subject of Badger culling was very much to the fore, so when she enquired as to where this accrual of body parts may end, I informed her we had Badgers willies arriving the next week! She didn't come in for any of those either.
In October we did something we had never done before: closed before our advertised time. A failure in the electricity supply, late in the day left us powerless (!) to do any other. We have had power failures before, but conveniently always during daylight. On these occasions we just unlock the cash draws on the tills and then note down sales amounts on a pad, to be rung into the tills when power is restored. This time however, we were plunged into darkness, so had no option but to close half an hour early. I have no doubt dad would have continued by candle light, but you know....health and safety!
Before we knew it, Christmas was once again looming, and plans were being made for the annual Christmas Fayre. With being on the outskirts of the town, the road closure has never come as far as us; the supermarket further into town always vetoing it on the grounds closing the road would adversely affect their trade, so leaving us and the other 'East Enders' (good name for a television programme that) feeling a bit left out.
This year however there was a new lady in charge, and she was not

to be trifled with, so she applied for the road closure to include our section, and then presented the situation to the supermarket as a fait accompli.
The other thing we always miss out on is the town's Christmas lights. Being deemed as not worthy of funding by our masters at the District Council, Holbeach has always had to pay for and erect its own lights, unlike the favoured son, Spalding.
It had always been felt a little unfair that as one of only three traders who help with the lights, I had never had them outside my shop (as is the case with the other two helpers, Nick & Graeham, for that matter, although they are a little more out of the way.) Lack of funds, and the reluctance of highways to let us use their structures for attaching the lights, has always prevented this.
A new, more amenable, person at highways, together with a bit of funding, gave the impetus to at last extend the run of lights as far as us; and very smart they looked too!
It's that community spirit again, as all the other helpers have nothing to gain from giving up two precious Sundays to erect and dismantle the lights, they do it purely because it is their town, and they want to do the best for its inhabitants they can.
Once again the Fayre was a great success, bringing a huge influx of people. Dozens of stalls line the streets, and street performers entertain the crowds. I suppose on the one hand these stalls suck some of the money out of the permanent shops, but on the other they are the main attraction for a lot of the visitors, so I suppose on balance they are a worthwhile addition.
It was a shame to hear on the run up to Christmas that a friend's wife had contracted shingles. I don't think it helped her mood any that he kept going into the bedroom and singing 'Shingle bells, shingle bells, shingle all the way....' (I made that last bit up!)
Wishing to provide a good service to our customers/being a money grabbing so and so, take your pick, we only close the two days when Christmas falls mid week, so on our return to work on the 27th I did a reconnoitre of other businesses in town, so I knew where I could send people who required something we didn't stock.

To my amazement, three of the shops were not going to re-open until January 2nd, and one of them was the baker! That seemed a heck of a long while for any retail business to be closed, and hardly helps the reputation of the town as a proper shopping centre. I know we all need a break, but we also have a responsibility to supply a reliable service: as dad would have said: 'There's no money coming through that door when it's closed boy', although I would take issue, as we do get the occasional cheque posted through the letter box!
Another hobby horse of mine is shops not adhering to their advertised opening times. I remember we once had a very good clothes shop in the town, but his opening hours were somewhat spasmodic. We once had one of his potential customers in the shop, who had really taken a shine to a jacket he had seen in the window. This was the third time he had made a purpose visit during the advertised opening hours, to try and purchase it, and he was completely exasperated by it all. He made it clear that this would be his last attempt at buying the jacket: not a good way to run a business, and perhaps partly why we sadly no longer have such an asset in the town.

Not long into 2014 we lost Alice's mother, and mine, now closing in on her 98th birthday, was not too good either. She does keep doing this however: showing all the signs of being on her last legs, and then before you know it, she is back from the brink, and asking for her playing cards! The last time she did this, we were so convinced we were going to lose her, that when she did yet another Lazarus, (as Jacquie calls it), I was moved to enquire if she was really some sort of alien! Although getting older is not something I particularly relish, I reckon that at least for now, it's better than the alternative.
What you do have to do with the onset of older age, and all it brings, is to guard against your inability to remember things: 30 years ago is fine, but what happened yesterday; no chance!
I have developed a number of little systems, like leaving my keys

against the shop fridge, so I don't forget the fish therein. I may spend a while trying to remember where I left my keys, but at least I don't go home without the fish!
In February the renewal notice arrived for the truck tax disc, and I happened to notice that the part about insurance had been re-worded, so I decided it was worth giving the on line system another go, and Hallelujah, they have at last sorted the anomaly with insurance out: quite impressive really, as they haven't even read my previous rant yet!
And that probably is as good a place as any for us to part company. It is difficult to know quite when to finish this journey: when Tony retired...or maybe when I eventually do? Really there is no tidy way; no Poirot like gathering of the suspects, no fat lady singing. I know there are still so many unanswered questions; like why is it always your big toe that pokes through the hole in your sock, even when you put it on the other foot, but for now this is the end of my story.

So; what of the future? I really don't know to be honest: like that bloke who lit the gas lamps, I thought I had a job for life, but now I'm not so sure. I know financially I would be far better off cashing in my assets and investing the proceeds, but it isn't quite that simple. To start with I am responsible for three other people's livelihoods, so I have them to consider; then there are our customers, some of whom have supported us across two generations; I owe them a bit of loyalty too.
Then there is the commitment required to keep going: it is pretty demoralising some days to look at the takings, and realise you have invested 10 hours of your life to be worse off than you were that morning!
The nature of the job means it is hard enough to survive giving it 100%, so there is no chance of easing back a bit; in fact I seem to be taking on more jobs within the firm the older I get! I do know however, that I am not as keen as I once was. In my far off younger days, after a week away I was well ready to be back at work; now

when we go to France, Alice nearly has to resort to sedation to get me on the plane home, even after a fortnights break.
That is the other thing of course; we love being out in France. The weather suits us, as does the way of life, and we now have a good circle of friends out there, including Joe and Liz from O'vineyards, who make some of the best wine you are likely to taste; so what's not to like?
I have a funny feeling that eventually something will happen, and that will be it: either the firm will no longer be viable, even in its current lean form, or some new bureaucratic imposition will persuade me I don't need the aggravation anymore; perhaps even something like the new Workplace Pensions, that will certainly be another nail in the coffin for many small businesses.
Until that day however I will try to serve my customers as well as I am able, while still trying to have a few laughs along the way. All I would ask on behalf of all shopkeepers, is that before you click that button to make an online purchase, just consider that you are actively contributing to the demise of the high street and with it *your* community. You may think that is not a problem; that retail shops are an outmoded way to buy things: I well remember a young customer, who when I enquired if I could help her, replied that she was just looking to see which size of dog toy she required, before ordering it, presumably a few pence cheaper, on the internet. Out of interest, I enquired what she would do when there were no longer any shops to use in this way. Her reply was unrepentant: she would face that problem when the time came, but for now we were here for her convenience, and that was all she cared about. She may well be right, but make no mistake, if the internet continues to grow at its current rate, many more shops will have to go: you can't have it both ways, and once they've gone, there will be no going back!
I do wonder what will happen then. As an example: a recurring problem has come to light with the igniters on a certain type of heater. Knowing this, I acquired a stock of these, so that if any of my customers had a problem I could sort it quickly, and at no cost to them; even though their heater may be out of warranty. The

people I have performed this service for have been delighted, and our Poppy Appeal collection box has benefitted as a result! I just wonder what those people would have done without their local retailer. I can't see some faceless internet trader popping over to sort the problems!

But enough of the doom and gloom! The question is: should any of you budding Arkwrights out there give it a go? Well, quite simply, if you have the necessary drive and tenacity to make a success of it, then you are not going to be deterred by me advising against such a venture: if you are that easily put off, you are not going to succeed anyway.

All I would suggest is you do your homework first: make sure you know how much it is going to cost each day to 'open the door'. By that I mean work out all your overheads; not just the obvious things, like rent and rates, but all the extras, like accountants fees, insurances, electricity, hire of PDQ terminals, bank charges, repayment of capital....right down to PAT testing, fire extinguisher hire, and in our case, even explosives and poisons licences!

When you have that figure, work out the likely overall gross profit margin, and then you can calculate how much you will need to turn over per year. Divide this figure by the number of trading days, and you will know how much a day you need to take to 'open the door'; if that doesn't frighten you, nothing will! I know there are many days when we don't achieve our target, and that's with no rent to pay, no bank loan and all the stock bought and paid for: if you were to add any one of those elements into the equation, that would be curtains for us, so marginal are trading conditions nowadays. I am not looking for sympathy; it is just a fact; and if you look at the remaining 'survivors' in the town, most of them are in a similar situation to us: long established businesses, who own their property and stock, and have no loans to service.

I really do feel sorry for anybody trying to start out now, what with the reluctance of the banks to lend, and the increasing legislative burdens being placed on businesses, it really is quite daunting. As

already mentioned, we have the spectre of Workplace Pensions looming, which will add yet more pressure, both administrative and financial. We have of course already paid for our pensions through our National Insurance contributions, but now, as with dental care, it appears we are going to have to pay twice. Let's hope the powers that be take better care of this chunk of money.
So; if after seeking psychiatric help, you still want to be a shop keeper, first make sure any significant others share your ambitions, (unlike my father!) as without their support things will be infinitely more difficult, and try to find a niche that the 'big boys' and internet have not already filled....best of luck with that one! You also need to have fun doing whatever it is you decide upon, because to succeed you will be living and breathing 'the job' nearly every waking hour; and on a few sleepless nights as well.
And finally: remember; the best way to make a small fortune out of shopkeeping.... is to start with a large one!

As a footnote, I have compiled a list of the numbers and types of business there were in the town when I was a teenager in the late sixties, early seventies, compared to what we have now, just to illustrate how the makeup of the town has changed.
I do not claim this to be completely accurate, but is near as I can get, as of March 2014. It is difficult to remember exactly when a certain shop closed, or changed trades, but I have consulted with a few of the 'old boys', and other shop owners, as well as referring to a trade guide from 1970, so I don't think it is a million miles out. There are also some anomalies, as I have only included businesses that are in the main body of the town: so for example, Holbeach Tyres is not included in the earlier figures, even though they were trading then, as they were not in the town as such.
We do also have Holbeach Market, on a Thursday and Saturday, which on occasion boasts stalls selling soft furnishings, plants, fruit & veg, watches, wet fish and eggs.
I am sure many other small towns have suffered the same fate as Holbeach, but it is still sad to see the way the town has changed

over the years.
Census figures show a population of 6,450 in 1971, and 7,346 in 2011.

Type of Business	Number then	Number now
Agricultural Merchant	2	0
Army & Navy Store	1	0
Baby Wear	1	0
Baker	3	1
Bank	4	2
Barber	4	5
Bike Shop	1	0
Book Maker	0	2
Book Shop	1	1
Bric-a-Brac	0	1
Builders Merchant	1	1
Building Society	0	1
Butcher	5	2
Cafe	2	2
Camera Shop	1	0
Car Sales	2	1
Card Shop	0	2
Charity Shop	0	5
Chemist	2	2
Chip Shop	5	3
Cinema	1	0
Coal Merchant	1	0
Cobbler	1	0
Computer Shop	0	2
Convenience Store	0	1
Dance Wear	0	1
Decorating Supplies	1	0
Delicatessen	1	0
Dentist	1	1
Discount Store (Multiple)	0	2

DIY	1	1
Drapers	2	0
Dry Cleaner	1	1
Electrical Sundries	0	1
Estate Agent	1	6
Flower Shop	1	2
Fruit & Veg Shop	5	0
Funeral Director	1	2
Furniture Shop	2	2
Garage	5	2
Garden & Pet Shop	1	2
Gift/Craft Shop	0	2
Hairdresser	5	11
Health Food Shop	0	1
Home Care Services	0	1
Hotel	3	2
Insurance Broker	1	2
Ironmongers/Hardware	3	1
Jeweller	2	0
Kitchen Shop	0	1
Ladies Outfitter	3	2
Laundrette	1	1
Library	1	1
Mens Outfitter	3	0
Monumental Mason	1	0
Motor Factor	1	0
Music Shop	1	0
News Agent	1	1
Optician	1	1
Plumbing Supplies	2	2
Polish Shop	0	3
Post Office	1	1
Pub	8	4
Independent Grocer	5	0
Radio & Television	2	0

Record Shop	1	0
Restaurants/Takeaways	0	3
Saddlers	1	0
Second Hand Shop	0	1
Seed Merchant	1	0
Services Club	1	1
Shoe Shop	2	1
Solicitor	2	2
Sports Shop	1	0
Stationer	1	0
Supermarket	1	2
Sweet Shop	3	1
Takeaways	1	10
Tattoo	0	1
Taxi Office	0	1
Tobacconist	2	0
Toy Shop	1	0
Travel Agent	1	0
Tyre Depot	0	1
Vet	0	1
Watch Repairer	1	0
Windows & Conservatories	0	1
Wines & Spirits	1	0
Wool Shop	1	0
Woolworths	1	0
Totals	129	120

On the face of it, a reduction of just nine shops does not seem so bad; but it is the *mix* of shops that is the problem: sixteen sources of 'fast food', and yet not a single greengrocer for example.

I look forward to being corrected on the above by sundry 'Old Boys and Gals'!

On the following pages are some pictures taken by dad in the early sixties, together with their 2014 counterparts.